T.J. COLES studies the philosophy of neu
the University of Plymouth, UK, with re
experiences of the blind and visually impaired. He is director of the Plymouth Institute for Peace Research (PIPR), editor and co-author of *Voices for Peace* and author of *The New Atheism Hoax* (both 2015, PIPR). His political writings have appeared in the *New Statesman*, *Lobster*, *Peace Review* and *Z Magazine*. He is also a columnist with Axis of Logic and in 2013 was shortlisted for the Martha Gellhorn Prize for journalism.

BRITAIN'S SECRET WARS

HOW AND WHY THE UNITED KINGDOM SPONSORS CONFLICT AROUND THE WORLD

T.J. COLES

CLAIRVIEW

Clairview Books Ltd.,
Russet, Sandy Lane,
West Hoathly,
W. Sussex RH19 4QQ

www.clairviewbooks.com

Published in Great Britain in 2016 by Clairview Books

A CIP catalogue record for this book is available from the British Library

Print book ISBN 978 1 905570 78 2
Ebook ISBN 978 1 905570 69 0

Cover by Morgan Creative
Typeset by DP Photosetting, Neath, West Glamorgan
Printed and bound by 4Edge Ltd, Essex

Contents

Introduction
Foreign policy – 'To pursue clandestine, illegal operations' 1

PART 1: THE MIDDLE EAST AND NORTH AFRICA
1. Syria – 'Illegal but necessary' 19
2. Libya – 'Orchestrated unrest' 27
3. Iraq – 'A momentary twinge of concern' 34
4. Iran – 'It's all about petrol prices' 52
5. Yemen – 'Put the fear of death into them' 60
6. Drones – 'We're talking about murder' 73

PART II: AND BEYOND
7. Ukraine – 'We saw this one coming' 83
8. Sri Lanka – 'Shining a light' 94
9. Colombia – 'The best business environment' 104
10. Papua – 'Starve the bastards out' 118
11. Somalia – 'Now I'm a real killer' 130
12. Bangladesh – 'Survival of the fittest' 145

Conclusion
Peaceniks – 'terrorist sympathisers' 155

Notes 164
Index 206

ACRONYMS

AI Amnesty International
BMENAI Broader Middle East and North Africa Initiative
BRA Bougainville Resistance Army
CIA Central Intelligence Agency (US)
DFID Department for International Development (UK)
EIJ Egyptian Islamic Jihad
EU European Union
FARC Fuerzas Armadas Revolucionarias de Colombia
FBI Federal Bureau of Investigation (US)
FCO Foreign and Commonwealth Office (UK)
FSA Free Syrian Army
GCHQ Government Communications Headquarters
HMG Her Majesty's Government
HRW Human Rights Watch
ICG International Crisis Group
ICU Islamic Courts Union (Somalia)
IMF International Monetary Fund
IS Islamic State (a.k.a., Daesh, ISIL, ISIS)
ISIL Islamic State of Iraq and the Levant
ISIS Islamic State of Iraq and Syria, a.k.a. Islamic State of Iraq and al-Sham
JFC Justice for Colombia
KLA Kosovo Liberation Army
LIFG Libyan Islamic Fighting Group
LNG Liquefied Natural Gas
LTTE Liberation Tigers of Tamil Eelam (or 'Tamil Tigers')
MEK Mujahideen-el-Khalq
MEPI Middle East Partnership Initiative
MI5 Military Intelligence, Section Five
MI6 Military Intelligence, Section Six
MoD Ministry of Defence (UK)
MSC Mujahideen Shura Council

NATO North Atlantic Treaty Organisation
PIL Public Interest Lawyers
PNG Papua New Guinea
RAB Rapid Action Battalion
RAF Royal Air Force
RAWA Revolutionary Association of the Women of Afghanistan
RIIA Royal Institute of International Affairs
SAS Special Air Service
SBS Special Boat Service
SNC Syrian National Council
TAPOL Indonesian human rights group
TFG Transitional Federal Government (Somalia)
USAID United States Agency for International Development
UN United Nations
UNGA United Nations General Assembly
UNHCR United Nations High Commission for Refugees
UNSC United Nations Security Council
UNSCR United Nations Security Council Resolution
WFP World Food Programme
WHO World Health Organization
WND *World Net Daily*

Introduction

Foreign policy – 'To pursue clandestine, illegal operations'

A few years ago, Britain's Defence Secretary, Liam Fox, said: 'If you want to keep a secret in the United Kingdom nowadays, the best place to speak it is in the House of Commons, as it is the least likely place to be reported'. Taking Fox at his word, this book consults government records in order to bring Britain's secret wars to public attention. The evidence presented here suggests that Britain has a greater role in world affairs than many realize. Secret wars are waged for the financial benefit of sectional interests (as internal records reiterate) and result in widespread crimes against humanity, including ethnic cleansing, torture and assassination.[1]

Domestic populations are generally pacifistic and responsive to humanitarian concerns. For that reason there is a concerted effort by governments to keep most wars secret. They do so by threatening libel, issuing directives to editors (D notices), and occasionally raiding offices to seize leaked files. A Royal Institute of International Affairs (Chatham House) book from 1997 explains: 'Much of our foreign policy is conducted on the sly for fear that it would raise hackles at home if people knew what we were pushing for'.[2]

The aims of this book are to raise awareness about what is happening by filling a gap in journalism and scholarship, and to encourage journalists, scholars, activists, and the tax-paying public to think more carefully about what Britain is doing in the world, rather than focusing exclusively on the crimes of other countries. An evidence-based framework is laid out in this Introduction in an effort to explain the motives behind the secret wars, drawing on government documents and policy briefings. Having contextualized contemporary British foreign policy here (the 'why'), Parts I and II address a number of secret wars taking place around the world (the 'where' and 'how').

The British Empire's notion of 'free trade' was of such benefit to a small number of monarchs, peers, merchants and traders that it became the ideal post-WWII model for global economic control. However, WWII wrought such damage to the global economy that an international system of regulated capital (Bretton Woods) was needed. In the 1970s, with Europe reconstructed along lines favourable to US businesses, the system was deregulated and 'free trade' promoted. This Introduction defines 'free trade' and illustrates how the Ministry of Defence uses violent methods to impose and maintain it where necessary.

'The New Trade Agenda'...

In building its Empire (circa 1583–1914), Britain invaded 'something like 171 out of 193 UN member states in the world today', writes historian Stuart Laycock, who omits, among others, the Falklands/Malvinas and Gibraltar, subjectively sticking to 'the more interesting' and 'unusual' invasions. It is also worth noting that Britain created many borders (directly and indirectly), such as the Durand Line (never recognized by the indigenous population), which separates Pashtuns in Afghanistan from their kinsfolk in Pakistan. Providing no evidence, Laycock asserts 'some truth' in the 'view' that to the majority of Britons, Empire was 'a force for good'. Other historians, notably Mike Davis and John Newsinger, provide ample documentary evidence to explode the myth of imperial beneficence. '[A]pologists', writes Newsinger, deny that 'imperial rule rests on coercion, on the policeman torturing a suspect and on the soldier blowing up houses'. Mike Davis documents the horrors of 'free trade' in India, which led to the deaths of 29 million people by famine.[3]

By the 1920s, the British Empire was all but over and the

American Empire (which denies that it is an Empire) was rising. For British policymakers, like the Milner Group, the logical conclusion was to integrate with the US. In 1920, Britain's main planners of the League of Nations stated their intention to use international force when desired: 'We wish to assist and develop the simple mechanism of international dealing ... without mortgaging our freedom of action and judgement under an international Covenant'. Lord Milner's publication, *The Round Table*, expressed the Group's desire to use 'the League to provide us with the machinery for United British action in foreign affairs ... A settlement based on ideal principles and poetic justice can be permanently applied and maintained only by a world government to which all nations will subordinate their private interests'.[4]

As the Milner groups were established, American money began pouring in to the Royal Institute of International Affairs (Chatham House), a think-tank (with ties to the Foreign and Commonwealth Office) whose American equivalent is the Council on Foreign Relations (CFR). Celebrating the 75th anniversary of Chatham House, director Sir Laurence Martin said: 'Seventy-five years ago the founders ... believed that a new world order was coming into being'. Noting the bourgeoning post-WWI relationship between the US and Britain, Martin explained that '[t]he core aim of the new Institute, and [the CFR] was ... to bring into this partnership politicians, businessmen and the more serious representatives of the media in ... confidential discussion and collaborative study'.[5]

At international bodies like the Word Trade Organization, the US, Canada, Japan, and the EU 'have set the agenda and ... been able to advance trade liberalization at a pace they are comfortable with', wrote future Trade Secretary, Vince Cable, in a 1996 paper for Chatham House. Cable outlined 'the new agenda for trade' across the world. Cable identified several factors that 'did immense damage to the nineteenth-century liberal economic order between 1914 and 1945'. They include the two World Wars, 'the intellectual respectability of state control' over economies, and 'economic autarky' (i.e. independence). State-intervention in the economy is fine for the powerful, but not for others. Britain's nineteenth century model of 'free trade' required a strong state to finance corporations and impose beneficial regulations, as well as 'gunboat diplomacy' to weaken state-controls in foreign markets.[6]

After WWII, the US and Britain shaped the international economic order with the Bretton Woods system of regulated international capital. This was essential for post-war reconstruction. Even in 'the relatively open' Organization for Economic Cooperation and Development economies, i.e., the rich countries, 'it took almost 30 post-war years of rebuilding the global economy to reach the level of integration through trade which existed in 1913'. Once the pattern had been laid, the Bretton Woods system was dismantled and the 'free trade' agenda of de- and un-regulated capital was back on the agenda.[7]

... Is the Old Trade Agenda

So what is 'free trade'?

The *Cambridge History of the British Empire* notes: 'The position of Britain in world affairs ... governed her attitude to imperial economic policy ... [and] made it difficult for her to contemplate any substantial change', hence the pursuit of status quo policies. 'Her sense of her own needs and interests had not changed. Free trade still seemed to her essential if she were to keep her position'.[8]

Historian Barrie M. Ratcliffe writes that, as Britain was the major power of the day, its policymakers could afford to adopt 'free trade', whereas other European countries, notably France, regarded Britain's 'free trade' mechanisms as 'a siren beckoning a less developed Europe to destruction'. French Prime Minister, Adolphe Thiers, 'described free trade as a weapon the British hoped to use to increase their domination of world markets', particularly in India, which Prime Minister Disraeli described as 'the jewel in the crown' of Empire.[9]

Prior to conquest, Indian and Chinese trade accounted for 60%

of global GDP. In 1600, 'a number of [English] merchants formed themselves into a society for their mutual benefit and protection', securing a charter 'for the security of their Eastern traffic'. British industrialists, traders, and politicians took control of quality Indian goods, including means of production, and reduced and eliminated domestic production. 'For the possession of these commodities, the manufacturers of Europe had been discouraged', a pro-'free trade' study continues, referring to the imposition of several manufacturing laws. This led to a decline in British and Indian living standards, killing 29 million Indians by famine in the last quarter of the nineteenth century alone, as documented by Mike Davis.[10]

In the 1950s, when 'decolonization' was inevitable, Gallagher and Robinson wrote that one of 'the most common political technique[s] of British expansion was the treaty of free trade and friendship made with or imposed upon a weaker state'. The authors cite treaties with Persia (1836 and 1857), Turkey (1838 and 1861), and Japan (1858), and 'the favours extracted from Zanzibar, Siam and Morocco, the hundreds of anti-slavery treaties signed with crosses by African chiefs', which enabled the British 'to carry forward trade with these regions', as in the case of the Dutch West Indies, whose former slave-owning sugar producers were undercut by slave-owning producers in Cuba and Brazil.[11]

'[B]y 1840 Britain could no longer produce enough food to sustain its population', writes historian Lawrence James. In the Dutch West Indies, for instance, sugar producers, who no longer benefited from slave labour, competed in deregulated markets, like British Guyana, which was 'parcelled into small-holdings for former slaves, who became subsistence farmers'. Historian Peter Harnetty notes 'the victory of free trade in 1846', advocated by economists of the Manchester School and pushed for by the British Board of Trade. 'In the age of so-called anti-imperialism, existing colonies were retained, new ones obtained, and new spheres of influence set up', writes Harnetty. 'It necessitated linking underdeveloped areas with British foreign trade ... [T]he general strategy of this development was to convert these areas into complementary satellite economies providing raw materials and food for Great Britain, and also provide widening markets for its manufacturers'.[12]

Defining 'Free Trade'

If we are to understand America's global objectives, and thus modern Britain's place in the 'new world order', it is necessary to understand 'free trade'.

In the latter part of its 'second empire' (post-1840), Britain 'artificially, and arguably unfairly,' allowed its producers to sell goods in foreign countries at prices lower than domestic producers. Known as 'dumping', the aim is to drive down profits to the point where competitors are destroyed. In industry, where in certain cases mass-production is more cost-efficient than specialization, and where overproduction is a problem at home, surplus products can be 'dumped' abroad, 'without affecting the monopolistic prices received at home', write economic historians Thompson and Magee. 'This is precisely the situation that the combination of British free trade and foreign protectionism provided for the foreign producer'.[13]

Harnetty writes that in India, 'free trade' advocates argued that 'duties must be abolished, thereby both enhancing the supply of cotton for British industry and enlarging the market in India for British manufactured goods'. In India, experimental cotton cultivation and railway construction were 'state interference'. The Governor-General Council 'appealed for the elimination of differential duties, whereby foreign goods entered India at a higher rate than British goods'. Ratcliffe concludes that the importance of 'free trade' was championed by publications like the *Economist*. '[T]ariff reductions coincided with the greater confidence generated by the re-establishment of stable regimes'. 'Stable regimes' was and is a code-word for governments who do what they are told by Britain and America.[14]

In short, 'free trade' relies on the labour of foreign and domestic working poor, especially foreign. It entails large tax-payer subsidies of otherwise failing industries and social engineering projects, like the railways of India, which were designed to maximize import/export efficiency for British producers. 'Free trade' is inherently non-competitive for state-protected businesses and highly competitive for foreign businesses and workers, often driving down wages. Since the financialization of the Euro-American economies in the 1970s, international organizations, notably the World Trade Organization (WTO), have been the vehicles through which 'free trade' is codified. Bi- and multi-lateral arrangements, including the Euro-American Transatlantic Trade and Investment Partnership, the US-Asia Transpacific Trade and Investment Partnership, and the Broader Middle East and North Africa Initiative are taking the place of the WTO as 'emerging' powers like China and India gain too much influence.

In whose 'National Interest'?

By 1997, the United States military felt powerful enough to commit America to a doctrine of global militarism known as 'Full Spectrum Dominance'. This involves America's orbiting of space weapons (like the X-37B), covering the skies of the world with drones (Predators and others), maintaining and constructing hundreds of large and small military bases (like Camp Anaconda in Iraq), expanding a global surveillance dragnet (Total Information Awareness, as they call it), and, perhaps most dangerously, threatening Russia with a missile system based in Europe.[15]

The aim is to 'to protect US interests and investment'. The Space Command's *Vision for 2020* document announcing these plans goes on to say that 'the globalization of the world economy' will create a two-tiered class structure of 'haves' and 'have-nots'. Full Spectrum Dominance aims to ensure Russian and Chinese compliance to 'free market' principles, hence America's 'Asia Pivot', a strategy designed to encircle China, and its construction of the missile system in Eastern Europe, pointed at Russia.[16]

When American policymakers refer to such actions as defending their 'national interests', they are referring to defending the interests of a narrow sector of the population, commonly referred to by activists as the 'one percent'. A report by the Carnegie Endowment says: 'U.S. wages have stagnated for the past three decades, while the workforce has also faced an erosion of job security, health care, and pension plans' for the poor, in contrast to the rich, who are richer now than at any time since the 1920s. 'This increasing economic insecurity has coincided with rapid globalization', as the Space Command documented predicted.[17]

The role of former powers, notably Britain and France, in this 'new world order' is to maximize their 'national interests' (meaning the interests of their wealthy sectors) without straying too far from America's overall strategy. Minus a brief spat in which President Jacques Chirac refused to commit troops to the invasion of Iraq, 'Relations between the United States and France are active and friendly. The two countries share common values and have parallel policies on most political, economic, and security issues', says the US State Department. Following 9/11, says the US Council on Foreign Relations, 'leaders on both sides of the Atlantic extol their common values and pledge solidarity between France and the United States'.[18]

Despite talk of the 'special relationship' between Britain and America coming to an end, the same sources say that '[t]he United States has no closer ally than the United Kingdom, and British foreign policy emphasizes close coordination with the United States' (State Department). Britain and America often work together on secret wars. Both train and arm the Rapid Action Battalion death-squad in Bangladesh, for instance, and both worked to overthrow the government of Somalia in late-2006. However, Britain's elite can and do pursue their interests independently, such as arming and training the Sri Lankan Army and invading the Falklands in 1982 – a move which found no significant support from the US.[19]

As in the case of training and organizing a proxy rebel militia to overthrow President Assad of Syria, the British and French also cooperate over shared interests, to the detriment of their populations. *Par exemple*:

Four years after the Anglo-French Treaty (2010), the French company Dassault and the Anglo-American BAE Systems announced that they had been awarded £120 million by the French and British governments to build a new drone to 'surveill[e], mark targets, gather intelligence, deter adversaries and carry out strikes in hostile territories'. Public opinion polls suggest that many members of the French and British publics alike agree that military spending should be reduced in favour of social spending.[20]

Foreign Policy as 'Necessary Exploitation'

In 1997, Chatham House published *British Foreign Policy: Challenges and Choices for the 21st Century*. The book was sponsored by numerous big businesses, including British banks and oil companies. Although it is available to the public, few copies were published. It was, rather, intended for policymakers and businesspeople. Its existence and concurrent obscurity implies much about how important books and documents are suppressed by the mainstream media.

The authors explain that 'a successful foreign policy requires a degree of secrecy and duplicity, a willingness to employ spies, engage in bribery, threaten, even use force, compromise principles, pursue clandestine, sometimes illegal, operations, and support dubious regimes'. The book appeared at a time when American 'humanitarian intervention' in Somalia (1992), Haiti (1994), and the US-British refusal to intervene in Rwanda (1994), was evoked to justify military interventions (i.e., invasions). 'Governments ... are expected to downplay the interests of humanity as a whole (except when those interests overlap with the national interest)', the authors explain.[21]

Ergo, Britain illegally bombed northern Iraq in the 1990s, supposedly to protect Iraqi Kurds, whilst simultaneously arming and training the Turkish military to ethnically cleanse Turkish Kurds across the border. With few exceptions, the media portrayed the bombing of Iraq as humanitarian intervention and suppressed Turkey's ethnic cleansing of Kurds.[22]

'[T]he issue is not "what does justice and the law require?", but "how much can we get away with?"', ask the Chatham House authors. '[P]ublic emotion' aroused by reports of poverty, inequality, starvation, etc., 'is not always a sensible guide to foreign policy-making'. The general public are 'inchoate, fickle, unreasonable, inconsistent', and express 'arbitrary' concerns. Noting the reality of child labour and the alliance with murderous regimes, such as those of Saudi Arabia, China, Nigeria, and Indonesia, the authors conclude that '[e]xploitation may be a *necessary* stage in the evolution of capitalism' (emphasis in original): 'capitalism' being an inaccurate description of 'free trade', which they refer to as 'the birth pangs of industrialization'.[23]

The Chatham House book informed the Blair government's *Strategic Defence Review* (1998). The latter explains that '[w]e depend on foreign countries for supplies of raw materials, above all oil', and that '[d]efence serves the aims of foreign and security policy', making Britain 'resolute in standing up for our own interests ... [T]here are opportunities to be exploited'. According to the *Strategic Defence Review*, the Royal Air Force, like the Navy, exists as 'a coercive instrument to support political aims'. By adopting 'humanitarian intervention' as an ideological justification for aggression, 'We now have a real opportunity to devise a security posture which will support and underpin all Britain's interests overseas, in a world where democracy and liberal economic systems continue to spread' – 'democracy' in the sense that Britain's allies, the Saudi monarchy, is democratic.[24]

Comparing the content of these documents to the ideas proposed in the nineteenth century demonstrates the similarity of today's policies with those of the past.

The *Defence White Paper* (2003) states that 'military force exists to serve political or strategic ends', which are not contingent on international law: 'we need to be realistic about the limitations of the UN and the difficulties of translating broad consensus on goals into specific actions, particularly where proactive military intervention is concerned'. These Blair-era policies continued to the Tory-Liberal 'coalition' government era and beyond.[25]

A 2010 UK Ministry of Defence white paper says: 'we cannot simply take a narrow, territorial-based view of our security. Our economy is exceptionally open to trade with many parts of the world and relies on the free passage of goods, services and information'. It notes that '[a] stable international order is essential if those interests are to prosper'. As noted above, 'stability' is code for regimes doing as they are told. The Egyptian regime, for instance, is highly unstable because it oppresses its population to the point of revolution. However, the regime grants Europe and America unhindered access to the important Suez Canal, hence it is a 'stable' regime.[26]

The MoD's *Future of Character of Conflict* (2010) paper says: 'The access to resources (energy, food or water) will drive states' security interests; control over these resources and their methods of distribution through the global commons will be a critical feature of conflict in the international system. It may dictate why we fight, where we fight and thus how we fight'. It goes on to note that by 2029, 'The UK will be critically dependent upon energy imports and securing them will be non-discretionary', hence wars in resource-rich and strategically important regions. The document defines 'globalization' as 'the spread of capital, trade, intellectual property, economic activity, wealth and resources', adding: 'It also encompasses the guaranteed access to and exploitation of these resources in developing states' – and for obvious reasons: a 'developed' state, like the UK, is not going to attack a peer, like France. Aggression (e.g., Iraq, Libya) and proxy wars (e.g., Syria, Sri Lanka) are limited to use against weak countries and groups within them.[27]

Preparing the *National Security Strategy* 2015, a high-level committee notes that '[t]he freedom that Britain has enjoyed to engage [in war has] ... been contingent on the fact that state-based threats to UK vital interests have been weak or non-existent'. The report refers to the situation as 'a nice problem to have: international politics has rarely been so benign at the major power level'. This is a rather different picture than the one presented by the media: that Britons are under constant threat of annihilation from terrorists.

The report concludes that 'economic globalization and interdependence ... produces relative power shifts', at which point it 'can actually be an underlying cause of war', hence the importance of bi- and multi-lateral 'defence' agreements, like Anglo-French Defence and Security Co-Operation Treaty (2010), signed around the time that both parties were training and arming the anti-Assad rebels in Syria and a year before both parties joined NATO's bombing of Libya. Britain supplied logistical help for France's unlawful bombing of Mali in 2012.[28]

How wars are sold

There are two types of war: open and secret. Sometimes they overlap, as in the case of Libya, where British special forces secretly trained rebels to overthrow President Gaddafi. When the rebels proved too weak, NATO provided them with air support under the pretext of humanitarian intervention. With open wars, there are two types of justification: self-defence and humanitarian intervention. In the post-9/11 era, Britain engaged in four open wars: Afghanistan (2001), Iraq (2003), Congo (2003), and Libya (2011). Two were launched under the banner of self-defence (Afghanistan and Iraq) and two as humanitarian interventions. With the exception of Congo,[*] these were big wars which required so much military power that they could not be concealed.

---

[*] The war in Congo is the worst in Africa, but Britain's role is comparatively small; it is not involved as much as it was/is in Iraq, for instance.

A Ministry of Defence projection out to 2040 (sponsored by oil companies and banks) says that the public must have 'perceptions of moral legitimacy' when it comes to war. Chatham House conferences held in 2010 by policymakers, scholars and business leaders from weapons companies, banks and the oil industry, culminated with a series of reports, concluding that voters 'will not actively call for a more effective foreign policy', therefore: 'The government should define its international mission as managing global risks on behalf of British citizens', hence the invocation of the alleged threats from 'al-Qaeda', the Islamic State, and so forth, by the media and policymakers. It is even better for the latter when wars can be waged in secret and by proxy.[29]

In the case of secret wars, the media remains silent. A few scattered articles about the SAS operating in Colombia have been published in the *Guardian*. The *Daily Mail* reported that Britain had trained a proxy force to overthrow the government of Somalia in late-2006. The BBC and others briefly covered revelations that Britain was training a death-squad in Bangladesh in 2011. There has been a culture of total silence about the fact that Britain armed and trained the Sri Lankan Army during its 2009 ethnic cleansing of 40,000 Tamils.

'Fickle' & 'Inchoate'?

Like most populations around the world, the British tend to oppose war unless they are exposed to media(ted) atrocities, like those of the so-called Islamic State, or panicked into self-defence, against for instance Saddam Hussein with his non-existent weapons of mass destruction. YouGov finds that 'polling since [summer 2014] has shown a steady increase in British support for airstrikes against ISIS, rising from 37% approve versus 36% disapprove in early August, to 58% approve versus 25% disapprove by early October [2014]'. Support for bombing occurred after 1) media horror stories of beheadings and 2) the use of drones, which a) protect British service personnel from harm and b) do not show the dreadful consequences of civilian casualties, thanks to a media-managed campaign. But fear-mongering doesn't always work: even at the second height of the cold war (in the 1980s), majorities thought that Britain should 'be more like Sweden and Switzerland' and pursue neutrality when it comes to international affairs.[30]

Support for the occupation of Afghanistan plunged to 22% in the final years of the war. Support for the invasion of Iraq in 2003 never peaked above 38% (to cite the most pro-war estimates), despite the fact that in the run-up to the invasion and in the following months, the majority of BBC coverage was pro-war, as it had been during the Gulf War of 1991. In 1999, the UK Ministry of Defence said that its propaganda campaign in Serbia ('information operations') would serve as a model for future wars, as it did in 2011, when the British were inundated with unsubstantiated claims about Muammar Gaddafi primed to commit 'ethnic cleansing'. Under half the British public supported the UK's role in the NATO bombing of Libya.[31]

The turning point came with Syria, when constituent pressure forced a no vote on the issue of bombing in 2013, even though the government had produced an atrocity video claiming that the regime of Bashar al-Assad had used chemical weapons (the validity of which is disputed by security experts). What the overwhelming majority of Britons don't know is that Britain has been at war with Syria since 2010, when it planned, and a year later instigated, a proxy army invasion. In Britain, the Armed Forces as an institution is respected, as are its servicepeople. Public attitudes toward the British Armed Forces is generally high, exceeding 80% in most polls. The primary reasons are a) respect for those who risk (and who are thought to risk) their lives for political decisions and b) the belief that the Armed Forces exist to keep the country safe. The internal documents analysed here paint a very different picture.[32]

Part I of this book is about the Middle East and North Africa. Chapter 1 exposes the thousands of terrorists organized by the US, Britain, and France in Syria with the aim of overthrowing President Assad. Chapter 2 documents how MI6 and the SAS hijacked Libya's

Arab Spring for the purpose of overthrowing President Gaddafi. Chapter 3 documents the evolution of the so-called Islamic State. Chapter 4 exposes the US-British-Israeli sponsoring of terrorists in Iran and argues that professed concerns over Iran's civil nuclear programme are a cover for opposing Iranian energy independence. Chapter 5 provides a brief history of the war in Yemen, revealing the British military's war against socialists in that country. Chapter 6 provides evidence that Britain is engaged in a secret drone war, of which counterterrorism is a low priority.

Part II is about the world beyond the Middle East. Chapter 7 argues that the situation in Ukraine, in which Britain is significantly involved, poses a grave danger to the world. Chapter 8 exposes Britain's culpability in the deaths of 40,000 Tamil civilians in Sri Lanka. Chapter 9 reveals the shocking levels of human rights abuses in Colombia, in which the UK is intimately involved, including chemical warfare. Chapter 10 uncovers British support for Indonesia's illegal annexation of West Papua. Chapter 11 explores the secret war against Somalia, in which the SAS trained Ethiopian rebels to oust a progressive government. Chapter 12 documents the use of death-squads in Bangladesh – trained by the UK – for social control.

Part I

THE MIDDLE EAST AND NORTH AFRICA

Chapter 1

Syria – 'Illegal but necessary'

This chapter is about how the British, French and American intelligence services conspired to wreck Syria. Their aim was (and continues to be) 'reform' in the country, meaning opening Syria's state-run economy to Euro-American investors. The Euro-American intelligence services employed disaffected young men (primarily) to do their dirty work. This demonstrates that, as the MoD document quoted below suggests, the deep state has no qualms about using terrorists when it suits them.

In August 2013, the British government was narrowly defeated in a Commons vote on a motion to bomb Syria. The human rights group Reprieve discovered that, beginning September 2014, British pilots 'embedded' with US forces bombed Islamic State targets in the north of the country, near the Turkish border, killing and injuring untold numbers of civilians. At least this time, the Cameron government waited until MPs said 'no' to war before bombing – in the case of Libya, the Cameron government voted on going to war two days *after* British bombs fell on Tripoli.[1]

The bombing of Syria is a violation of international law, as codified in the UN Charter (1945), which allows for military intervention under two conditions: individual and collective self-defence (Article 51) and with UN Security Council authorization. Kings College professor of War Studies, and international law expert, Theo Farrell, points this out, but concludes that the US bombing is 'probably illegal but ... necessary', in keeping with Ministry of Defence doctrine quoted in the Introduction: that we will act illegally when we want to.[2]

In the case of Syria, the closest thing to authorization is UNSCR

2170, which condemns the human rights abuses of all opposition forces, including the Islamic State, but gives no green-light to bomb. The bombing followed numerous statements by military experts that using violence against the Islamic State was not the solution. Former counterterrorism head at MI6, Richard Barrett, said that bombing will 'play to the [jihadist] narrative that these bad regimes [i.e., Assad's] are being supported by outside powers and, therefore, if you get too close to overthrowing them, the outside powers will come and beat you up'.[3]

Because ISIS appears to receive its ideological support from the regime of Saudi Arabia – whose brutality it mimics – W. Patrick Lang, former head of the Middle East and South Asia division at the US Defense Intelligence Agency, said: 'If you wish to really go after the Islamic State, a group of [Islamic] scholars [in the Middle East] can launch a campaign and denounce them for their view of Islam. You could attack this thing by undercutting its foundations'. Reporting on an anti-IS summit held by the Muslim World League in 2015, the *Atlantic* notes US opposition to a consistent narrative, citing 'the divergence in messaging from Washington and Mecca'.[4]

Even the now-weakened US-UK-French allies, the Free Syrian Army (FSA), agree. FSA spokesman, Hussam al-Marie, said: 'Airstrikes against ISIS inside Syria will not be helpful. Airstrikes will not get rid of ISIS. Airstrikes are like just tickling ISIS'. Metin Turcan, formerly of the Turkish military, said: 'I don't think the US air attacks will produce definitive results. They may disrupt IS operational capacity temporarily, but will not eliminate it'.[5]

Still, the media overlook the bigger picture: that Britain, France and the US have been at war with Syria, in secret, since 2010, and that the huge 'al-Qaeda'-linked terror network created by the secret services to depose Gaddafi and Assad gave IS a much-needed boost (see Chapter 3). This proxy war is also illegal, as it violates the sovereignty of Syria: and we needn't wonder how Britain would react if Assad organized an armed militia comprised of, say, far-right extremists to overthrow the Cameron government. Britain's secret proxy war has led to the destruction of much of the country, the creation of 4 million external refugees (adding to the 5 million Palestinian refugees and 2 million external Iraqi refugees in the region), and the deaths of 210,000 civilians.[6]

The New Middle East: 'Manufacturing Democracy'

In a document from 2005, US intelligence predicted that Arabs would rise to overthrow their largely unelected regimes, as they did in late-2010/early-2011, later known as the Arab Awakening or Arab Spring. One military document even predicted the date. This happened in Egypt's Tahrir Square. The uprisings were a result of decades of oppression and joblessness. They coincided with an EU-US plan to model the Middle East and North Africa on the European Union. The US military-linked Rand Corporation even published a plan for hijacking genuine reform movements, notably Egypt's *Kifaya* (Enough!) and steering them to US interests. As certain regimes (notably Mubarak's of Egypt and Ben Ali's of Tunisia) were no longer following US plans to denationalise resources and lower tariffs for export, Euro-American businesses wanted to get rid of them.[7]

Documents from the US Congress, the Carnegie Endowment, and the US military provide the evidence. The 2005 military document notes that, following the destruction of Iraq, the US had lost such standing in the 'Muslim world' that internal revolutions, as opposed to US-led military regime changes, could be fomented in the region by 'manufacturing democracy', in their words, and creating a 'domino effect', where one former ally would fall after another. Long before the Arab Spring, Carnegie Endowment scholars wrote: 'Except in Syria and Libya, economic liberalization has been an integral part of the policies of Arab governments at least since the early 1990s'. It later emerged that Tunisia's Ben Ali and Egypt's Mubarak had halted reforms.[8]

A 2010 British House of Commons document says that Syria's President, Bashar al-Assad, 'was thought to be a reformer ... Economic reforms were enacted ... but the economy is still dominated by the state'. The 'state' means not dominated by European and American corporations. This, says the document, hampered Euro-Syrian trade, the kind of which is essential for the New Middle East project. Oil journals said the same about Gaddafi: that Gaddafi post-2004 'reform process was highly orchestrated, in effect an affair of marginal and cosmetic rather than radical or wholesale changes'.[9]

The Proxy War: 'Difficult to Control'

So that 'manufactured democracy' would triumph over real democracy, regime change necessitated collaboration with extremists. In early-2010, before the civil war, the UK Ministry of Defence admitted that terrorist proxies would be used to fight future wars and that they may get out of hand: '[states] *will* seek to distance themselves by use of proxy forces, cyber-attack, as well as covert and clandestine methods ... [Many] are *likely* to employ irregular tactics including terrorism, while concealing and refuting links to state sponsors in order to preserve their freedom of action and maintaining a degree of deniability for the state ... [They] are *likely* to prove difficult to control over time' (emphases in original). As we shall see in Chapter 3, the growth of IS is a prime example of how terrorist proxies can get out of control.[10]

It has long been known that in the late-1970s, the British and American secret services created an extensive network of Muslim terrorists from Afghanistan, Algeria, China, Egypt, Pakistan, the Philippines and elsewhere, to 'draw the Russians into the Afghan trap', in the words of President Jimmy Carter's National Security Advisor, Brzezinski. These terrorists were later called 'al-Qaeda' by the same organizations that created them (see Chapter 5). To create a New Middle East, the secret services appear to have organized a contemporary network on a comparable scale.

By 2012, there were three major opposition forces fighting in Syria: 'al-Qaeda' (as 'Al-Nusra Front'); the Islamic State (an 'al-

Qaeda' offshoot); and the comparatively secular Free Syrian Army. The majority of opposition fighters, foreign and domestic, are Sunni. The majority of foreign fighters (approximately 10,000) entered Syria through Iraq and Turkey. 'Turkish authorities have reportedly made no effort to halt that flow', says the UK House of Commons Library. According to the international press (notably not the British press), Assad accused Turkey of sponsoring the extremists, thereby hampering a UN ceasefire in the battle for Aleppo.[11]

It is unclear who, but many terrorists are trained in Turkish, Jordanian, and Libyan camps. Foreigners include Muslims from Afghanistan, Albania, Algeria, Australia, Azerbaijan, Belgium, Bosnia-Herzegovina, Britain, Cambodia, Chechnya, China (Uighurs/ Turkmens), Denmark, Egypt, France, Germany, Iraq, Ireland, Italy, Jordan, Kosovo, Kyrgyzstan, Lebanon (Sunnis), Libya, Macedonia, Montenegro, the Netherlands, Norway, Pakistan, Philippines, Saudi Arabia, Serbia (the Sandzak region), Sweden, Tajikistan, Tunisia, the USA and Uzbekistan. The extent of US-British support to Islamic State elements is unclear.[12]

Referring to events in 2010, prior to the Arab Spring, former French foreign minister, Roland Dumas, said: 'top British officials ... confessed to me ... that they were preparing something in Syria ... Britain was organizing an invasion of rebels into Syria'. It was later revealed in the British media that MI6 drafted a plan to invade Syria with a 'rebel army' of 100,000 fighters, indicating the breadth of MI6's terrorist connections. Dumas's allegations were not reported in the British media (save a single *Guardian* article by Nafeez Ahmed, whose 'Earth Insight' blog was later 'ended'). Media coverage of the rebel invasion plan was spun to suggest that humanitarian concerns against Assad's brutality were the prime motive.[13]

As a result of what appears to be a botched SAS operation in Libya, and subsequent media damage-limitation, we know that MI6 had been training anti-Gaddafi terrorists in Libya since October 2010, four months before the start of the Libyan Arab Spring. The *Daily Mail* reported on one 'Tom Smith', an MI6 agent who had been living on a farm and facilitating contacts between anti-Gaddafi terrorists and the SAS. This is important for Syria because Libya has been a conduit through which arms have flowed to the anti-Assad terrorists.[14]

As the plans for Syria were implemented, British politicians facilitated diplomatic support for the rebels. In October 2011, the UK's Middle East Minister, Alistair Burt, said: 'The establishment of the Syrian National Council' (SNC, which opposes Assad and whose military wing is the Free Syrian Army, FSA), 'marked a positive step in bringing together a broad range of Syrian opposition [sic] representatives'. Burt met with SNC representatives to discuss 'the importance of establishing a shared vision for the future of Syria and a credible plan of how to move peacefully to an alternative political system'.[15]

The Elite UK Forces website published details of the 'peaceful' transition:

> Reports from late November [2011] ... state that British Special forces have met up with members of the Free Syrian Army ... The apparent goal of this initial contact was to establish the rebel forces' strength and to pave the way for any future training operations. More recent reports have stated that British and French Special Forces have been actively training members of the FSA, from a base in Turkey. Some reports indicate that training is also taking place in locations in Libya and Northern Lebanon. British MI6 operatives and UKSF (SAS/SBS) [UK Special Forces (Special Air Service/Special Boat Service)] personnel have reportedly been training the rebels in urban warfare as well as supplying them with arms and equipment. US CIA operatives and special forces are believed to be providing communications assistance to the rebels.[16]

This was not reported in the British (or international) media. Whilst committing war crimes, including the indiscriminate killing of women and children, and terrorism, including car bombings, the FSA took Aleppo (and is struggling to hold it) and Idlib (before it fell to 'al-Qaeda's' Nusra Front) in Northern Syria, near the Turkish border.[17]

The British House of Commons Library says that, 'One Libyan/ Irish fighter [Mahdi al-Harati] heads the Umma Brigade ... [which] now numbers about 3,000 and is particularly strong on communications, logistics and heavy weaponry. The brigade is made up mainly of Syrians, with the Libyans in command and training roles'.[18] Al-Harati allegedly acquired €200,000 from the CIA. The *Sunday World* reports that Irish police officers were called after thieves took the money from al-Harati's apartment. Asked where he acquired such a sum, al-Harati said 'he had travelled to France, the United States and Qatar the previous month [October 2011] and that representatives of an intelligence agency in the States had given him a significant amount of cash to help Libya's efforts to topple [Gaddafi]'.[19]

One month later, the *Telegraph* reported that '[a]t the meeting' between the SNC and the UK-installed Libyan puppet government, 'the Syrians requested "assistance" from the Libyan representatives and were offered arms, and potentially volunteers'. A Libyan source said: 'There is something being planned to send weapons and even Libyan fighters to Syria'. An SNC campaigner, Wissam Taris, said: 'The Libyans are offering money, training and weapons to the Syrian National Council'. 'The Libyans' is code for the extremists organized by MI6 and the SAS (see Chapter 2).[20]

MI6 facilitated the armament of anti-Assad terrorists. '[A] secret agreement reached in early-2012 between the Obama and [Turkish Prime Minister] Erdoğan administrations ... was responsible for getting arms from Gaddafi's arsenals into Syria', says Seymour Hersh. '[F]unding came from Turkey, as well as Saudi Arabia and Qatar'. It was organized by 'the CIA, with the support of MI6 ... A number of front companies were set up in Libya, some under the cover of Australian entities'. Hersh goes on to note that '[r]etired

American soldiers, who didn't always know who was really employing them, were hired to manage procurement and shipping. The operation was run by [CIA director] David Petraeus'. Hersh notes that '[t]he involvement of MI6 enabled the CIA to evade the law by classifying the mission as a liaison operation'.[21]

In March 2013, the *Guardian* reported: 'Jordanian security sources say [a] training effort is led by the US, but involves British and French instructors ... [A] small number of [British] personnel, including special forces teams, have been in the country training the Jordanian military'. As we shall see, many anti-Assad rebels trained by the US in Jordan and Turkey defected to IS. According to details that emerged from a court case, one Bherlin Gildo of Sweden was arrested on terrorism charges while travelling from Copenhagen to Manila. He is accused of attending training camps between August 2012 and March 2013. The defence, led by Henry Blaxland, argued that pursuing the case would make information public concerning the extent of the British secret service's contacts with extremists, so it was dropped.[22]

Britain, France, and America have succeeded in turning Syria into what the Home Secretary, Theresa May, describes as 'an unprecedented concentration of the terrorist threat'.[23]

Chapter 2

Libya – 'Orchestrated unrest'

Following a similar plan to that which was implemented in Syria, MI6 invoked a blueprint which they had attempted to implement in the mid-1990s, to stir 'orchestrated unrest' in the less secular parts of Libya by working with terrorists and revolutionaries. The purpose was to denationalize Colonel Gaddafi's oil resources. After the attempted coup, Gaddafi made 'cosmetic' reforms, as did Assad in his country. By 2010, with regional change plotted by the Euro-American secret services, MI6 began training terrorists to hijack the democratic reforms sweeping the region, known as the Arab Spring. Here, we document how they did it and how forcing change led, in part, to the so-called 'Islamic State' group becoming more powerful.

The 2011 Parliamentary debate about whether to bomb Libya happened two days after the bombing had started, in keeping with Whitehall's centralized idea of democracy. During the debate, the leader of the Labour Party, Ed Miliband (former Energy Secretary), told Parliament: 'We do not seek commercial gain or geopolitical advantage, and we are not intending to occupy Libya or seize her natural resources'. Two years earlier, his brother David, then Foreign Secretary, told Parliament: 'With the largest proven oil reserves in Africa and extensive gas reserves, Libya is potentially a major energy source for the future. We work hard to support British business in Libya, as we do worldwide'.[1]

As NATO bombs fell on Libyan children, Prime Minister Cameron, said: 'Libya is ... one of the richest [countries] in Africa. Its proven oil reserves are the ninth largest in the world and in relation to their GDP, bigger than Saudi Arabia'. The British House of Commons Library report, *Energy Security*, which predicts a 'new scramble for Africa', states: 'African oil 2005: Proven reserves: 114 billion barrels; 9.5% of world total – concentrated in Libya, Nigeria and Algeria'.[2]

After the invasion of Iraq in 2003, Gaddafi capitulated and relinquished Libya's chemical and biological stockpiles. In 2004, Tony Blair led the famous deal in the desert, wherein BP and other oil and gas companies won contracts to explore in Libya for the first time since 1969, when Gaddafi came to power and nationalized the resources. Secular Gaddafi's Islamist enemies, the leaders of the Libyan Islamic Fighting Group, were betrayed by their former allies, the British and Americans, and turned over to Gaddafi's secret police for torture. However, energy journals lamented that by 2010, Gaddafi's privatization pledge was merely cosmetic, and his brand of socialism (the *Jamahiriya*) remained intact.[3]

In the name of stopping ethnic cleansing, for which no evidence was ever presented, NATO, by its own records, bombed over 3,400 civilian targets. The destruction killed 50,000 people, wrought $200 billion-worth of damage to the infrastructure, provoked an actual ethnic cleansing of tens of thousands of black Libyans by rebel forces supported by the West, caused the deaths of hundreds of boat refugees, and fractured the political structure in favour of Muslim gangsters – many allied to the US and Britain.[4]

As with Syria, the proxy rebel invasion and bombing were violations of international law. UNSCR 1970 forbade providing material support to the rebels, which Britain had as early as October, 2010. UNSCR 1973 was widely reported as legitimating NATO action, but nowhere does the resolution grant NATO authorization to bomb (or do anything in Libya). Indeed, experts advised a Parliamentary committee that NATO's role was illegal: 'the use of NATO air power to support offensive operations by rebel forces against those of Gaddafi falls outside UNSCR 1973's authority, and thus do not appear to comply with international law'.[5]

Background

In 1994, after fighting in Afghanistan, where the CIA and MI6 had created a terrorist network which it later called 'al-Qaeda', one Abd al-Baset Azzouz left Libya, his home country, to live in London, where he appears to have been protected by the British government. In 1995, MI6 learned of a Libyan coup plot against Gaddafi. At that point in history, Gaddafi remained an enemy of the state, so Britain supported the coup. The plot was readied for February 1996 and devised by secular colonels within Gaddafi's military circle. A leaked MI6 report says: 'It would begin with attacks on a number of military and security installations including the military installation at Tarhuna. There would also be orchestrated civil unrest in Benghazi, Misrata and Tripoli'. The report notes that '[c]oup plotters are not associated with Islamic fundamentalists', like Azzouz, 'who were fermenting unrest in Benghazi'. However, the coup plotters 'had had some limited contact with the fundamentalists, whom [MI6 informant 'Tunworth'] described as a mix of Libya veterans who served in Afghanistan', i.e., likely to be old CIA-MI6 contacts, 'and Libyan students'.[6]

There were two coup plots: a secular one led by Gaddafi's inner circle and an Islamic one led by extremists in Benghazi. In 2010, when MI6 started training anti-Gaddafi rebels, Benghazi was a major base for the operation, indicating that Benghazi was a hotbed of extremism. The MI6 report on the 1996 coup says that the plotters wanted to see Libya decentralized and federally run.[7]

Richard Bartlett and David Watson were MI6 agents, allegedly involved in the operations. Watson is said to have worked with the Libya contact, 'Tunworth', who provided information from within the Libyan Islamic Fighting Group (LIFG), the organization referred to in the MI6 report as the Benghazi-based extremist group. In 1995, MI6 chose to work with the extremists in Benghazi, which had close connections with Osama bin Laden through its leaders, Abu Abdullah al-Sadiq (a.k.a. Belhaj, who was later betrayed by MI6) and Anas al-Liby. The British government protected al-Liby, who is described by the US Congress as 'the builder of al-Qaeda's network in Libya'. MI6 financed the anti-Gaddafi LIFG to the tune of £100,000. The coup failed and Gaddafi launched attacks on the extremists, culminating with the infamous Abu Salim prison massacre.[8]

A more efficient version of the 1996 coup was orchestrated by the CIA and MI6 in 2010, completed in 2011, leading to the bombing of Libya by NATO.

Khalifa Haftar led the anti-Gaddafi rebellion in 2011. The *Jamestown Monitor* notes that in 1998, 'with strong backing from the Central Intelligence Agency', Colonel Haftar founded the National Front for the Salvation of Libya's armed wing. For nearly 20 years, Haftar was an ex-pat, living near the CIA headquarters in Langley, Virginia. In 2001, Libya's head of intelligence, Moussa Koussa, allegedly started working for MI6 and the CIA as a double-agent. In late-September 2001, former NATO commander, General Wesley Clark, saw a memo which read: 'we're going to take out seven countries in five years, starting with Iraq, and then Syria, Lebanon, Libya, Somalia, Sudan and, finishing off, Iran'.[9]

Classified documents reveal that MI6 'monitored LIFG members since their arrival in Britain following a failed attempt to kill Gaddafi in 1996, and understood their aim was the replacement of his regime with an Islamic state', says the *Guardian*. The document (dated 2005) says that in Libya, 'The extremists are now in the ascendancy, ... pushing the group towards a more pan-Islamic agenda inspired by AQ ['al-Qaeda']'. Ergo, British intelligence was perfectly aware that sponsoring extremists may lead to the push for a caliphate in the Levant. As will be documented in the next chapter, the rise of extremists in Libya and Syria transformed the Islamic State of Iraq from a weak, moribund phantom menace into a multinational terror force.[10]

Working with 'Al-Qaeda' in Libya

In 2006, having been protected from jail on potential terrorism-related charges by the British government for 12 years, Azzouz (mentioned above) was arrested in Manchester but released on bail. In 2009, he travelled to Pakistan, where he allegedly met Ayman al-Zawahiri, bin Laden's second-in-command, who ordered Azzouz to go to Libya and establish a jihadi training college in Derna. As we saw in the previous chapter, the *Daily Mail* reported on 'Tom, a British man who had been working on [a farm in Libya] as its administration supervisor for the past five months', i.e., beginning October 2010, months before the Arab Spring in Libya. '[I]t now seems certain that Tom, if that is his real name, is in fact an MI6 agent'.[11]

The *Daily Mail*'s evidence, and that of Roland Dumas and the UK MoD (both quoted in the previous chapter), is bolstered by the reaction of the UK's then-Secretary of Defence, Liam Fox, who told Parliament: 'It would simply be untrue ... to say that any policy-maker in the western world has been on top of the speed at which events have happened in the Middle East and North Africa'. Notice that Fox said that planners were not on top of the 'speed' of the uprisings, not the uprisings themselves.[12]

Terrorists from all over Libya, particularly Benghazi, began an armed uprising in February 2011. When Gaddafi sought to defend his country from Islamic extremists sponsored by the West, the propaganda machine claimed that Gaddafi was about to launch an 'ethnic cleansing' in Benghazi. The 'ethnic cleansing' was invoked to justify NATO's air support. When SAS troops invaded Libya in 2011, MI6 agent 'Tom Smith', who had been living on a 'farm' (training camp) and working with anti-Gaddafi rebels since October 2010, 'was there to collect them in his boss's Toyota pick-up and take them to the farm. The eight-man unit's mission was to link up with rebels fighting Colonel Gaddafi'. The article notes that 'Smith had converted a small conference room in the farm compound into what appeared to be a nerve-centre for the undercover SAS unit'.[13]

Beginning April 2011, with the armed uprising underway, former State Department worker Sidney Blumenthal, who maintained close connections with agents in the Middle East, emailed Obama's

Secretary of State, Hillary Clinton, to advise her that MI6 was 'game playing' in Libya. High-ranking associates of the Libyan National Council (LNC) told Blumenthal that Britain was 'using its intelligence services in an effort to dictate the actions of both the LNC and the Qaddafi regime'. The purpose was to tacitly support Gaddafi in case the rebels failed to overthrow him.[14]

'[D]espite early indications that they would provide clandestine military support to the rebels, neither the French nor the British government would provide enough equipment and training to defeat Qaddafi's forces', says Blumenthal. 'French, British and other European countries would be happy with a stalemate that leaves Libya divided into two rival entities'. Weighing all options, 'MI6 prepared to move [Gaddafi] to [Equatorial Guinea], which does not recognize the International Criminal Court' (*Telegraph*).[15]

Mohamed al-Guirtili, Ali Sallabi and Salem al-Shiki are alleged by Blumenthal to be 'leading Islamic figures who have taken refuge in London (and are close to the Moslem Brotherhood)'. They drafted 'a roadmap for organizing the role of the Islamist movement in the transition to a post-Qaddafi Libya'. Blumenthal tacitly alleges that the Islamists are ex-LIFG/'al-Qaeda' affiliates. The regime in Egypt (the Army) had a brutal internal record of crushing Muslim Brotherhood supporters, but played its own divide-and-rule game by training and arming anti-Gaddafi Islamists in Libya's East, helping to establish political structures.[16]

The emails also claim that the rebels were acquiring sophisticated anti-tank missiles from contacts in Niger and Mali. Blumenthal acknowledges that, 'While *Qaddafi's regime has been successful in suppressing the jihadist threat* in Libya, the current situation opens the door for jihadist resurgence', as indeed it did, with 'al-Qaeda' gaining ground in Libya, followed by the rise of the Islamic State (emphasis added).[17]

In May 2011, MI6 and the SAS began Operation Mermaid's Dawn, an anti-Gaddafi rebellion in Libya's capital, Tripoli. The

Telegraph reports that 'groups of young male volunteers ... travelled to Benghazi to learn the art of insurgent warfare from an international force of covert units composed of the British SAS and MI6 agents and troops from the French, Qatar and United Arab Emirates special forces'. As we have seen, Benghazi was the major centre of Islamic extremism. 'As well as training the rebels, the British government also covertly supplied 1,000 sets of body armour, advanced telecommunications equipment and night vision goggles ... Libyan volunteers were taught weapon training, street fighting and sabotage in a series of disused compounds', the report continues. 'While the rebels trained, hundreds of weapons, tons of ammunition and communications equipment were smuggled into Tripoli and hidden in secret arms dumps'.[18]

It was later reported (by Blumenthal) that 'al-Qaeda' came into possession of weapons intended for the anti-Gaddafi rebels. In 2013, MI6 informed the British Prime Minister Cameron, 'that up to 3,000 surface-to-air missiles have gone missing in Libya and could fall into the hands of al-Qaeda-linked groups. British intelligence agencies fear Libya is becoming the "Tesco" of the world's illegal arms trade', the *Sunday Times* reported, 'with Islamist terrorist groups able to obtain an array of sophisticated weaponry'.[19]

A US Defense Intelligence Agency report says that in 2011, and apparently under the instruction of Zawahiri, Azzouz established the Al-Tawhid (Oneness of God) College in Derna, Libya. The College was approved by Libya's Muslim Brotherhood-linked Undersecretary of Education, Fathi al-Ka'ary, whom the US and Britain helped to power. The College trained fighters of the Brigades of the Captive Omar Abdul Rahman (BCOAR), a militia led by Azzouz. On 11 September 2012, BCOAR supposedly attacked the US Embassy in Benghazi, killing two officials – many believe in order to silence US officials who discovered that 35 CIA operatives were using the Embassy to smuggle weapons to anti-Assad terrorists in Syria.[20]

Chapter 3

Iraq – 'A momentary twinge of concern'

Iraq has been the UK's favourite punch bag for nearly two centuries, ever since trading ships, backed with armed boats, sailed the Tigris and Euphrates rivers. In the 1920s, Britain installed the Hashemite kingdom of Iraq which, by the 1930s, it ruled indirectly under the guise of independence. In the 1950s, a revolutionary, Abdel Kassem, threatened the status quo by nationalizing the country's vast oil reserves. Kassem was overthrown in a US-British coup and eventually replaced by Saddam Hussein, who was armed by the US and Britain for years, even during the times of his worst massacres. Thirteen years of an economic blockade devastated Iraq, reducing it from the living standard of Greece to Burundi. The Gulf War and sanctions softened the country for full Anglo-America occupation in 2003. In this chapter, we document how secular Iraq was transformed into a hub of terrorism, eventually leading to the creation of ISIS.

It was understood by the Anglo-American invaders that oil-rich Iraq would not be allowed to develop its own resources, but rather, that the Saddam Hussein regime would be replaced by a similar proxy. 'Iraqi security forces . . . could present a plausible façade of stability, at least in the short-term, and appear to guarantee the independence of the state from regional intervention', wrote government advisor, Charles Tripp (an Oxford academic) in 2002, a year before the invasion. Tripp was right about a 'short-term' 'façade of stability'. He continued: 'The fact that it would look remarkably like one of the precursors to the regime which produced Saddam Husain [sic] – and would emerge out of similar circumstances – might only cause a momentary twinge of concern'. For Sunnis, the Shia-led al-

Maliki government certainly resembled Saddam Hussein, with torture chambers and chronically reduced living standards.[1]

Seven years into the occupation, the British Foreign Office described Iraq as a 'bonanza of contracts for western companies'.[2]

Iraq: 2003–2005

In 2003, the Anglo-American occupiers faced a dilemma familiar to imperial powers, namely how to pacify a hostile population. The initial effort was 'shock and awe', which the US military describes as the 'delivery of instant, nearly incomprehensible levels of massive destruction directed at influencing society writ large, meaning its leadership and public'. As intended, this 'non-nuclear equivalent of the impact [of] the atomic weapons dropped on Hiroshima and Nagasaki' had devastating effects, killing 100,000 Iraqis, according to the famous British medical journal, the *Lancet*. A few years later, the *Lancet* reported that 650,000 Iraqis had died. This was followed by a survey from Opinion Research Business, that 1.03 million Iraqis had perished. A recent poll found that just 6% of the British population knows that a million or more Iraqis died. 59% think that the toll is 10,000 or less.[3]

The million Iraqis who perished from 2003 to 2008 join the million or more who died as a result of the blockade, which was enforced by the Royal Navy and lasted from 1990 to 2003. In the years of sanctions, everything was banned from Iraq: chemicals for water sanitation, women's pads, surgical equipment, painkillers, even children's toys including pencils (under the pretext that the graphite might be used to make weapons of mass destruction). Iraq's living standards thus declined from that of Greece to Burundi.[4]

Returning to the question of how to pacify a hostile population, the US and British occupiers subjected the most courageous resistance, namely the city of Fallujah, to nuclear attack. According to peer-reviewed Western epidemiologists, there were higher levels of radiation found in Fallujah than in Hiroshima in 1945. The kind of foetal and infant deformities suffered by children and their parents are unique in scale and character, eclipsing even the tragic children of Vietnam, many of whom continue to be born with severe health problems and deformities as a result of America's use of dioxin.[5]

But nuking the rest of Iraq was not a feasible pacification strategy. The occupiers created a phantom menace, namely 'al-Qaeda in Iraq' (AQI), supposedly led by a Jordanian, Abu Musab al-Zarqawi, who had contacts with former Afghan War fighters in Iraq's north, Kurdistan. The US military explained that religious extremists were not really a problem in Iraq, but rather, Saddam loyalists. Colonel Derek Harvey explained: 'The long-term threat is not Zarqawi or religious extremists, but these former regime types and their friends'. Harvey also acknowledged that '[o]ur own focus on Zarqawi has enlarged his caricature, if you will – made him more important than he really is, in some ways'. A US military document uncovered by the *Washington Post* states: 'Through aggressive Strategic Communications, Abu Musab al-Zarqawi now represents: Terrorism in Iraq/Foreign Fighters in Iraq/Suffering of Iraqi People (Infrastructure Attacks)/Denial of Iraqi Aspirations'.[6]

A RAND corporation report from 2008 funded by the US military explained: '*Divide and Rule* at the strategic level [against Salafist *jihadis*] would be an inexpensive way of buying time for the United States ... Today in Iraq such a strategy is being used at the tactical level, as the United States now forms temporary alliances with nationalist insurgent groups that it has been fighting for four years by exploiting the common threat that al-Qaeda now poses to both parties and providing carrots in the form of weapons and cash'. The RAND document essentially describes the military's Zarqawi plan. According to US military experts, the strategy appears to have worked. US Army spokesman, Major General Rick Lynch, said: 'What we're finding is indeed the people of al-Anbar – Fallujah and Ramadi, specifically – have decided to turn against terrorists and foreign fighters'.[7]

For propaganda purposes, anyone who resisted the occupation was 'al-Qaeda', as Col. Harvey infers. This was dramatically demonstrated with the US-British nuclear assault on Fallujah, where Zarqawi was alleged to be hiding. 'AQI' appears to have been a small number of foreigners from Jordan, Pakistan, Saudi Arabia and elsewhere, and Anglo-American special forces. The US ran Task Force Black, which incorporated Special Ops 626 (mentioned in the military's Zarqawi document, quoted above) and the British Joint Support Group, whose specialty, according to the *Guardian*, was setting off car-bombs in Northern Ireland during the so-called Troubles. Elite UK Forces reports on an incident in Basra in 2005, where two British 'soldiers were disguised as Arabs and . . . weapons and communications gear was found in their car'. The report goes on to note that '[p]ictures released to the media showed C8 CQB carbines, a mini PARA, a LAW rocket launcher, radios and medical kit'. The website continues: 'These items cause some to speculate the SAS were really on a sabotage mission, posing as terrorists and acting as agent provocateurs. Some even went as far as to suggest that their mission was to plant bombs in order to create a 'false-flag' terrorist attack'.[8]

ISIS: A 'Virtual Organization'

As a reminder of the fallacy of 'al-Qaeda in Iraq', recall Jon Lee Anderson's 2003 article in the *New Yorker*. Anderson accompanied US forces into opposition strong-holds and found 'that many Americans in Iraq had started to make references to Al Qaeda terrorists when they talked about the attacks on US soldiers, although there seemed to be no evidence for the claims'. Quoting US military personnel, the *New York Times* (NYT) reported in 2008 that 'the overwhelming motivation of insurgents is the need to earn a paycheck'. An official said that anti-occupation sentiment among Sunnis and hatred of their Shia-Kurdish opponents 'are being rivaled by the economic factor, the deprivation that exists'; due in no small part to the 13 years of sanctions, one might add. IS and AQI were financing themselves with oil revenues.[9]

Major Kelly Kendrick estimated the presence of 'no more than 50 hard-core "Al Qaeda" fighters in Salahuddin, a province of 1.3 million people that includes Baiji and the Sunni cities of Samarra and Tikrit'. Notice also the astonishing admission: the NYT writer actually put 'al-Qaeda' in quotation marks. This suggests that indeed 'al-Qaeda' is a brand name given to US enemies (and often allies), even though said groups may not call themselves 'al-Qaeda'. Kendrick 'said most fighters were seduced not by dreams of a life following Mr bin Laden, but by a simpler pitch: "Here's $100; go plant this I.E.D. [improvised explosive device]... Ninety percent of the guys out here who do attacks are just people who want to feed their families'.[10]

In October 2006, the NYT reported that an organisation calling itself the Mujahideen Shura Council (MSC) established an 'Islamic state' in Anbar province. MSC was 'an umbrella group for insurgents. The Council had recently announced the creation of an Islamic state in the area, independent of the Iraqi government'.[11]

According to the US military, the communications of AQI were led by Khalid Mashhadani, who 'helped create a virtual organization, called the Islamic State of Iraq, on the Web in 2006'. Mashhadani is said to have created an Iraqi leader called al-Baghdadi in order to give an Iraqi face to a foreign (i.e., AQI) organization. US Brigadier General Bergner said: 'The rank-and-file Iraqis in (al Qaeda in Iraq) believed they were following the Iraqi al-Baghdadi, but all the while they have actually been following the orders of the Egyptian Abu Ayyub al Masri'. The US military reasoned that the Iraqi resistance against the US occupation is reluctant to follow foreigners, i.e., AQI, whose leaders are primarily Pakistani and Saudi. Ergo, AQI created a new 'virtual' group that appeared to be led by Iraqis, hence the name of its alleged leader, al-Baghdadi.[12]

This explication is highly dubious because, as we have seen, there was no 'al-Qaeda in Iraq' prior to the invasion, and post-invasion 'AQI' was led by Zarqawi, whom US intelligence admits was largely – if not a total – fabrication. Ergo, if 'AQI' did not really exist, who was the Islamic State (IS)? The first mention of the

Islamic State of Iraq in the NYT appears on 2 February 2007. The US Joint Chiefs of Staff alleged that the downing of a US helicopter was an action taken by this hitherto unknown group, which the military had previous described as 'a virtual organization'. According to an IS statement: 'On the morning of this blessed day, Friday, 2 Feb. 2007, an air defense battalion of the Islamic State of Iraq was able to gun down an Apache [helicopter] . . . The Apache was completely burned. We will show the filming of this soon'.[13]

On 7 February 2007, the NYT reported the downing of a US cargo helicopter. '[A]ccording to news reports, military officials suggested that the crash [of the CH-46 Sea Knight] was probably caused by a mechanical failure', yet it was blamed on IS, which appeared to take credit for the crash. 'Video images of the aftermath of the crash, broadcast by the BBC, showed bright red flames and thick black smoke billowing from the wreckage of the helicopter in an open field. The BBC did not say how it obtained the video'. Despite this, media reported the events as authentic. 'An Internet message from an insurgent group calling itself the Islamic State of Iraq claimed credit for shooting down the helicopter, the latest in a string of crashes that the group has claimed credit for'.[14]

Where did the US acquire IS's statements? Apparently, the only organization in the world able to track and translate the IS web statements is SITE, Search for International Terrorist Entities. SITE is a private, US-based intelligence-gathering firm run by Rita Katz, a former Israeli Defence Forces officer. In a previous book, this author provides evidence to argue that Katz's book, *Terrorist Hunter*, contains inaccurate information concerning alleged extremists. In addition, Arab groups have taken legal action against Katz on defamation grounds. Ergo, SITE claims concerning IS are dubious at best.[15]

'Al-Qaeda' defeated, Al-Baghdadi fake

On 12 August 2008, it was reported by the NYT that IS had taken Baqubah, declaring it as its capital, following a defeat in Anbar by

Sunnis. Little was heard from IS until 28 April 2009, when the NYT reported that Abu Omar al-Baghdadi, the alleged leader, had been arrested. The newspaper said that the Iraqi government 'has not provided proof of his capture ... beyond showing a photograph of a man with a trimmed beard wearing a black T-shirt'. The newspaper reminded readers that, 'In 2007, Iraqi officials announced twice that Mr Baghdadi had been captured and killed. A spokesman for the United States military, which has suggested that he might not exist, said ... that the military could still not confirm his arrest'.[16]

On 9 July 2009, the newspaper reported on an internet statement 'attributed to Abu Omar al-Baghdadi', saying that 'attacks on American forces should continue despite the withdrawal from Iraqi cities by United States combat troops last week. ... It was impossible to verify the authenticity of the statement', but, as happened many times with reporting on IS, it was published anyway.[17]

By August 2009, IS appeared to be running swathes of Kurdistan, northern Iraq, like the mafia. An Iraqi soldier from Kurdistan said: 'We have three governments up here: the central government, the Kurdish government and the Islamic State of Iraq government ... We are lost in the middle'. Maj. Gen. Robert L. Caslen Jr., commander of American forces in Northern Iraq, said: 'Al Qaeda in Mesopotamia had now teamed up with ... the Islamic State'. Earlier, we saw that the NYT, usually quoting the US military, called IS an 'offshoot' of AQI, but here the story changed.[18]

Until then, it seemed as if the Islamic State had been defeated. 'In Diyala Province, which has remained restive even as other parts of the country have become relatively stable, a body was found riddled with bullets. A note pinned to the victim read: "We are coming back. The Islamic State of Iraq."' At that point, Bashar al-Assad, President of Syria, whom the US and UK wanted to depose, appeared to be – or at least was accused of – protecting IS in Syria. In late August 2009, a bomb blast added to the civilian toll and drove further wedges between Iraqis. Government spokesman, Ali al-Dabbagh, said that two suspects (Mohammed Younis al-Ahmed and Sattam

Farhan) were living in Syria, just as IS claimed responsibility via the web. IS (or US intelligence) made clear their opposition to Iran, calling the Shia al-Maliki government agents of Shia Iran. 'Rarely is there any firm evidence of who is responsible for major attacks in Baghdad. The government will routinely play heavily edited video confessions from those they claim took part in attacks, but the statements are impossible to verify', the NYT acknowledged.[19]

The next reports came in early 2010, with IS allegedly posting internet statements claiming that it would disrupt Iraq's election. The message was translated by SITE (the US private firm linked to Israeli intelligence) and appeared to come from al-Baghdadi, the fictional leader: 'O people, these elections are illicit in the legislation of our Lord'. Al-Maliki again announced that Baghdadi was dead: his 'demise has been reported at least three times before . . . [I]t has become a macabre joke about the murkiness of Iraq's security and government credibility', the NYT reported. Senior Iraqi military spokesman, Major General Qassim Atta, said that 'officials had deliberately falsified reports to mislead the insurgents'. The paper also reported on the alleged killings of two 'terrorist' leaders in April 2010: Al Qaeda's military commander, Abu Hamza al-Muhajir (the Egyptian also known as Abu Ayyub al-Masri) and IS commander Hamid Dawud Mohamed Khalil al-Zawi, a.k.a. Abu Omar al-Baghdadi.[20]

In 2010, the fictional Baghdadi supposedly died and was replaced by an MSC operative, Ibrahim al-Samarrai, who went by the name Abu Bakr al-Baghdadi. Al-Samarrai had been captured and interned in Bucca Camp by the US occupiers in 2004.[21]

On 4 June 2010, the NYT reported that US and Iraqi forces killed or captured 34 out of 'al-Qaeda in Iraq's' 42 leaders, 'cutting off the terrorist organization from its foreign sponsors and raising questions about whether it can reconstitute'. US commander Ray Odierno said: 'I think they're struggling now, and I think it's going to be difficult for them to continue to recruit'. As for the leaders still at large, Odierno said: 'we're not even sure if there's actually people behind those names ... We picked up several of their leaders that did the financing, that did planning, that did recruiting'. Odierno admitted: 'We were able to get inside of this network'.[22]

With AQI supposedly weakened and certainly infiltrated, IS (or US-British special forces) bombed a Syrian Catholic Church in Baghdad. The bombers supposedly identified themselves as IS fighters. Fifty-one worshippers and two priests were killed. Shortly after, General Lloyd J. Austin III said that IS has 'minimal support from some elements in the population ... But they have shown creativity in replenishing their operations and financial resources even after traditional sources have dried up or been cut off by military raids'. As we have seen, those resources include illicit oil revenues. 'He noted a series of bank robberies and attacks in recent months targeting gold markets – as well as a series of bloody attacks, especially in Baghdad'. After 24 January 2011, reporting on IS in the NYT drops significantly until February 2012, except for one minor article.[23]

Support for ISIS

In the previous chapters, we documented how the Anglo-American-French intelligence services transformed Syria and Libya into epicentres of modern terrorism. A US Defense Intelligence Agency (DIA) report says: 'There was a regression of AQI in the Western provinces of Iraq during the years of 2009 and 2010; however, after the rise of the [anti-government] insurgency in Syria, the religious and tribal powers in the region began to sympathize with the sectarian uprising'.[24]

The first significant mention of AQI/IS in Syria in the NYT is 12 February 2012, which says: 'Not so long ago, Syrians worked to send weapons and fighters into Iraq to help Sunnis fighting a sectarian conflict; suddenly, it is the other way around ... Others collected money to send aid and weapons to the fighters opposing President Bashar al-Assad's government across the border'. The report concludes that 'Al Qaeda in Iraq, also referred to as the

Islamic State of Iraq, has stated, "a lot of Syrians fought side-by-side with the Islamic State of Iraq, and it is good news to hear about the arrival of Iraqi fighters to fight with their brethren in Syria." '[25]

By 7 July 2013, the NYT was referring to IS as 'the new Syria-based affiliate of Al Qaeda', which appeared to oppose the US-UK-French-backed Free Syrian Army (FSA). However, further reporting revealed temporary alliances: a Syrian government base was besieged by a FSA brigade, North Storm, and 'joined by fighters from the Islamic State of Iraq and a group calling itself Jaish al-Muhajireen wal Ansar', mostly comprised of foreigners from Chechnya and elsewhere. 'In Latakia, the [IS-led] rebel offensive ... accelerated what had been a gradual rebel push into a province whose government-held central city has been a relatively secure haven for displaced Syrians from war-torn areas'. As we shall see, the leader of Jaish al-Muhajireen wal Ansar was trained by US special forces and went on to join IS.[26]

In northern Syria in Kobane, near the Turkish border, Kurdish fighters held off IS strongholds. In October 2014, the US military 'accidentally' armed IS when it air-dropped a cache of weapons, including grenades, intended for the Kurdish fighters. According to the *Washington Post*, 'Airdrops of food and water to religious minorities trapped on mountain cliffs in northern Iraq in August hit the mark about 80 percent of the time, Pentagon officials said' – meaning that 20% of US arms drops could have ended up in IS hands.[27]

On 8 August 2013, a NYT article revealed a brief, tacit alliance between IS and the US. A correspondent in Raqqa interviewed a Syrian IS commander, Abu Omar. 'He did not speak of attacking the United States. But he threatened Russia, and he spoke of a broad-based battle against Shiite-led Iran'. The reporter notes that Omar 'said Sunnis from across the world were justified in flocking to Syria to fight because of the government's reliance on Shiite fighters from Lebanon and Iraq'. On 21 October 2013, a US official commented on the tacit alliance: 'By challenging moderate Syrian rebels, the group, the Islamic State of Iraq and Syria, has forced them to fight on two fronts and divert resources from their battle with the government of President Bashar al-Assad'.[28]

Turning to Libya, US intelligence insiders told Fox News that 'the new support base for ISIS in eastern Libya is now providing "tangible assistance" in the form of training camps around the city of Derna, in addition to a growing number of Libyan fighters joining the terror group in Syria and Iraq'. In the previous chapter, we noted that Derna was an important centre for Libyan jihadis, where Azzouz, who was protected by the British, allegedly established a terrorism training college. '[O]ne of the alleged leaders of ISIS in North Africa is Libyan Abdelhakim Belhadj, who was seen by the US as a willing partner in the overthrow of Libyan dictator Muammar Gaddafi in 2011', the report continues. As we saw in the previous Chapter, Belhadj was a high-level member of the Libyan Islamic Fighting Group – tied to Osama bin Laden via its then-leader, Anas al-Liby – which received £100,000 from MI6 to help the Libyan Army in a coup against Gaddafi. The intelligence source said: 'Now, it's alleged he is firmly aligned with ISIS and supports the training camps in eastern Libya'.[29]

For decades the Turkish military and political leadership has harshly oppressed its Kurdish population, going so far as to commit ethnic cleansing in the 1980s and '90s, with American and European military and diplomatic support. In 2008, Turkey even invaded Kurdistan in Northern Iraq to battle Kurdish fighters. The Turkish regime has considered IS a potential ally because IS opposes the Iraqi Kurdish leadership. A US invasion of Syria in July 2015 yielded 'undeniable' intelligence connecting Turkey to IS, particularly via the latter's oil smuggler, Abu Sayyaf.[30]

The Turkish governments, Arab governments of Iraq, and Alawite governments of Syria have long considered the Kurds a problem because no homeland was created for them when Britain and France drew the borders of the modern Middle East. There are high concentrations of Kurds in eastern Turkey, northern Iraq, and northeastern Syria, clustered together yet separated by artificial state borders. In the 1980s, Saddam Hussein engaged in *al-Anfal*, a genocide in which 100,000 Kurds were murdered with Anglo-American arms, including chemical weapons. In the 1990s, policy towards Saddam shifted, so much so that as 'no-fly zones' were imposed on northern Iraq to protect the semi-autonomous Kurdish region (Kurdistan), Britain and America trained and armed the Turkish military as it continued its ethnic cleansing of Kurds across the border.[31]

Today, IS has carved almost a straight line across northern Syria and Iraq, as if to separate the Kurdish regions from the rest of the countries. Indeed, UK bombing of alleged IS targets in Iraq is mostly confined to Kurdistan, according to Ministry of Defence statements. In June 2014, the Iraqi government ordered the Iraqi Army (an Arab majority army) to stand down as IS took the Kurdish towns of Tikrit and Mosul. The Iraqi Army was trained and is armed by Britain and America, and the Iraqi government is controlled by the US. The US State Department says, for instance: 'Since 2005, the Department of State has approved more than $18.6 billion worth of Foreign Military Sales (FMS) with Iraq. The Iraqi Government has financed the vast majority of these government-to-government transfers of military systems and equipment using their own national funds'. The decision to order the Iraqi Army to stand down appears to be a tactical move against the Iraqi Kurds, whose Peshmerga force essentially fought IS alone. A Peshmerga spokesman, Brig. Gen. Halgurd Hekmat, said: 'the sudden collapse of the Iraqi army has left us with no option but to fill some areas with our forces because we can't have a security vacuum on our border'.[32]

In June 2014, a Shia Iraqi government minister told *World Net Daily* (WND) that the Obama administration 'has been aware for two months that [the group IS] that has taken over two Iraqi cities and now is threatening Baghdad was training fighters in Turkey'. According to the source, 'knowledge of ISIS actions was to be coordinated with the Saudis. Riyadh, he said, had paid some $3 billion to the jihadist group to overthrow Maliki. "Plan B" was to split Iraq into three states, for Kurds, Sunnis and Shiites'. The source also alleged that 'Iraqi officials told him the US Embassy in Baghdad had known since June 2 of the attack on Mosul but declined to inform Maliki'.[33]

Cynically, the Turkish government was facilitating IS for its own strategic interests against the Kurds. In July 2014, *Newsweek* quoted a former IS technician as saying: 'ISIS commanders told us to fear nothing at all because there was full cooperation with the Turks'. He added that 'they reassured us that nothing will happen, especially when that is how they regularly travel from Raqqa and Aleppo to the Kurdish areas further northeast of Syria because it was impossible to travel through Syria as YPG [National Army of Syrian Kurdistan] controlled most parts of the Kurdish region'. The individual identified as 'Omer' said: 'ISIS saw the Turkish army as its ally especially when it came to attacking the Kurds in Syria. The Kurds were the common enemy for both ISIS and Turkey. Also, ISIS had to be a Turkish ally because only through Turkey were they able to deploy ISIS fighters to northern parts of the Kurdish cities and towns in Syria'. Former counterterrorism analyst at the US Treasury Department, Jonathan Schanzer, told *Business Insider*: 'You have a lot of people now that are invested in the business of extremism in Turkey ... If you start to challenge that, it raises significant questions of whether the militants, their benefactors, and other war profiteers would tolerate the crackdown'.[34]

WND reported that '[t]he Kingdom of Jordan says it caught more than a dozen members of ISIS who disclosed during interrogations that they received training from NATO member Turkey'. In addition, an Egyptian security source told WND that 'Turkey is providing direct intelligence and logistical support to [IS]'. The source alleged that 'Turkish intelligence is passing to ISIS satellite imagery and other data, with particular emphasis on exposing to ISIS jihadists the positions of Kurdish fighters and the storage locations of their weapons and munitions'. In conclusion, 'The official confirmed reports that Turkey released ISIS terrorists from jail in a sweeping deal ... that saw the release of 49 hostages from the Turkish embassy in Mosul who were being held by ISIS'. The source alleged that the number of released IS prisoners was 700, and included British *jihadis*.[35]

Turkey has also been a location for border crossings of extremists into Syria, blurring the distinction between the 'moderate' terrorists organized by the US, Britain and France, and the extreme terrorists supposedly organized by no one. A former Syrian resident turned smuggler in Turkey, 'Abdullah', told a McClatchy newspapers reporter: 'A lot [of rebels smuggled into Syria] were Muslims who had come to support the revolution against Bashar Assad from every country. So many from Europe, Russia, Germany, France ...', he said (ellipsis in original). 'Only later did Abdullah realize that the network that funneled these men to him was the beginnings of the Islamic State'. However, many began as Free Syrian Army or affiliated groups, making the extent of US-British-French involvement in training IS unclear:[36]

Connections with the West

As we have seen, former US-British ally, Belhadj, allegedly went on to lead IS in Libya at Derna, where training camps were established by a man apparently protected by the British secret services, Azzouz. We have also seen instances of 'accidental' armament of IS by the US military. An 'informed' Jordanian official told WND that Syrian rebels who would later join the Islamic State of Iraq and the Levant, or ISIS, 'were trained in 2012 by US instructors working at a secret base in Jordan'. The reporter noted 'that at least one of the [IS] training camps ... is in the vicinity of Incirlik Air Base near Adana, Turkey, where American personnel and equipment are located'.[37]

In 2015, McClatchy newspapers, citing Georgian defence officers, alleged that Tarkhan Batirashvili (a.k.a. Abu Omar al-Shishani), a Chechen rebel opposed to the Russian government, was trained by the US before going on to join Jaish Mujahireen wal-Ansar in Syria and then IS. 'Abdullah', the Syrian smuggler living in Turkey, did not realize that 'one of the 15 [extremists he allegedly smuggled] would turn out to be the most important non-Arab figure in the Islamic State hierarchy', namely the 'former American-trained non-commissioned officer in the special forces of the nation of Georgia', Batirashvili, 'who'd led his men heroically during the 2008 Russian invasion of his homeland', referring to the Georgian invasion of the Russian 'protectorate' South Ossetia in 2008, triggering the Russo-Georgian war.[38]

'Since [Batirashvili] swore allegiance to the Islamic State in 2013, thousands of Muslims from the Caucasus have flocked to Syria to join the extremist cause'. After the Saudis radicalized Sufi Chechens by turning them into Salafists by financing the construction of a mosque, hundreds of young, impoverished Chechen men became cannon fodder for IS. 'They all started leaving for Syria', said a Chechen community elder. 'Things are safer here now because all the radicals – our children – have gone to Syria'. An anonymous Chechen fighter in Turkey told the reporter: 'Once the jihad in Syria began', which, as we have seen was organized by the US, Britain and France, 'people began to tell us, "Come to Syria, there's fighting and paychecks and wives." So we started leaving by the hundreds'.[39]

Batirashvili, from the Sufi-majority Chechen region, appears to be a mercenary more than a Salafist fanatic. The Georgian defence official said: 'The only reason he didn't go to Iraq to fight alongside America was that we needed his skills here in Georgia' during the 2008 war with Russia. It was Batirashvili who allegedly 'helped the Islamic State get many Russian-speaking recruits from Chechnya, Dagestan, Uzbekistan, Tajikistan and even Afghanistan', the official continues. 'He was responsible for bringing them in through a network that I think was controlled by al Qaida'.[40]

Turning to the UK, one Syrian-born Omar Bakri, who emigrated to the UK in 1986, appears to have utilized Sakina Security Services, 'an Islamist security organization with extremely close links to al-Muhajiroun and Supporters of Sharia. Sakina sends people overseas for jihad training with live arms and ammunition', Andrew Dismore MP alleged in 2001. 'I regret that the [UK] Department of Trade and Industry has done nothing to close the company'. (Interestingly, a 7 July 2005 bomb suspect, Mohammad Sidique Khan, once worked for the Department of Trade and Industry.) 'Bakri ... boasted that al-Muhajiroun sent Muslim youths on jihad training courses ... [Quoting Bakri:] "some went to Kashmir, and others to Chechnya and to Kosovo before that. Some remained in Britain because they were not fully trained ideologically."' According to Ron Suskind, a security source told him that Bakri 'helped MI5 on several occasions'. Bakri left the UK for Lebanon, where he was later arrested. In 2015, *The Times* alleged that Bakri's son, Mohammed Fostok, travelled to Syria to join IS.[41]

The murderer of journalist James Foley is alleged to be Mohammed Emwazi, a Kuwaiti-born Briton. It was reported in the British media that MI5 'spent five years talking to Emwazi before he left the country for Syria'. Provocateurs appear to have drawn him into terrorism. Emwazi said: 'An MI5 agent known as "Nick" knew everything about me; where I lived, what I did, the people I hanged around with'. After Emwazi declined to join MI5, 'Nick' said, 'You're going to have a lot of trouble ... you're going to be known ... you're going to be followed ... life will be harder for you' (ellipsis in original). Following the harassment and recruitment drive, Emwazi allegedly joined IS.[42]

According to the Asian News Network, MI6 and the CIA 'intercepted conversations on mobile phones, e-mails that show that several former British Army officials have joined the ranks of the Islamic State of Iraq and Syria (ISIS)'. Citing a 'defence source', the news network adds that 'agents linked to the ISIS have also revealed that people with English accents and a military background are now training the members of the terrorist organization in Iraq and Syria'. The report is unclear as to whether the personnel 'served in the regular British army or in the Territorial Army'. A source alleged 'that the recruits who join the ISIS are given a "pretty decent" degree of military training before they are allowed to take part in battles'. The report concludes that '[t]hey are not just taught to fight but also to save ammunition, fire aimed shots, plan ambushes and carry out day and night operations. Those who excel at handling weapons are also taught to use sniper rifles and other longer-range weapons. Almost 600 British citizens have joined the organization so far'.[43]

According to the French government, about ten military personnel defected to the Islamic State. The *Telegraph* reported: 'Most of the ex-soldiers ... including former paratroopers and French foreign legionnaires [sic], are said to be fighting on behalf of Islamic State of Iraq and the Levant'. The newspaper goes on to report the 'presence of an ex-member of France's elite First Marine Infantry Parachute Regiment, considered one of Europe's most experienced special forces units'. It would also appear that the Canadian secret services are trafficking *jihadi* brides.[44]

In 2015 it was reported by the *Daily Mail* that three British teenage girls, Shamima Begum, Amira Abase and Kadiza Sultana, 'are believed to be in Syria after flying to Turkey in February'. A foreign spy was arrested in Turkey 'on suspicion of helping [the] schoolgirls travel to Syria to join the Islamic State'. The individual is believed to have been 'working for the Canadian intelligence service ... Turkish foreign minister Mevlüt Çavuşoğlu earlier said the suspect works for the intelligence agency of a country that is part of the US-led coalition fighting ISIS but did not identify the country, saying only that it was not the United States or a member of the European Union'. Later, a Turkish newspaper 'reported that the spy was working for the Canadian government'.[45]

Finally, Russia joined with Iran and the Lebanese Shia group, Hezbollah, to prop up the Assad regime in Syria by bombing Free Syrian Army strongholds under the pretext of targeting IS, before Putin admitted that the real aim – surprise, surprise – was propping up Russia's major Middle Eastern ally, Assad. Had Russia stepped in earlier, perhaps 200,000 Syrians or more may still be alive, but as there appears to be no morality in international affairs, Russia's aims are as self-interested as Britain's and America's. As Syria becomes a second proxy battle ground between US and Russian interests, Ukraine being the first, the world is pushed ever-closer to the threat of terminal nuclear war (see Chapter 7).[46]

Chapter 4

Iran – 'It's all about petrol prices'

By 2016, an international agreement had been reached on Iran's enrichment of uranium for civilian nuclear energy, which the US, Europe and Israel claims, without evidence, is being enriched for the purpose of building a nuclear weapon. Praised as a triumph of international diplomacy, the 'deal' has been a disaster for Iran. It was imposed after years of rejection by the West of Iran's negotiation offers, Euro-American sanctions (admittedly less severe than those imposed on Iraq), the murder of Iran's civilian nuclear engineers, and the support by Britain, Israel, and the US of Sunni and Shia terrorist groups. Like Iraq, Iran has also endured a century of Western interference.

Much like Iraq, when it comes to Iran there appears to be no end to Anglo-American duplicity. The UK is assisting the Israeli Mossad and the US CIA in a dirty war. Geostrategically, Iran is in a position to build pipelines to India (through Pakistan) and China (through Afghanistan) and supply both countries with inexpensive gas and oil, thereby threatening Anglo-American energy interests. Numerous British and American intelligence projections emphasize that 'containing' Iran by encircling it with military bases is the best long-term strategy. MI6, the CIA, and the Mossad also seek to destabilise the Shia theocracy by supporting secular movements across the country and Balochi Sunnis on the border with Pakistan.

In 2012, MI6's then-head Sir John Sawers acknowledged that 'covert operations by British spies' had been taking place in Iran since at least 2008, though details, of course, were not forthcoming. Before examining the secret war, it is necessary to look at a little history.[1]

Brief history

Anglo-Persian Oil (now BP) began life under Churchill during WWI. Iran had been under the thumb of Shah Pahlavi and the Prime Minister, General Ali Razmara. In 1951, after Razmara's assassination by the Devotees of Islam, a branch of the Iranian Muslim Brotherhood, the Shah appointed the Western-educated Mohammed Mossadeq as Prime Minister. Mossadeq made the same error as Iraq's Kassem and Libya's Gaddafi, namely nationalizing the oil – a mistake also made in Egypt by Nasser with regards to the Suez Canal, arguably the most important strategic route in the world, and a major cause of Egypt's woes today.[2]

As part of Operation TPAJAX, MI6 and the CIA set about overthrowing the secular Mossadeq. In doing so, they worked with Islamists (ulema), including Ayatollah Khomeini's mentor and godfather, Ayatollah Kashani. Khomeini himself, whom the US portrayed as their arch-enemy during the late-1970s and 1980s, was a CIA asset who participated in the coup against Mossadeq. In deposing Mossadeq, the ulema committed many atrocities against Iran's progressive communists, the Tudeh Party.[3]

In 1953, Mossadeq was overthrown and Shah Reza Pahlavi installed as Iran's ruler. Under his SAVAK secret police force, tens of thousands of Iranians were either killed, tortured, or disappeared, earning SAVAK a reputation as the world's worst human rights violator.[4]

Calling the Shah 'one of the world's most far-sighted statesmen', Prime Minister Thatcher ensured that the UK's £1.2 billion weapons contracts, which included tanks, were still valid, aiding the Shah's murder, torture, and general terrorization of the Iranian population. Political analyst William Engdahl writes: 'During 1978, negotiations between the Shah's government and British Petroleum were underway for renewal of the 25-year oil extraction agreement. By October 1978', Engdahl continues, 'talks collapsed over a British "offer", which was actually a demand for exclusive rights on Iran's future oil output'.[5]

Like Mossadeq before him, the Shah had to go. Engdahl continues: 'the British Broadcasting Corporation sent dozens of Persian-speaking BBC "correspondents" into even the smallest villages to drum up hysteria against the regime with exaggerated reports of incidents of protest against the Shah. The BBC gave Ayatollah Khomeini [a] propaganda platform'.[6]

Former Chatham House Fellow, Mark Curtis, observes that by April 1980, British special forces were training between 28 and 30 of Khomeini's men. Tactics included counter-communist operations (torture and murder). During its long, bloody war with Iraq, in which a million people on both sides were killed, Britain supplied weapons to the Ayatollahs and the secular Saddam Hussein regime, including chemical and biological weapons. Israeli intelligence provided information to Iran. The US was caught in the famous Iran-Contra Affair selling weapons to the regimes in order to finance its State-terrorism in tiny Nicaragua.[7]

Friendly terrorists

Similar deceptions continue.

Despite 12 nautical miles of the Strait of Hormuz being Iranian territorial waters, Britain 'sent a huge armada to protect the key oil route', the UK *Daily Star* reported a few years ago, quoting a British intelligence aide: 'It's all about petrol prices ... The CIA and our people, MI6 and GCHQ, are out there in force. They have also recruited locally'. *Haaretz* specialist, Yossi Melman, revealed in 2010 that 'the mysterious assassination in Tehran of a top Iranian nuclear scientist and the wounding of another ... are part of ... endless efforts by the Israeli intelligence community, together with its Western counterparts[,] including Britain's MI6 and America's CIA'. In 2007, the *Telegraph* revealed that 'America is secretly funding militant ethnic separatist groups in Iran in an attempt to pile pressure on the Islamic regime'. A CIA agent said: 'Funding for their separatist causes comes directly from the CIA's classified budget but is now "no great secret"'. What is a secret is Britain's involvement.[8]

Also quoted was former State Department counter-terrorism official, Fred Burton, who said that the '[terrorist] attacks inside Iran fall in line with US efforts to supply and train Iran's ethnic minorities to destabilize the Iranian regime'. In 2008, *The Times* reported that then-MI6 head, John Scarlett, met his Mossad counterpart, Meir Dagan, in 'an intelligence-sharing process … building on long-standing cooperation between MI6 and Mossad, both of which have extensive spy networks in the Middle East'. Commenting on the meeting, Israel's Defence Minister, Ehud Barak, said: 'We're doing a lot of things about Iran, … but the worst thing to do at the moment is to talk'.[9]

When Britain's UN Ambassador John Sawers 'rejoined' MI6 in 2008 in order to head the organization, the BBC acknowledged that, as '[a]n Iran specialist and scientist, his press briefings on the status of Iran's nuclear programme have been known to resemble seminars on nuclear physics'. In an unprecedented public address, Sawers said that '[s]topping nuclear proliferation cannot be addressed purely by conventional diplomacy. We need intelligence-led operations'. Within 12 months of Sawers's statement, Iranian civilian nuclear physicists were targeted for death.[10]

At the time of writing, five Iranian nuclear experts appear to have been murdered. They are: Mostafa Ahmadi-Roshan, Masoud Alimohammadi, Ardeshir Hosseinpour, Darioush Rezaeinejad and Majid Shahriari. Can you imagine Britain's reaction if its leading civilian nuclear engineers, many of them university staff, were being blown up and shot on the streets by Iranian terrorists, citing Britain's violation of the Non-Proliferation Treaty as a justification?[11]

Another terrorist group targeting Iran is the Mujahedin-e-Khalq (MEK), also known as the People's Mujahideen of Iran. In this case, Britain has gone very far to support it, including removing it from the arbitrary Terrorism Act 2000. The MI6-CIA Operation TPAJAX led to the formation of the leftist National Council of Resistance of

Iran (NCRI), of which MEK is the paramilitary wing. MEK attempted to destroy the incumbent Iranian theocracy.

Allowing its leadership to operate from their country, the French authorities recognized MEK in 1986 when the organization was attacking Iran from bases in Iraq. The US Council on Foreign Relations explained that, 'Despite MEK's violent tactics, the group's strong stance against Iran have won it support among some US and European lawmakers ... and there has been an ongoing, vigorous campaign by its supporters in the US Congress to have it removed from the terrorist list'.[12]

During the US-UK occupation of Iraq in 2003, 'coalition forces detained the group and provided protection to prevent the Iraqi government from expelling MEK members to Iran', according to the RAND corporation. 'The MEK was allowed to establish a liaison office on the coalition's nearby forward operating base (FOB) rather than at Camp Ashraf [in Iraq], to hang its propaganda posters in recreation areas at the FOB, and to hold conferences to promote its agenda'.[13]

In the 1990s, The British Charities Commission closed a MEK sham charity, Iran Aid, after finding no 'verifiable links between the money donated by the British public', approximately £5 million annually, 'and charitable work in Iran'. The RAND study continues: 'The MEK is widely believed to have assisted Saddam in the suppression of the Shia and Kurdish uprisings in Iraq in the aftermath of the Gulf War of 1991'. The situation wasn't black and white. Typical of divide-and-rule tactics, the US attacked MEK bases in Iraq to demand MEK's cooperation in attacking the Iranian regime.[14]

RAND adds: '[T]here have been no patrols of the camp itself since 2003. Although individual housing units are fenced, there is no external fence around the 15-square-mile camp'. The study further notes that, 'Large numbers of local workers come and go each day without being stopped by coalition guards outside the camp's main entrance ... [T]here are buildings at Camp Ashraf that no American has ever searched'. In 2003, US forces claim to have raided and disarmed MEK headquarters at Camp Ashraf in order to grant its members 'protected persons' status. The real reason appears to have been to disarm MEK in order to dilute its autonomy, thereby making the organization dependent on US authorization for further attacks on Iran. Any MEK attacks on Iran not approved by Washington could have disturbed the fragile Iran-Iraq alliance (particularly in Basra), which is favourable to US energy interests.[15]

The UK appears to have aided MEK's Iraq base. In 2005, Adam Price MP raised concerns about 'reports ... of Mujahideen-e-Khalq offices or safe-houses being operated in Basra', the validity of which the Armed Forces Minister, Adam Ingram, neither confirmed nor denied. In 2006, Foreign Affairs and Commonwealth Secretary Kim Howells informed Parliament that, 'Multi-National Forces in Iraq (MNF-I) currently provide perimeter security at the camp [Ashraf]', where four thousand MEK were disarmed. In Iraq, 'coalition forces detained and provided security for members of the Mujahedin-e Khalq' from 2003 to 2009.[16]

According to the British government, 'The [Iraq-based] MEK undertakes cross-border attacks into Iran, including terrorist attacks. It has assassinated senior Iranian officials and launched mortar attacks against government buildings in Teheran and elsewhere'. Despite this, 'The organisation was removed from [Britain's] list of proscribed organisations in June 2008 ... [and] was removed from the EU list of proscribed terrorist organisations on 26 January 2009'. Parliament adds that, 'There is no *acknowledged* MEK presence in the UK, although its publication MOJAHED is in circulation here. The National Council for Resistance in Iran undertakes fund-raising in support of the MEK, demonstrates, and produces and distributes anti-regime propaganda in support of MEK objectives' (emphasis added).[17]

The failure of the British government to explain why it removed MEK from the arbitrary List of Proscribed Organizations led to a Foreign Affairs Committee recommendation 'that the Government

... sets out fully why it has resisted the decisions of both the High Court in the UK and the European Court of Justice that the People's Mujahideen of Iran (PMOI), also known as the Mujahedin-e-Khalq (MEK), should no longer be listed as a terrorist organisation'.[18]

Ergo, the British political establishment has violated European Court of Justice and even domestic High Court rulings in order to back Iraq-based terror attacks in Iran.

Balochis

As well as supporting terrorism, Britain is also fomenting anti-regime activity in Iran. Adam Werritty, the 'unofficial advisor' to former Defence Secretary, Liam Fox, allegedly had 'regular contact with dissident groups who wanted regime change' in Iran. 'Werritty is a self-proclaimed expert on Iran and has made several visits', the *Daily Mail* reported. 'He has also met senior Israeli officials, leading to accusations that he was close to the [Israeli Mossad]'.[19*]

According to a Chatham House report on Iran's neighbours, 'Iran fears the risk of an irredentist movement among its own Baluch minority in southeast Sistan province' on the border with Pakistan, 'and is reluctant to further inflame its six million Sunnis, who are also concentrated in southeastern regions, where they are said to be mobilizing under the leadership of the militant Sunni group, Jundullah, and looking for Western ... support against the Shi'a regime'.[20]

Destabilizing the Balochi region is imperative to Western interests because of the Iran-Pakistan pipeline, which undermines Britain and America's Turkmenistan-Afghanistan-Pakistan pipeline monopoly.

Foreign Policy cites declassified CIA memos revealing Mossad's role in recruiting Balochi Sunnis from the Pakistan border region linked to Jundullah, a terrorist organization (recognized as such in the US), which has murdered dozens of Iranian civilians. Mossad's

---

* This is not a suggestion, however, that Liam Fox knew about the alleged Iran plot.

activities were conducted with at least tacit MI5-MI6 approval: 'Israel's recruiting activities occurred under the nose of US intelligence officers, most notably in London', reports *Foreign Policy*. 'US intelligence services have received clearance to cooperate with Israel on a number of classified intelligence-gathering operations focused on Iran's nuclear program'.[21]

Chapter 5

Yemen – 'Put the fear of death into them'

The Saudi war crimes being committed in Yemen in the former's efforts to fight Houthi rebels are actually US-British-Saudi war crimes, given the amount of weaponry and training supplied to Saudi Arabia by the US and Britain. According to (very few) mainstream media reports, the US and Britain blocked UN efforts to investigate Saudi war crimes in Yemen in 2015. In this chapter we explore the background to two conflicts taking place in Yemen: 1) a socialist uprising in the south, crushed by the UK-backed government and 2) the Houthi uprising in the north. A few years ago, the Yemeni government was committing war crimes in its own fight against the Houthis, until former President Saleh sided with the Houthis in an effort to oppose the Saudis. As usual, ordinary people are the victims of power-politics.

Aden, now Yemen, was part of the British Empire and 'the site of a massive British Petroleum refinery which dealt with the oil production from Kuwait', Dr Stephen Dorril notes in his partly-censored history of MI6. In the North, an uprising led by the Nasserite nationalist, Colonel Abdullah al-Sallal, deposed the British-backed Imam. Backed by Saudi and Jordanian forces, both of which were trained by the SAS, loyalists initiated a civil war. Egypt's President Nasser invaded Northern Yemen in order to back the new government.[1]

Former Chatham House Fellow Mark Curtis unearthed heavily censored, partly declassified files in which UK Foreign Office Ministers, including Alec Douglas-Home, complained that if Yemen fell from the sphere of British influence, other sheikhdoms, like Oman and the UAE, would be inspired to revolt, and Britain's 'credibility' would be damaged. In response to the Radfan rebellion, High Commissioner, Sir Kennedy Trevaskis, suggested to the British mercenary forces that they 'put the fear of death into the [Yemeni] villagers' with air raids, which they did. Prime Minister Harold Macmillan wrote that 'it would not suit us too badly if [Yemenis] were occupied with their own internal affairs during the next few years'. As we shall see, this divide and conquer strategy operates today.[2]

After 'Al-Qaeda'

From 1962, Britain ran a covert mercenary war in Yemen, in which a staggering 200,000 people died in an eight year period, many from chemical weapons – phosgene – produced by the tax-funded Porton Down laboratories (the UK's biochemical warfare plant). The operations were run by MI6 head, Dick White, and former MI6 Vice Chief turned banker, George Young, via the latter's Mossad-allied proxy, Neil McLean.[3]

By the late-1970s, the CIA and MI6 were training fascistic Yemeni collaborators to 'draw the Russians into the Afghan trap', in the words of US President Jimmy Carter's National Security Advisor, Zbigniew Brzezinski. The plan worked. The Soviet invasion of Afghanistan in December 1979 led to the deaths of around 1 million Afghans and drove a flood of refugees into Pakistan (some of whom later became the Taliban). These were just 'a few stirred-up Moslems' (Brzezinski). According to New Labour's Foreign Secretary, Robin Cook, 'al-Qaeda' exists in name only and means 'the database' or 'computer file' of tens of thousands of Arab *mujahideen* terrorists whom the US Navy SEALS, Green Berets and CIA, and the UK SAS and MI6 were training in Afghanistan throughout the 1980s.[4]

Yemen's unification under the leadership of President Saleh in 1990 galvanized former *mujahid*, Tariq al-Fadhli, 'a descendant of the British-appointed Sultan of Abyan . . . [whose] family acquired large land holdings during the era of British rule'. Historian Gordon

Waterfield notes that al-Fadhli set up 'training camps in southern Yemen for "Afghan-Arabs" – Arabs who fought in Afghanistan – and his fighters attacked the PDRY government, which had nationalized his family's lands'.[5]

The PDRY refers to the People's Democratic Republic of Yemen, or the socialist South, which, under Saleh, was united with the North in 1990. Al-Fadhli 'was linked to a series of bombing attacks targeting socialist officials in November 1992', Waterfield continues. Since 1990, Southerners have become increasingly marginalized by the central government, with many losing their jobs, pensions and state-rights, which were already severely restricted in Yemen.[6]

As we saw in Chapter 1 (on Syria), banks and oil companies associated with the European Union and the US want to pursue 'development' in Yemen, but on their own, narrow terms. Genuine socialism is not acceptable. Added to which, Yemen is on the Gulf of Aden, which, as we shall see in Chapter 11 (on Somalia), is considered one of the most important trading routes in the world. Under the guise of counterterrorism, the UK Ministry of Defence trained Yemen's Minister of the Interior in repression.

As we have seen, the CIA and MI6 created what is now called 'al-Qaeda'. 'Al Qaeda in Yemen's leader, Nasir al-Wuhaishi, has publicly expressed support for the Southern Movement', writes Human Rights Watch. However, as the organization also suggests, this is black propaganda put out by the CIA or related agencies designed to associate socialists with terrorists.[7]

HRW notes: 'Al-Wuhaishi may have been speaking only for his Yemeni groups, since comments by a global al-Qaeda leader made one month later distanced the group from supporting secession of southern Yemen'. In June 2009, Mustafa Abu al-Yazid, 'al-Qaeda's general chief in Afghanistan' and a member of its high Shura Council, 'denied al-Qaeda's support for southern secession ... Some Yemeni political analysts and two foreign diplomats Human Rights Watch met dismissed claims of direct links between the

[Yemen] Southern Movement and al-Qaeda. One European ambassador called such allegations a "red herring" put out by government officials'.[8]

For the advocates of financial neo-liberalism, it is necessary to counter socialism in Yemen, and indeed everywhere, especially as '[t]here are an estimated 100,000 military and civil employees in the south who were forcibly retired after 1994, and their pension arrangements were at the core of the original protests in 2007', Human Rights Watch continues. As one of the few organizations to document the events, HRW forms the bulk of the following research.[9]

Counter-revolution

The Southern secessionist movement is a loose association of interests, including the Yemeni Socialist Party, local branches of the Islah party, Nasserites and Baathists, using 'grassroots networks to mobilize support for the movement'. 'Since 2007', HRW continues, 'southern Yemenis have conducted sit-ins, marches and demonstrations to protest what they say is the northern-dominated central government's treatment of them, including dismissal from the civil and security services'.[10]

In its *Annual Accounts 2006–07*, the UK MoD published a map of then-current deployments, including this one-line revelation: 'Yemen: Training support to forces of the Minister of Interior'. A map published in the 2009–10 report confirms that training continued. As we shall see, Parliamentary statements not reported in the media confirm Britain's training of the Yemeni military as late as November 2011, when President Saleh's anti-demonstration violence was peaking. HRW's reports provide an indication of the Yemeni security services and their operational procedures, and in doing so reveal both Britain's direct and proxy involvement:[11]

'There are many security agencies in Yemen answering to different parts of the executive. Their remits overlap, leading to public uncertainty about which agency might be responsible for a particular human rights violation'. According to HRW, 'Central Security is officially under the Minister of Interior's direct authority. This agency has been heavily involved in the use of force against southern demonstrators. Also under the Interior Ministry are the Criminal Investigation Department'.[12]

Since 2007, the security forces and especially the Central Security, one of the organizations trained directly or indirectly by the UK MoD, 'have carried out widespread abuses in the south – unlawful killings, arbitrary detentions, beatings, crackdowns on freedom of assembly and speech, arrests of journalists, and others'. As in Colombia (see Chapter 9), 'These abuses have created a climate of fear, but have also increased bitterness and alienation among southerners, who say the north economically exploits and politically marginalizes them'.[13]

HRW also reports that '[d]uring a 21 May [2009] protest in Aden, security forces on several different occasions opened fire without warning or provocation, wounding 23 protestors ... Protestors responded by throwing rocks at the security forces, who again responded with deadly force'. Britain provides not only training for these atrocities, but weapons, as we shall see.[14]

'Security forces have made it increasingly difficult for wounded persons to obtain medical care by ordering public hospitals not to treat persons wounded at protests, stationing officers from the Political Security Organization (PSO) and other security agencies at hospitals, and even carrying out attacks inside hospitals or seizing wounded patients from their beds', HRW continues.[15]

In April and May 2009, 'Armed clashes in the Ahmarain mountains', northeast of Aden, 'left several soldiers dead and civilians wounded'. This illustrates the blurring distinctions between internal 'security' and outright domestic war. 'In July 2009 a clash between followers of Tariq al-Fadhli', Britain's former *mujahideen* ally, 'and security forces in Zinjibar, the capital of Abyan province, left at least 12 persons dead in the wake of a "festival" promoting southern demands'. Al-Fadhli reportedly turned against President Saleh in the years prior. However, as the British officials stated in the 1960s, internal conflict services the UK's divide and rule interests, and thus al-Fadhli's could be a staged opposition.[16]

'On 28 April [2009], the Yemeni army began moving new troops into the Ahmarain mountains ..., establishing military positions overlooking villages in the area and erecting new checkpoints'. HRW also notes that in order to frighten Southern demonstrators and block information from other Yemenis that might lend support to the cause, 'The authorities have ... launched a frontal attack on the independent media, suspending publications, blocking websites, arresting journalists, and even shooting up the offices of the largest independent newspaper'.[17]

In the UK, we hear a lot about Russia's and China's use of state-internet censorship, including its persecution of bloggers. When it comes to the UK's allies, however, we have our own media blackout, as little of the above has been reported in the UK, much less about Britain's ties to the Saleh regime. 'On 4 May, 2009 the [Yemeni] Ministry of Information suspended from publication eight daily and weekly independent newspapers over coverage they had given to events in the south', HRW reports, including: *Al-Ayyam*, *Al-Masdar*, *Al-Watani*, *Al-Diyar*, *Al-Mustaqilla*, *Al-Nida*, *Al-Shari* and *Al-Ahali*.[18]

'Also in May, the government created a new court to try journalists'. Except for *Al-Ayyam*, 'all other [newspapers] print on government presses, which makes it easier for the authorities to interfere with their publication'. President Saleh sent envoys to *Al-Ayyam*, asking the editors 'to tone down' their coverage of the protests and the government's brutal UK-trained and armed crackdowns. Yemeni officials conceded that Saleh 'was worried the images would be used as evidence against him at the International Criminal Court in the Hague'. As always with victor's justice, those who provide the training and weapons needn't fear.[19]

'Following deadly protests in January 2008, the Yemeni authorities also blocked several websites, apparently after they posted graphic video footage of security forces firing "unprovoked at the crowd [of protesters]," according to the Committee to Protect Journalists'.[20]

That's the South.

Northern Civil War

In the North, a civil war has been fought intermittently since 2004 against Houthi 'rebels', whose 'political aims ... are not clear. The group originated as a religious movement – the "Believing Youth" (al-shabbab al-mu'min) – in the mid-1990s, mainly to promote religious education in Sa'da governorate', writes HRW. 'Yemenis in Sa'da overwhelmingly follow the Zaidi branch of Shia Islam'. Indeed, then-President Saleh is a Zaidi, whose people 'ruled large parts of Yemen for a thousand years under a religiously legitimized imamate until 1962, when a military-led coup eventually ushered in republican rule'.[21]

The 'Huthis object to what they say is the government's failure to end Saudi-inspired Sunni Islamic missionary activities in Sa'da, which they say clash with traditional Zaidi doctrine'. In the 1990s, the 'Believing Youth' established schools to teach the Zaidi code. However, the Yemeni government, 'which originally supported these schools[,] decided around [the year] 2000 that they represented a Zaidi revival that might threaten its power base'.[22]

In 2006, Britain exported £7.5 million-worth of weapons to Yemen, which, as we shall see, were used to deadly effect. They included: 'weapon day and night sights', 'armoured all wheel drive vehicles', 'components for combat helicopters', 'components for combat aircraft', and 'components for military surveillance aircraft'. Since 2007, international aid agencies have sought access to the northern Sa'dah governorate. As the military operations intensified, the Yemeni authorities 'severely restricted humanitarian access to tens of thousands of civilians in need'. Over the years, the war has intensified. 'After a fifth round of fighting erupted in May 2008',

HRW continues, 'the government blocked the movement of all commercial goods, including staple foods and fuel, an act that appears to constitute an illegal collective punishment'.[23]

On the civil war issue and the human rights abuses, the British media were largely silent, and on the issue of Britain's involvement, totally silent. HRW further notes that between February 2007 and July 2008, Saleh 'imposed a total information blackout on Sa'da governorate' and 'clamped down on media coverage, banning local and international journalists from traveling anywhere in the governorate, threatening journalists covering the conflict, and arbitrarily arresting internet webmasters and others with information on civilian casualties' – as the regime had in response to the Southern secessionist crisis. Further isolating people, 'The government cut off most mobile phone subscribers, allowing only a few government-vetted individuals access to the network'.[24]

HRW also reports that Saleh blocked access to the World Food Programme and the Yemeni Red Crescent, two organizations upon which thousands of people's lives depended. In 2008, the conflict spread beyond Sa'dah governorate into 'Amran, Hajja, and Jawf governorates, and in June 2008 briefly reached Bani Hushaish, on the outskirts of Yemen's capital, San'a'. Fighting started again in August 2009, after the military launched Operation Scorched Earth – all the while, Yemeni soldiers and senior offices were trained in the UK.[25]

In 2009, Britain exported 'Night vision goggles', 'body armour' and 'components for body armour' to the Yemeni military.[26]

Violence erupted around Hasama, near Malahit and Razih on the border with Saudi Arabia, and in Saqlain, south of Sa'dah town. The Yemeni Armed Forces attacked Houthi rebels by 'using fighter jets, artillery and tanks. Houthi fighters mainly use small arms and some artillery. No official casualty counts exist, but Yemen's news outlets give almost daily reports of dozens of civilian and Houthi fighter casualties', HRW continues, noting 'the government's air strike on

Adi, in the Harf Sufyan District, killing over 80, including displaced civilians'.[27]

The independent Yemeni newspaper *Al-Masdar* reported that on 15 October, government aircraft bombed the market at Razih. One of HRW's 'well-informed sources' testified that villagers took 16 casualties, including a dead infant, to their local Ministry of Health clinic. Government aircraft were reported to have bombed five villages in the Wasit District. A Yemeni from Silah village informed HRW that Houthis took over the area three months before the start of Ramadan, during which time government aircraft bombed Silah 'and at least three other nearby villages – Shaqih, al-Haira and Wadi 'Ayyan"'.[28]

After August 2009, the start of the war's 'sixth round', shelling by both sides, coupled with government aerial bombing, resulted in the deaths of hundreds of civilians and the razing of 'entire villages'. By February 2010, aid agencies were struggling to help even a fraction of the 265,000 displaced civilians, most of whom were women and children. 'At a high-level meeting on Yemen in London in January 2010, UK Foreign Secretary David Miliband' noted Britain's 'commit[ment] to non-interference in Yemen's internal affairs'.[29]

On 12 February 2010, Saleh and the Houthis 'agreed on a truce that ended the sixth round of fighting in a five-year-long war that has devastated the lives of hundreds of thousands of people'. Exemplifying Britain's 'commitment to non-interference', MoD training continued, as did government-approved weapons exports. In 2010, Britain exported £250,000-worth of weapons to Yemen, including 'military firing sets', 'military helmets', and 'technology for the use of military cameras'.[30]

Crushing the Arab Spring

HRW also reports that in November 2009, Saudi Arabia, which receives the biggest arms shipments in the region from the UK, including pathogens, nuclear-grade materials, aircraft, and tanks, entered the war by sending jets into Yemen's airspace to bomb Houthi-held positions. In that month, 'following what it said was a cross-border raid on its territory, Saudi Arabia engaged the Huthis in sustained hostilities, including airstrikes, and established a "buffer zone" inside Yemen along the Saudi border'. In addition to the above admission considering British MoD's training of Yemen's Minister of the Interior, the MoD noted its 'Training support to Saudi Armed Forces', which has been going on since at least the 1960s.[31]

As the Arab Spring was getting under way in early-2011, the *Observer*, one of the only newspapers to cover the following, which it did by citing counterterrorism and counter-Iran strategies as a justification, noted: 'The courses are organised through the British Military Mission to the Saudi Arabian National Guard, an obscure unit that consists of 11 British army personnel under the command of a brigadier'. Beginning in the early-1960s, Britain has sent 'up to 20 training teams to the kingdom a year', including training snipers, or 'urban sharp shooters'. HRW reports that 'Saudi Arabian secret police ... arrested Yemenis blogging from Jeddah for websites featuring news about the Southern Movement, and secretly rendered [prisoners, including] Ali Shayif to Yemen in May or June, 2009'.[32]

In 2000, the British Parliament noted 'British personnel on secondment, assistance and advice on training, and joint exercises' to the regimes of Bahrain, Kuwait, Oman, Qatar, Saudi Arabia, and the UAE, explaining that 'Bahrain is a regular port for British ships from the Armilla patrol', while 'Saudi Arabia provides one of the UK's largest defence markets'. More generally, Britain's objectives are 'to preserve stability and guarantee the West's oil supplies [which] remains a key issue'. Numerous human rights organizations have documented the Saudi elite's brutality, including floggings, beheadings, crucifixion, limb amputations, torture and general fear meted out to those who insult the Kingdom, Islam, change their religion, practice homosexuality, etc.[33]

In 2008, a year before the Saudi invasion of Yemen, Britain exported £101 million-worth of weapons to the Kingdom, including: 'ammunition for wall and door breaching projectile launchers', 'armoured all-wheel drive vehicles', 'assault rifles', 'components for projectile launchers', 'equipment for operation of military aircraft in confined areas', 'gun mountings', 'gun silencers', and 'military devices for initiating explosives'. In 2010, a year after the attack, Britain exported £339.9 million-worth of weapons to Saudi Arabia, including: 'components for air-to-surface rockets', 'components for bombs', 'small arms ammunition', and 'sniper rifles'.[34]

After the invasion of Northern Yemen, Liam Fox, Britain's then-Secretary of State for Defence, 'visit[ed] the Kingdom ... [H]is programme included an insight into the training given to Saudi pilots by the [UK] RAF'. The MoD further reported that the Saudi regime 'signed an agreement in 2007 for the supply of 72 Typhoon aircraft to the Royal Saudi Air Force worth £4.43bn'. The Salam ('Peace') Project 'is supported by substantial weapons, infrastructure, training and logistics support packages from the UK. The first 12 Typhoons have been delivered and have already built up extensive flying hours', the MoD trumpeted.[35]

As with Saudi Arabia, human rights groups have long noted the Bahraini regime's use of torture and general intimidation. As the only newspaper to cover the story, the *Independent* reported that 'British police have helped to train their counterparts in Bahrain, Libya, Abu Dhabi, Qatar and Saudi Arabia through schemes run by the National Policing Improvement Agency', also noting 'the long-standing connection between the UK military and Arab regimes that send scores of officers through training at Sandhurst. Five Arab heads of state are Sandhurst alumni, including the King of Bahrain, Sheikh Hamad bin Isa al-Khalifa, who ordered the violent crackdown' on demonstrators in Bahrain, beginning in 2011. 'Other Arab rulers who have been through officer training in Britain include King Abdullah of Jordan, the Emir of Kuwait, Sheikh Saad al-Abdullah al-Salim Al Sabah, the Sultan of Oman, Qaboos bin Said al Said, and the Emir of Qatar, Sheikh Hamad bin Khalifa Al Thani'.[36]

A year before the Arab Spring, Britain exported over £5 million-worth of weapons to Bahrain, including: 'rifles', 'shotguns', 'small arms ammunition', 'sniper rifles', and 'submachine guns', which, along with the UK's training, was put to deadly effect. In 2011, Amnesty International reported that 'hundreds of people were arrested, detained and prosecuted for participating in anti-government protests'. By 17 March 2011, 'Seven protesters were killed and others were injured, some due to the use of live ammunition and shotguns at close range by the police and army. In March 2011, as the protests continued', Amnesty documents, 'Saudi Arabian troops were dispatched to Bahrain and on 15 March the King declared a state of emergency. The next day, Bahraini troops stormed the Pearl Roundabout and the Financial Harbour where protesters were gathered, causing further deaths and injuring many'. Many more Bahrainis died at the hands of the regime.[37]

These examples are important in themselves, but also relate to Yemen, given the similarity of abuses. In Yemen in 2011, Amnesty further reports, 'protesters were killed when security forces attacked them during prayer ... [S]ecurity forces opened fire on the protest camp [al-Tagheer Square] during the early morning prayer'. Amnesty goes on to state that '[t]he most serious incident of violence against protesters was an apparently co-ordinated attack on the same protest camp' in Sana'a, in March 2011, which left 52 people dead and hundreds more injured. Imagine if during Occupy London, Yemeni-trained British snipers using Yemen-supplied rifles and bullets, slaughtered dozens of peaceful demonstrators.[38]

In November 2011, Richard Burden MP 'ask[ed] the Secretary of State for Defence ... what the training is which is being provided to Yemeni officers in the UK'. Nick Harvey, Minister of State for the Armed Forces, confirmed that 'Yemeni officers are currently undertaking training on courses at the following establishments within UK', as they have been doing since at least 2007, probably earlier: 'Royal College of Defence Studies: strategic development and training for senior officers. Joint Services Command and Staff College: staff training for middle ranking officers. Britannia Royal Naval College: Navy initial officer training. Royal Military Academy Sandhurst: Army initial officer training. Defence School of Languages: English language training'.[39]

As we shall see, the dilemma for Britain's elite in Somalia and Yemen alike is the strategic importance of the Gulf of Aden, and thus the prevention of socialist development in either country. As we saw in the Introduction, analysts understand that, if foreign policy has to be presented to the public, it must be framed as if Britain is responding to threats to national security.

In 2010, the UK's Yemen Ambassador Tim Torlot was allegedly targeted by a suicide bomber. However, this author conducted a press analysis at the time and found that the only sources making the claim were the Yemeni Security Forces – no independent journalists verified the incident. In 2010, it was widely reported that a bomb from Yemen had been found on a cargo plane bound for the UK.[40]

In a single episode of the BBC's *Newsnight*, a UK Government official confirmed that there was no bomb on the plane – it was the only time that the event was reported as a hoax. Ratedesi archived the snippet online as 'UPS Yemen Bomb Scare is a Hoax BBC Confirms No Explosives'.[41]

Chapter 6

Drones – 'We're talking about murder'

The US is committed to a global control system, which it calls Full Spectrum Dominance. The events of 9/11 were used by the Bush II administration to justify war and technological expansion, including drones. In a document published before 9/11 (Rebuilding America's Defenses) *by future-administration officials, we learn of the US's efforts to project US power with drones in an effort to ensure US primacy. In this chapter we document Britain's drone wars, which began in Kosovo and are now such a regular part of foreign policy that they are being used to murder civilians, including British suspects on foreign soil.*

We noted in the previous chapter that many 'terror' threats emerging from Yemen are likely exaggerations, in keeping with the government agenda to portray foreign policy as 'managing risks on behalf of British citizens' (Chatham House, quoted in the Introduction).

In 2015, the *Guardian* reported that GCHQ shared intelligence with the US National Security Agency on Yemen. It 'was a "great opportunity" for UK agents to focus on any leads they had in the country. Given the domestic terror threat to the UK as well as internal conflicts in the country, GCHQ has multiple reasons to be monitoring individuals in the country'. The newspaper adds that '[a] secret 2009 legal briefing suggests that British military lawyers believe that some US operations beyond traditional battlefields may be unlawful'. Despite this, in 2010, following the incredible story of Umar Farouk Abdulmutallab, the alleged, suspected, failed, Nigerian, Yemen-based 'underpants bomber', whose father had warned the CIA of his son's increasing radicalization, Britain,

Australia, and America initiated a major surveillance and assassination programme in Yemen: Operation Overhead. One geolocation tracking team was called 'Widowmaker'.[1]

But how did it come to this?

'Full spectrum dominance'

The majority of civilians in Europe and America believe that unmanned aerial vehicles (drones) are being operated abroad – particularly in the Middle East and North Africa – in order to defeat 'al-Qaeda' and the Islamic State: hence the popularity of drone warfare (with lower support among women).[2]

However, in 1997 (i.e., before 9/11), the US Space Command committed America to a doctrine called Full Spectrum Dominance: military superiority over 'land, sea, air, space and information' by the year 2020. A year before 11 September 2001, the Project for the New American Century, whose members soon became the George W. Bush administration, stated their objectives: 'the preservation of a favorable balance of power in Europe, the Middle East and [the] surrounding energy-producing region, and East Asia'. The document goes on to suggest that drones 'will make it much easier to project military power around the globe ... [Drones] ... will allow not only for long-range power projection but for sustained power projection' – in keeping with the Full Spectrum Dominance doctrine.[3]

In 2015, the Bureau of Investigative Journalism revealed that since the armed drone campaign began in 2002, 2,500 people had been killed by drone operators. The tacit implication that US forces – Army and/or Central Intelligence Agency personnel – are targeting 'terrorists' does not withstand legal scrutiny. In 2010, Philip Alston, the UN Rapporteur on Extra-judicial Killings, published a landmark General Assembly Resolution in which he outlined the legality of drone operations.[4]

Even if the United States is permitted or even asked to engage in drone warfare in another country, 'A State killing is legal only if it is required to protect life (making lethal force *proportionate* [emphasis in original]) *and there is no other means, such as capture or nonlethal incapacitation* [emphasis added]'. In no case of drone murder has a victim been in the process of attempting to cause harm to US civilians. Alston concludes that, 'rather than using drone strikes, US forces should, wherever and whenever possible, conduct arrests, or use less-than-lethal force to restrain [suspects] … [I]t was legally incorrect for the US Bush [and subsequent Obama administrations – TC] to claim that [their] right to conduct targeted killings anywhere in the world was part of [the] "war on terror".'[5]

Human Rights Watch concurs. In its public letter to Obama, HRW states: 'The notion … that the entire world is a battleground in which the laws of war are applicable undermines the protections of international law'. The letter concludes that '[t]he deliberate use of lethal force can be legal in operations involving a combatant on a genuine battlefield, or in a law enforcement action in which the threat to life is imminent and there is no reasonable alternative'. Thus, the current campaign is illegal.[6]

The evolution of Britain's drones

The first explicit reference to Britain's use of drones in warfare came from then-Secretary of State for Defence, John Spellar, in 1999 (i.e., pre-9/11). When asked what role drones will play in future combat missions, Spellar replied: 'The planned Airborne Stand-Off Radar, ASTOR, programme, together with the in-service Phoenix unmanned aerial vehicle and future UAV programmes, such as SENDER and SPECTATOR, will form an important part of our integrated Intelligence, Surveillance, Target Acquisition and Reconnaissance, ISTAR, capability'.[7]

Spellar was asked the question in Parliament in March 1999, at a time when SAS forces were secretly operating in Serbia, shortly before NATO illegally bombed Serbia under the pretext of preventing the very 'ethnic cleansing' that other parliamentary records confirmed was not happening. Spellar concluded that '[l]ong range surveillance and reconnaissance assets, such as ASTOR and longer range radar and UAVs, will help to cue and subsequently direct medium and short range reconnaissance and target acquisition assets, such as Phoenix, to identify, prioritize and engage enemy targets from long range before they can inflict damage on our and friendly forces'.[8]

In July 1999, with the bombing of Serbia underway, Lord Kennet spoke about Britain's drone developments and asked: 'What of the opportunities given to defence firms to test their new systems? Some Kosovo weapons are already being hotly marketed. To some, the war was a commercial opportunity'. Toward the end of the year, Spellar confirmed that British Phoenix surveillance drones, under the command of the Royal Artillery, had been used in Serbia from bases in Macedonia.[9]

The new chapter to the *Strategic Defence Review* proposed in 2002 (i.e., *post*-9/11) involved 'looking at the extent to which [drones] require that offensive capability, as well as the reconnaissance aspect that they already enjoy', according to Geoff Hoon (Secretary of State for Defence). Britain began to shift from design, development and testing of surveillance drones – from Phoenix to Watchkeeper – to offensive drones, hence the UK's acquisition of (to date) five Reapers. Britain fired its first missile from a drone, a Hellfire, in Afghanistan in May 2008. Reapers remain under the control of RAF 39 Squadron, based at Creech Air Force Base, Nevada. The Ministry of Defence says that the 'UK Reaper is normally armed with 2 × GBU-12 500lb laser guided bombs and 4 × AGM-114 Hellfire missiles, although this number can be changed to suit particular missions ... RAF personnel have flown more than 44,000 hours providing essential support to NATO ground forces in Afghanistan'.[10]

In 2008, the 39th Squadron fired 27 missiles from its Reapers: 44 in 2009, 70 in 2010, 102 in 2011, and 120 in the following year. Trying to obtain information on fatalities is extremely difficult. Tom Watson (Labour) asked 'the Secretary of State for Defence what the *(a)* type, *(b)* circular error probability and *(c)* blast radius is of each variant of the Hellfire precision guided missile employed by the UK Reaper ... and if he will make a statement'. Philip Dunne, the Parliamentary Under-secretary of State for Defence, replied: 'I am withholding the information requested as its release would, or would be likely to prejudice the capability, effectiveness or security of the armed forces'.[11]

According to the *Guardian*, the MoD says 'only four Afghan civilians have been killed in its strikes since 2008'. '[I]t does everything it can to minimise civilian casualties, including aborting missions at the last moment. However, it also says it has no idea how many insurgents have died because of the "immense difficulty and risks" of verifying who has been hit', which of course contradicts the statement that 'only' four civilians have been murdered. We may raise more than eyebrows if the government of Afghanistan were targeting *jihadis* formerly trained by the SAS and MI6 in the 1980s, now living in London and Manchester, and killed 'only' four British civilians in their counterterrorism programme.[12]

Complicity in US crimes

The US is currently running two drone programmes: a military operation (headed by the Air Force and Army) and a civilian operation (run by the CIA). The first recorded murder of civilians by drone operators occurred near Khost, Afghanistan, on 4 February 2002. Pentagon spokeswoman, Victoria Clarke, said: 'We're convinced that it was an appropriate target, although we do not know exactly who it was'. The appropriate target turned out be civilians gathering scrap metal: Jehangir Khan (age 28), Mir Ahmed (30), and Khan's cousin, Daraz (31). In November of that year, a CIA Predator operater fired a missile from the US drone base in Djibouti, killing at least six civilians, all of them 'al-Qaeda' suspects, led by Qaed Salim Sinan al-Harithi.[13]

According to the Bureau of Investigative Journalism, it is possible that SAS troops laid the groundwork for US drone operations in

Yemen by providing details on the whereabouts of alleged 'al-Qaeda' members. British media reported in the previous year that the Ministry of Defence had plans for the SAS to conduct 'pinpoint' attacks on 'al-Qaeda' camps in Yemen, in preparation for US authorization. In March 2002, the *Scottish Herald* published reports suggesting that the US did indeed seek the SAS's 'unrivaled expertise' and 'to defuse growing anti-American feeling' among Yemeni warlords, some of whom the SAS and CIA had trained in the 1980s. 'The reports marked the first of many claims that British Special Forces were carrying out counter-terror operations in Yemen', says the Bureau of Investigative Journalism. Here's what we can prove:[14]

In 2012, as part of Operation Overhead, Britain and Australia provided information to US military personnel for drones. The giant listening post at RAF Menwith Hill, Yorkshire, has long been known to gather intelligence on every citizen across the UK, Europe and beyond, including their telephone calls, emails, visited web-pages and keystrokes. According to the Edward Snowden leaks, which expanded on what we already knew, GCHQ provides the US with details about the locations of individuals targeted for death.[15]

In 2012, intelligence memos (known as Comet News) confirmed that Anglo-Australian intelligence had likely led to the killing of two Yemenis, one unnamed, the other identified as Usama Khalid. The attack also killed a 60-year-old civilian, Mohamed al-Saleh al-Suna, and induced shrapnel injuries in six children playing nearby. (Whether we like it or not, 'al-Qaeda' members are all, technically, civilians under international law – in the same sense that criminals are civilians – because they do not abide by the Geneva Conventions. The 'controversy' is over the fact that the US has classified them, and thus all suspects, as combatants, essentially applying the Laws of War to everyone.)[16]

In the same year, the family of a Pakistani elder, Noor Khan, took the British government to court for alleged complicity in his death. The barristers said that GCHQ operatives could be 'accessor[ies] to murder'. The judges twice ruled a no verdict, for fear that details would compromise British security. (In Chapter 1, we documented similar courtroom behaviour in the case of terror suspects apparently trained by the secret services.)[17]

In 2013, the *Daily Mail* reported that Bosh Global Services 'is openly recruiting US security-cleared staff to work on American military operations from Britain', at RAF Waddington, Lincolnshire. It was revealed that RAF Croughton, Northamptonshire, is also used as a base. The latter provides a super-fast, BT-supplied telecommunications link to Camp Lemonnier, Djibouti, from which US Predator operators murder civilians in Somalia and Yemen. In March 2012, the *Telegraph* reported that US-UK drone attacks against Yemen had murdered 516 people, in what *Alternet* counted as 125 attacks since 2002. 'Nationwide the figures are comparable to those in Pakistan', which are causing large numbers of civilian casualties. The *Telegraph* acknowledged that the operations are conducted from the US base in Djibouti.[18]

In 2013, *Wired*'s David Axe confirmed that at least 112 Somalis had been murdered in drone and other US strikes, again from the British-linked Djibouti base, since June 2011. 'Under the guise of tracking Somali pirates, the Pentagon negotiated permission to base people and planes on the Indian Ocean island nation of the Seychelles', Axe reported, one of many locations from which drone attacks are mounted. The US Navy 'also deployed one of its five RQ-4 Global Hawks – Northrop-built spy drones with the wingspan of a 737 airliner – to an unspecified Indian Ocean base to, among other duties, provide air cover for the 5th Fleet off the Somali coast'. The 'unspecified Indian Ocean base' is probably Diego Garcia, from which Britain expelled the indigenous population in the late-1960s and '70s to make way for a US military base.[19]

In 2014, Tom Watson, Labour MP of the All-Party Parliamentary Group on Drones, commissioned Jemima Stratford QC to advise the group on the legality of British intelligence-gathering for the US drone programme(s). Stratford writes: 'In our view, if GCHQ transferred data to the [US National Security Agency] in the knowledge that it would or might be used for targeting drone strikes that transfer is probably unlawful'. Anna Thomas, an author for the group, paraphrasing Stratford's conclusion, says that the government must 'ensure British data and facilities are not used to support activities which would be unlawful in the UK, including drone strikes against non combatants [sic]'. Tory MP, David Davis, says: 'The phrase extra-judicial killing is a euphemism. What we are talking about here is murder. It may be that you are murdering terrorists and the people are villains, but it is still murder'.[20]

Part II

AND BEYOND

Chapter 7

Ukraine – 'We saw this one coming'

The drone agenda documented in the previous chapter is bolstered by an even more ominous weapon: intercontinental nuclear warheads. By expanding its global control agenda into Russia's next-door neighbours, the US is playing a potentially catastrophic game. Ukraine is the key to Russia's ability to easily export oil and gas to Europe, a key market. Controlling Ukrainian politics is the key to controlling the Russian energy spigot in Europe. In this chapter we document Britain's little-discussed role, including indirect collaboration with neo-Nazis.

Since declaring independence from the Soviet Union in 1991, Ukraine has been a proxy battleground for US and Russian strategic influence. Russia's interests are obvious: about 17% of the population is ethnic Russian, with high concentrations in the East (Donbas); nearly 50% of Russia's trade (mainly oil and gas) is with the EU, and Ukraine is Russia's corridor to Europe; and the geographical proximity of Ukraine, important for Russia's security in the same way that Mexico is important for the US or Ireland for the UK.[1]

NATO acknowledges that '[j]ust four months after Ukraine's declaration of independence', in 1991, 'NATO invited its representative to an extraordinary meeting of the North Atlantic Cooperation Council, the body set up to shape cooperation between NATO and the states of the former Warsaw Pact'. The NATO-Ukraine Charter on a Distinctive Partnership (1997) 'set out a wide range of areas for potential cooperation, including civil emergency planning, military training and environmental security'. In *The Grand Chessboard* (1997), Jimmy Carter's National Security

Advisor, Zbigniew Brzezinski, describes the American takeover of and influence over Eurasian governments, trade routes and energy systems as essential to US global primacy. Brzezinski describes Ukraine as a 'geostrategic pivot' – the gateway between Russian energy and Europe.[2]

The UK, rightly or wrongly, considers itself the arbiter of Europe's security, bragging that at a time of austerity it is the only European NATO power meeting its 2% of GDP defence spending pledge. Ergo, Britain has particular interests in Ukraine. In 1994, the US, UK, Ukraine and Russia signed the Budapest Memorandum, Article 3 of which states that signatories 'reaffirm their commitment ... to refrain from economic coercion designed to subordinate to their own interest the exercise by Ukraine of the rights inherent in its sovereignty and thus to secure advantages of any kind'. This was followed four years later by Ukraine's first Partnership and Cooperation Agreement with the European Union and 'a new Agreement ... [which] looks forward to an EU-Ukraine Free Trade Area, negotiations on which will start when Ukraine has joined the [US-dominated] World Trade Organisation', said the House of Lords a few years before the revolution in 2014.[3]

'Doomsday'

Evidence submitted to a Parliamentary committee on the UK's *National Security Strategy* (2015) warns that the prospect of 'major power conflict', meaning direct confrontation between nuclear powers (for instance, the UK and Russia, or the US and China), 'dwarfs that of other contemporary security concerns such as terrorism'. The author notes the murder of 52 people in London by terrorists on 7 July 2005, before pointing out that, by comparison, 'the last time that the UK was engaged in military confrontation with another major power', namely the Soviet Union, it 'could have left Britain a smoking, radiating ruin if one of its multiple crises had escalated'. Despite – or because of – this ominous fact, public attention is drawn to lesser threats, particularly terrorism.[4]

Britain is not only ignoring the threat of nuclear Armageddon, as the author acknowledges, but is acting in ways that increase it. The author of the report errs in thinking that the people in power are unaware of this trend. In 2007, the Ministry of Defence noted casually the possibility of a 'doomsday scenario' out to 2036 and beyond, resulting from technological developments and state-policies. In 2015, the hands of the Bulletin of the Atomic Scientists' Doomsday Clock were moved from 5 to 3 minutes to midnight. The closest they have ever been is 2 minutes to midnight, after the Soviets tested the hydrogen bomb.[5]

NATO is expanding its presence in and around Ukraine, provoking a potentially catastrophic reaction from Russia, which sees America's involvement as further proof of US imperial designs, as John Sawers, former head of MI6, acknowledges: 'Putin's actions are ones of a leader who believes his own security is at stake'. The House of Commons Library says that '[t]he Alliance's eastwards expansion is seen by many in Russia as evidence of the West's continuing determination to take advantage of Russian weakness and to contain and encircle Moscow. The conflict in Georgia', over the Russian 'protectorate' Ossetia in 2008, led 'to a breakdown in NATO-Russian relations'. UK MoD documents anticipate that 'nuclear possession may lead to greater adventurism and irresponsible conventional and irregular behaviour, to the point of brinkmanship and misunderstanding'.[6]

The British government would express more than concern if Russia had sponsored a coup in, say, Ireland, basing troops there, training the Irish military, and conducting military exercises in the Irish Sea. Yet when the US and Britain do the same with Russia's next door neighbour, where a significant number of Russians live, the media go into overdrive to report Russia as a danger to world peace, totally inverting the values. The media also took the politically-motivated step of reporting Russian manoeuvres near UK territorial waters, despite the fact that Russian forces regularly fly near the UK. Typical of nationalist propaganda, nothing is reported about the UK's threats to Russian airspace as part of its NATO Baltic Air Policing Mission.[7]

'A [US] State Department cable from April 2009 said Russia had warned it would take countermeasures, including putting "missiles" in Kaliningrad, in response to expanded U.S. missile defenses in Europe', the Atlantic Council reported in 2010. 'US officials believe ... movements of Russian tactical nuclear weapons took place in late spring. In late May [2010], a US Patriot missile battery was deployed in northern Poland, close to Kaliningrad, sparking public protests from Moscow'. In early-2013, US forces began preparations for nuclear strikes on Russia. Operation Global Lightning 14 was conducted in May 2014. 'Units included in the exercise are bomber wings that will fly approximately 10 B-52 Stratofortresses and up to six B-2 Spirit bombers to demonstrate flexibility and responsiveness in the training scenarios throughout the continental US.'[8]

Russia began its own nuclear war games. '[T]he exercise was devoted to coordinating actions of various units in countering a large-scale missile- and air-attack.' Also, the exercise checked the procedures for launching a 'massive launch-on-warning ... missile strike and countering a nuclear attack by the means of the Moscow missile defense system', according to the Russian Forces website. 'As part of the exercise, the Strategic Rocket Forces launched a Topol/SS-25 ICBM [intercontinental ballistic missile] from the Plesetsk test site to the Kura test site in Kamchatka. The warhead was reported to have successfully reached its target'. Such operations may have been prohibited by the US-Russian Antiballistic Missile Treaty 1972, had the US not withdrawn from the Treaty in 2002.[9]

Documents not reported in the media reveal that Britain had no qualms about training and arming both pro- and anti-Russian regimes in Ukraine. The pro-Russian forces used weapons, possibly UK-supplied rifles and ammunition, against demonstrators, while the pro-EU forces have shelled and tortured civilians.

Hard power & soft power

For years, the UK had quietly supported Ukraine's ousted President Viktor Yanukovych, including arming and training the Ukrainian military. The hope was that Yanukovych would facilitate Euro-American energy and pipeline companies and liberalize Ukraine's financial sector.

According to the House of Lords, the pro-Russian Ukrainian President, Leonid Kuchma, was ousted in the US-backed Orange Revolution 2004, which 'tore [Ukraine] out of Moscow's sphere of influence'. Viktor Yushchenko was elected in 'the anti-Kremlin victory' of October 2007. Russia 'had backed' his opponent, Yanukovych, 'in an unprecedented way'. In a blow to Europe and America, the pro-Russian Yanukovych was elected in February 2010. A year later, a report published by the US Army War College predicted that in the event of US 'soft-power' operations, like backing coups and revolutions, Russia would split Ukraine by annexing Crimea, which it did in March 2014. '[T]he prospect of a new political spasm, similar to the orange revolution [sic] ... is perceived as fairly high, particularly as the devastating economic crisis generates massive discontent', the report continues. 'Such a replay of the West-sponsored coup against pro-Russian elites could result in a split, or indeed multiple splits, of the failed Ukraine, which would open a door for NATO intervention', thus furthering the risk of terminal nuclear war.[10]

Britain has no qualms about arming and training the Ukrainian military under both pro-Russian and pro-European governments. In 2014, the House of Commons Library noted that, 'Since April 2009 the Ministry of Defence (MOD) has spent approximately £3.9 million supporting Ukraine through the Defence Assistance Fund and the Conflict Pool', the latter being a hard-soft-power matrix of Foreign Office, MoD and Department for International Development spending. 'Many of the activities funded through these mechanisms support command, control and communications capabilities (C3), to a greater or lesser extent, including through the provision of joint exercising, military education and contributions to NATO coordinated activities'.[11]

The Wire: The Magazine of the Royal Corp of Signals states: 'Since Autumn [2010, the 7th Armed Brigade HQ & Sig Squadron (207)] has seen it's soldiers [sic] sent to all corners of the UK's glorious training areas, ... such as the Ukraine, Czech Republic and Marseille'. The MoD's *Annual Report and Accounts* states: 'In Serbia, Ukraine, Georgia and Armenia we have continued to provide advice on improved governance and Defence reform. Throughout 2012–13, MOD has assisted in the development of the Armed Forces of partner nations, by providing defence education and training to twelve countries through the Security Sector Education programme'.[12]

This, despite a Foreign and Commonwealth Office report from 2012 stating: 'Selective justice and rule of law remained concerns in Ukraine. The December [2011] EU Foreign Affairs Council conclusions made clear that progress on the proposed Association Agreement depended on Ukraine acting in accordance with EU values'. The report also notes that the EU 'called on Ukraine not to implement proposed legislation that would discriminate against the LGBT [Lesbian, Gay, Bisexual, Transgender] community'. Amnesty International's Heather McGill said in November 2013: 'Every year thousands of Ukrainians are beaten by the police to extract confessions for crimes'. Despite this, Britain's arms flows, training and support for the Yanukovych regime continued.[13]

Energy is Britain's principal interest in Ukraine. Cheap labour and goods are secondary concerns. UK Foreign Office Minister, Jeremy Browne, said: 'Ukraine is of immense geo-strategic importance, as it borders four European Union member states and, of course, Russia. We must also consider the size of the Ukrainian market, coupled with its near double-digit gross domestic product potential'. He went on to note that Ukraine offers 'significant opportunities to UK exporters and investors ... Ukraine is a major part of the European energy security jigsaw. It is an important transit route from the east to Europe, with 80% of Russian gas sold to EU customers transiting through Ukraine'. Browne concluded that 'Ukraine's closer integration with the EU offers the surest way of ensuring that not only Ukraine's long-term interests, but ours and those of our European partners are met'.[14]

The UK's trio of subversive institutions has been working hard to oppose democracy in Ukraine. They are the Westminster Foundation for Democracy (WFD), the British Council and the Department for International Development (DFID). The British Council notes that under Yanukovych's predecessor, Yushchenko, the UK issued 'strategic grants and connected capacity building which aims to make links within NGO/CSO [civil society organizations] communities, between NGOs and other CSOs and public institutions, and with other wider stakeholders, including the media and the general public'.[15]

Also under Yushchenko, the WFD trained NGOs in 'how to develop well-evidenced policy recommendations and present them professionally to MPs and parliamentary committees, and how to work with the media when running advocacy campaigns'. Can you image what would happen if Ukrainian propagandists were in Britain advising the three main parties and the BBC on how to report elections? A Yanukovych-era DFID report discusses Britain's '"mentor" role . . . , more of which can be done from a distance using video-conference and email'. Another states: 'Thomson Reuters Foundation ran a competition for journalists who had taken part in [Parliamentary] courses to encourage excellence in parliamentary reporting' – meaning that journalists keep to party-political trivia, *à la* UK media.[16]

The subversion appears to have had some effect. In 2012, the Yanukovych government reported that 'British businessmen note improving investment climate in Ukraine. This was stated by a member of the Parliament of Great Britain, Jack Straw', former Foreign Secretary under whose watch torture was allegedly committed (namely the UK's role in America's 'rendition' programme), 'during a working lunch with [the] Prime Minister of Ukraine'. The report went on to state that Straw said that 'the British businessmen were convinced that the investment climate in Ukraine has improved radically[, noting] the possibility of intensification of investment ... In particular, ... the issue of attracting investment in agriculture, in particular the cultivation of sugar beets'.[16]

But, like Gaddafi in Libya and Assad in Syria, both of whom refused to agree to the Broader Middle East and North Africa Initiative, Yanukovych refused to sign a crucial liberalization deal. In 2014, an article on the 2014 revolution/coup in Ukraine, subtitled 'Why we saw this one coming', was published by the Jean Monnet Centre of Excellence, King's College London. The author notes that, 'Under pressure from [Russia], Yanukovych decided to abandon the plans to sign the Association Agreement ... represent[ing] a huge blow to the Ukrainian relations with the EU'.[17]

Civil war

McGill's Amnesty report on Yanukovych's state-brutality preceded the massacre of dozens of demonstrators in Kiev. Beginning November 2013, a growing number of activists began demonstrating against Yanukovych's decision to reject the EU-Ukraine deal in favour of a more lucrative Russian contract. The mainly Kiev-based protests, which spread throughout the country, were known as EuroMaidan, or Europe Square. The demonstrators appear to have had an economic interest in Europe. According to an empirical investigation led by Harvard-Oxford specialist, Olga Onuch, 'the "median protester" was middle class, with a new level of linguistic cosmopolitanism and a relative lack of partisanship'. The majority of protestors advocated a Europeanization of Ukraine: 'fully two-thirds (67 percent) of our *Kyiv* survey's respondents were in fact older than 30, with an average age of almost 36. Nearly a quarter of all *Kyiv* respondents were older than 55'.[18]

Both the UK Ministry of Defence's training of the Ukrainian

military and the Department of Business Innovation and Skills' weapons exports were put to use. 'Over 100 people were killed [by police] as the EuroMaidan protest reached its bloody conclusion in February [2014]', says Amnesty. A year before, Britain had exported £22.4 million-worth of weapons to Yanukovych, including 'sniper rifles', 'weapons sights', and 'components for air-to-air missiles'. The Foreign and Commonwealth Office's *Annual Report and Accounts 2013–2014* reiterates UK complicity in working with the dictator. It states: 'Our Rapid Deployment Teams (RDT) were activated on seven occasions to France, Kenya, Philippines, South Sudan, Ukraine and Egypt (twice)'.[19]

In February 2014, Crimean and Russian forces blocked Ukrainian military posts in Crimea, the ethnic Russian-majority peninsula of Ukraine. The Crimean Parliament voted to cede to Russia, which annexed Crimea in March, in violation of international law.[20]

Amnesty cites 'credible reports of abductions and beatings carried out by volunteer battalions operating alongside regular Ukrainian armed forces'. In August 2015, a security guard in the 50% ethnic Russian Luhansk region 'was seized by several dozen armed men who arrived in vehicles flying Ukrainian flags. At least one was marked "Battalion Aidar" '. In an article titled, 'Ukrainian nationalist volunteers committing "ISIS style" war crimes', *Newsweek* cites 'over 30 pro-nationalist, volunteer battalions similar to Aidar, such as Ukraina, DND Metinvest and Kiev 1, all funded by private investors'. It alleges that Aidar 'is publicly backed by Ukrainian oligarch Ihor Kolomoyskyi, who also allegedly funds the Azov, Donbas, Dnepr 1, [and] Dnepr 2 volunteer battalions, operating under orders from Kiev', following the ousting of Yanukovych. The author notes that a warrant for Kolomoyskyi's arrest 'was issued in Russia . . . for "organising the killing of civilians," through his sponsorship of volunteer militants'.[21]

Norway's Channel TV2 broadcast footage of the Azov Battalion 'flying flags with the symbols of Ukraine's neo-Nazi party

[Svoboda]'. The *Newsweek* report concludes that 'numerous powerful paramilitary groups are reportedly involved in the Ukrainian conflict such as Patriot of Ukraine, Right Sector and White Hammer'. Meanwhile, the Ukrainian Army held off pro-Russian movements in Donbas, on the Russian border. Yanukovych fled the country after a warrant was issued for his arrest. An interim President was sworn in and in May 2014, Petro Poroshenko was elected President. The billionaire Poroshenko was Minister of Trade and Economic Development and head of the Council of Ukraine's National Bank.[22]

Human Rights Watch reports that in Donetsk, a pro-Russian stronghold, 'both Ukrainian government forces and the Russia-backed rebel forces have unnecessarily endangered civilians by locating military objectives and using explosive weapons with wide-area effect in populated areas, including near school buildings, in violation of international humanitarian law'. More than 300 civilians had died in that region alone since fighting began. About 4,000 people had died by 2015 in the civil war.[23]

The extent of British covert operations is difficult to ascertain. The *Mirror* reports that, 'British teams have been moving around the country [Ukraine] covertly monitoring border crossing points and towns where Russian support is strongest to "clarify [Russian President Vladimir] Putin's intentions"'. The *Independent* quotes Ukrainians who claim to have found evidence of CIA and MI6 involvement.[24]

Amnesty interviewed eyewitnesses escaping war near Alchevsk, Donetsk, Kramatorsk, Krasnyi Luch, Lisichansk, Lugansk, Rubizhne, Pervomaisk and Slovyansk. Interviews were conducted with Ukrainian refugees in Rostov, Russia. 'Civilians from these areas told Amnesty International that the Ukrainian government forces subjected their neighbourhoods to heavy shelling. Their testimonies suggest that the attacks were indiscriminate and may amount to war crimes'. The House of Commons Library notes the UK's escalation of the violence, namely 'the deployment of a 70-

strong UK military training team to the country. The decision to deploy a team of military advisers to Ukraine has been interpreted by some as the UK government putting "boots on the ground", in breach of the 1994 Budapest Memorandum'. The aim is to prevent pro-Russian forces from gaining ground in a long-term, potentially catastrophic strategy to keep Ukraine tied to Europe. Defence Secretary Michael Fallon said: 'The infantry training package will focus on protective measures to improve survivability, and the intelligence capacity building team will provide tactical-level analysis training' to Poroshenko's forces.[25]

Summarizing Fallon, news agencies reported that Britain was escalating the war by sending 'up to 1,000 troops to a high readiness force and deploy four RAF Typhoon jets for air policing in the Baltic States to boost NATO's collective security', or Russian's insecurity. Fallon announced that 'the UK will be the lead nation in the Very High Readiness Joint Task Force (VJTF) in 2017 and then on rotation thereafter'. The VJTF 'will see the UK contributing manpower to two regional headquarters in Poland and Romania and to force integration units in the three Baltic States, Poland, Romania and Bulgaria'.[26]

Chapter 8

Sri Lanka – 'Shining a light'

The Government of Sri Lanka's 2009 ethnic cleansing of 40,000 Tamil civilians is one of the most shameful episodes of the modern age. The outrage was widespread, including in the UK. What has remained a secret, however, is Britain's role in the atrocities. As the UK condemns Sri Lanka for its war crimes, no one in the mainstream or even in the dissident media (with two exceptions, one of which includes this author) is talking about the UK's role. Here, we document Britain's participation of war crimes and outline some of the background to the conflict.

In September 2015, the United Nations Human Rights Council adopted a resolution to launch an inquiry into abuses committed by the Sri Lankan government during its nearly three decades-long war against the Tamil Tigers. No thought was given to investigating the role of British politicians and military personnel.

In response to the UN announcement, Hugo Swire, Minister of State for Asia, said that he 'warmly welcome[s]' the Resolution, adding: 'the United Kingdom pushed hard for a UN process that would shine a light on a traumatic period in Sri Lanka's history … [F]or Sri Lanka to fulfil its enormous potential it must address the difficult legacy of its past'. Naturally, Britain could not address the 'difficult legacy' of its own recent involvement. Reuters (which also fails to report the UK's involvement) notes how the US 'softened' the resolution in a 'balancing act needed to keep Sri Lanka's new reformist leadership on board while making a credible attempt to end a culture of impunity over what the UN calls the mass killings of tens of thousands of people'.[1]

The 'culture of impunity' is such that even 'dissident' journals in the UK refused to publish this author's findings: that Britain had provided weapons that had been used in the 2009 ethnic cleansing, which led to the deaths of 40,000 Tamil civilians. This author eventually published the findings in an academic journal in the USA. In 2012, a book-length study was accepted by peer-review in the UK by a university press, but eventually pulled following a board-level decision. Were it not for the cowardice of the editors and board, the information could have reached the public several years ago. Eventually, five years after the fact, the International Human Rights Association, Bremen, published a pioneering report by Phil Miller of Corporate Watch, *Britain's dirty war against the Tamil people, 1979–2009*, which was brought to public attention in the UK by SpinWatch. This chapter is based on independent research conducted prior to Miller's important work.[2]

A little history

Global Security reports that 'Sri Lanka's oldest and most enduring military relationship has been with Britain ... [Its] own indigenous armed forces were organized, trained, armed, and led by British military personnel'. This is confirmed by a British House of Commons Library Note, which acknowledges that, 'From a military perspective relations between the UK and Sri Lanka are historically well established'.[3]

Britain invaded Ceylon (now Sri Lanka) in 1796, bringing Indian Muslim labourers to the predominantly Buddhist island. The ethnic majority Sinhalese were transformed into workers for imperial export markets, mainly as tea growers. Power was given to the minority Tamils, eliciting anti-Tamil sentiment among the general population. Britain's colonial subjugation reduced progress for centuries to come. The World Bank reported that in 1993 a Sri Lankan 'child from the poorest household was 3.7 times more likely to be stunted. By 2000, this ratio had more than doubled to 7.7'. The country 'has run persistently large budget deficits (averaging 7.8% of GDP per year between 1990 and 2009)', the British House of Commons Library confirms. '[W]ith much of its public spending devoted to the military[,] ... its debt burden remains relatively high, at around 80% of GDP'. The military expenditure is thus not only a fatal problem for the Tamils, but for the country's poor in general.[4]

In 1965, following some genuinely socialist reforms that may have freed the then-newly 'independent' country from postcolonial colonialism, the Bandaranaike Government reinstated pro-Western initiatives, including goodwill visits to several Western countries to ensure the resumption of 'aid' (i.e., neoliberal investments) from the World Bank. The liberalization of the economy disenfranchised the sons and daughters of plantation workers, who were enjoying free higher education. The 1971 uprisings led by the nationalist-Marxist Janatha Vimukthi Peramuna (People's Liberation Front) were crushed by the 'brutal counterinsurgency efforts' of the supposedly 'leftist' Sri Lanka Freedom Party, which killed 2,000 to 3,000 people.[5]

The national crises of the early-1970s led to the further oppression of the Tamil minority. The Tamil United Liberation Front's Constitution (1972) formally called for an independent Tamil State. Job and cultural discrimination, exemption from employment in the civil services, lack of access to higher education and the difficulties of communicating to Sinhalese-speaking officials all provided support for Tamil nationalism. The major factors leading to calls for Tamil secession appear to be demographic and migratory.[6]

The Sinhalese population grew by 650 percent in Tamil-majority areas in the post-'independence' era, which the Tamils saw as a deliberate colonization effort. Populations tend to increase in conditions of poverty. Thousands of Sinhalese migrated to the northern Tamil-majority areas. Tamils migrated southwest to Sinhalese-majority areas. According to the specialist Robert Kearney, the Dry Zone, in which the majority of Tamils reside, expanded in population density from 130,000 to 850,000 in less than forty years. Violence against Tamils soon increased.[7]

'Pogroms were reported in 1977, 1978, 1981, 1982' and, in July

1983, on a 'massive scale'. In 1981, Tamil-owned shops and stalls were 'looted and burned throughout the Sinhalese areas', writers Bryan Pfaffenberger. 'Expenditure on arms purchases has been truly colossal', says Kumar Rupesinghe. 'In Sri Lanka the military response to domestic conflict has led to an over 500% growth in real terms since 1981', the year of the pogroms against the Tamils. Up to that point, Tamil terrorism had been very limited, mostly targeting political and military personnel. By 1982, however, a civil war was underway.[8]

At that point, President Junius Jayewardene requested assistance. The UK Special Task Force was established as a counterterrorist unit in Sri Lanka, 'not as a military force but rather a highly-specialised police unit'. British Special Air Service (SAS) officers, 'under the auspices of the private firm of Keeny Meeny Services [KMS] were instrumental in training Sri Lankan troops in counterterrorist and counterinsurgency techniques', *Global Security* reports. Playing the divide and conquer card, KMS and Israeli special forces were secretly training the nascent Tamil terror group, which opposed the Sri Lankan Government.[9]

The civil war rapidly intensified. An article in the Welsh *Western Mail* reported that '[a] band of mercenary soldiers recruited in South Wales is training a Tamil army', going on to claim that '[a]bout 20 mercenaries were signed up after a meeting in Cardiff, and have spent ... two months in southern India' – a country also involved in training Tamil insurgent groups – 'preparing a secret army to fight the majority Sinhalas, in the cause of a separate Tamil State'. The article which reprinted the story notes that, 'According to [then-] recent Indian press reports, the LTTE [Tamil Tigers] is now being equipped with Stinger missiles diverted from former Afghan mujahideen stocks' – *mujahideen* who were also trained by the SAS.[10]

Britain's involvement with the Tamils was raised at a press conference in 1985: a reporter asked Britain's Prime Minister Margaret Thatcher if it was 'true that your government has refused to cooperate with us in eradicating terrorism in Sri Lanka?' Thatcher replied: 'When it comes to supplying arms, that is a matter which is dealt with according to each issue and we do not give details ever'. K. T. Rajasingham reported that 'British pilots were seen flying helicopter gunship and airplanes to bombard and attack innocent Tamil civilians in the Northern province, especially on the Jaffna Peninsula. These British mercenaries were paid a monthly salary of around 2,500 British pounds per person and other fringe benefits in order to actively participate in killing and maiming innocent Tamil civilians'.[11]

As this was going on, their colleagues were training the Tamil Tigers opposition force.

Rise of the Tigers

In 1987, the All Ceylon Buddhist Congress supported the Sri Lankan government's efforts to 'wipe out terrorism' by whatever means, Bruce Matthews reported. In that year, a British government official confirmed that the UK government had authorised mercenaries to train the Sri Lankan counterinsurgents. 'Tamil militants fighting for a separate homeland in the east and north of this island nation have alleged that British mercenaries were directly aiding Sri Lankan troops', notes the Associated Press. In Sri Lanka in April 1987, Minister of State David Waddington informed the AP of 'the 20 British nationals employed here', going on to identify the service in question as Keeny Meeny Services.[12]

The British arms and training were used to devastating effect. As many as 40,000 Sri Lankans were killed in the late 1980s, 'when the United National Party (UNP) was in power, most through murder and disappearance by [British-armed and trained] security forces and government death squads', the oil company-financed International Crisis Group (ICG) reported. 'Counterinsurgency campaigns under the UNP government in 1989-1990 and then under President Chandrika Kumaratunga in the late 1990s killed thousands of Tamil civilians with impunity and were largely perceived by that community as a continuation of the violence of 1983'.[13]

In 1989, 'many left-wing Sinhalese activists were targeted by government death squads and ultra-nationalist groups'. The ICG further notes that 'While thousands of Sinhalese died at the hands of the LTTE, as many have been killed by other Sinhalese'. The JVP-inspired uprisings between 1987–1990 and the 'brutal counter-insurgency efforts in response were two of the deadliest periods in modern Sri Lankan history'. Members of the British government continued covert divide and rule action in the country. Future-Defence Secretary Liam Fox said: 'since 1996, when I was a Foreign Office Minister, I have been involved in attempts to help resolve the conflict in Sri Lanka ... As the war with the Tamil Tigers drew to a close I worked with a number of others in business, banking and politics'. Fox concluded: 'It was my aim to create a mechanism that would allow reconstruction funding to occur through the private sector. This was called the Sri Lankan Development Trust'.[14]

Fox went on to admit a secret meeting with the Sri Lankan President in the Dorchester Hotel (London) in December 2010. Fox also revealed that his 'friend' was Tamil former Foreign Minister, Lakshman Kadirgamar, who was assassinated by the Tigers. CorpWatch alleges that the British mercenary firm DSL 'has provided counter-insurgency training for security forces in Sri Lanka'. SourceWatch alleges that Britain's Sandline International also had 'contracts' in Sri Lanka. It was noted in a House of Commons report that the elite Royal Military Academy Sandhurst has hosted training for Sri Lankan Army officials every year since at least 1997.[15]

In 2000, having won major ground, the Tigers declared a ceasefire, which the government rejected. A Tiger attack on the Bandaranaike Airport in 2001 changed the power dynamics. 'Tourism vanished overnight, trade collapsed, and Sri Lanka's economy slumped', threatening food imports. After the attack threatened long-term economic prospects by destroying the main airport, Lloyds insurance underwriters insisted that the airport adopt war risk surcharges.[16]

The lowering of the surcharges was conditioned on the government hiring the British-based Trident Maritime corporation and Rubicon, the former being a start-up of former Sandline mercenary, Tim Spicer. Sri Lanka's High Commissioner in London, Mangala Moonesinghe, 'was instructed to open negotiations, not with the Tamil Tigers, but with [London's insurance] brokers', Sri Lanka's *Sunday Times* alleges. It wasn't until 2001 that the UK designated the Tigers a terrorist organization.[17]

The *Sunday Times* (Sri Lanka) alleges that Spicer's associates have, 'in the past, mounted coups, guarded British, US and Arabian dignitaries and ambassadors, engaged in civil wars, and run sabotage and terror activities from behind hostile lines'. The majority of the 15 names on Spicer's list of Trident Maritime employees, 'were retired British Special Forces and Intelligence Officers', the most prominent of whom was allegedly Harry Ditmus, an MI5 agent. Ditmus assisted in Britain's occupation of Northern Ireland.[18]

In 2001, Britain's New Labour government exported £15.5 million-worth of weapons to Sri Lanka, including 'components for sniper rifles', 'equipment for the use of weapon night sights, flash suppressors, grenade launchers, gun mountings, illuminators, laser range finders, military aeroengines', 'small arms ammunition, sniper rifles', and 'stun grenades'.[19]

The arms flowed to Sri Lanka and the Sandhurst training continued, even after the Army's Bindunuwewa Rehabilitation Camp Massacre in 2000, which the UK Foreign Office acknowledges, 'brought the Sri Lankan government international condemnation for not providing adequate security to those who surrendered or to the detainees. Twenty-seven of the camp's 41 inmates were murdered in the massacre'. During the 2002 'ceasefire', British arms continued to flow. In 2002, Britain exported £1.5 million-worth of weapons to the country, including 'components for combat helicopters', 'components for heavy machine guns', 'components for naval light guns', 'projectile launchers, small arms ammunition, sporting gun ammunition', 'toxic chemical precursors', and 'weapon cleaning equipment'.[20]

The massacre

In 2004, the Tigers split when the eastern commander, Vinayagamoorthy Muralitharan (aka Colonel Karuna), defected. The nascent Tamil Eelem People's Liberation Tigers, led by Karuna, fought the Tamil Tigers, killing around 6,000 members. It would seem that Karuna was a British agent. The House of Commons reported: 'He had entered the UK in September 2007, allegedly on a false diplomatic passport, but was arrested. The Crown Prosecution Service announced that it was investigating whether it should also bring war crimes charges against him but ultimately decided that there was insufficient evidence to do so'.[21]

By 2004, Sri Lanka suffered high inflation, national debt, and a devalued currency. The tsunami killed around 30,000 Sri Lankans and left one million homeless. Under the pretext of concern over human rights abuses, Britain withdrew 50% of a £1.5m relief pledge. The claim about human rights was a cynical farce: leaving aside the fact that genuine aid relief for civilians has nothing to do with factional fighting, in that year Britain exported £4.3 million-worth of weapons to Sri Lanka, including: 'components for demolition devices', 'linear cutting explosive charges', 'technology for the use of military utility helicopters', 'technology for the production of combat helicopters', 'semi-automatic pistols', 'technology for the use of semi-automatic pistols', 'hand grenades', and 'NIGHTVISION goggles'.[22]

In 2005, 'a team of British intelligence officials attached to MI6 had met STF [Special Task Force] counter-terror experts in Colombo', the same group that their SAS colleagues helped to create in 1983. In August 2005, Foreign Affairs Minister Lakshman Kadirgamar, Fox's associate, was assassinated. The death was blamed on the Tigers, which denied responsibility. Martial law was imposed in Sri Lanka.[23]

Once again, British arms and training were put to deadly use. The years 2005–6 saw a major escalation of violence, with the Tigers blocking the main Jaffna-Colombo road. 'In August [2006] a Sri Lankan air-force attack on a camp in Mullaitivu left at least 61 school children dead', the House of Commons reported. 'Official Sri Lankan defence expenditure reportedly rose by 30% in 2006 ... In July 2007, the Sri Lankan Government announced that the defence budget for 2007-8 would increase by 45% on 2006–7 and that the size of the army was to be increased by 50,000 to 168,000'.[24]

It was clear that the Tigers had served their purpose and that the World Bank and IMF wanted a return on their investments. The following years saw severe clampdowns on Tamil civilians in an effort to destroy the Tigers. UK arms sales shot up, with £8.5 million in arms sold to Sri Lanka in 2006, including: 'armoured all wheel drive vehicles', 'components for general purpose machine guns; components for heavy machine guns', 'revolvers', 'semi-automatic pistols', 'small arms ammunition' and 'weapon cleaning equipment'.[25]

Malcolm Bruce, Chair of the International Development Committee and a member of the Select Committee on Arms Export Controls, acknowledged that 'Britain's sales did violate the EU Code of Conduct'. In 2007, the UK Foreign Office reported that: 'The situation in Sri Lanka remains grave, with human rights abuses manifested as both a symptom and ongoing factor in the conflict – abuses by government forces, the Tamil Tigers and the Karuna faction are reported'. That didn't stop the Sandhurst training and weapons exports (£1 million in 2007, including 'combat shotguns' and 'semi-automatic pistols').[26]

What followed has been widely reported, and summarized in the opening paragraph of this chapter, namely one of the most disgraceful episodes of modern times. The remaining 1,000 Tigers were killed, putting an end – at least formally – to the terror group, at the expense of 40,000 Tamil civilians.[27]

In 2010, after the widely-reported atrocities (which omitted Britain's involvement), the UK government exported nearly £1 million-worth of weapons to Sri Lanka, including: 'demolition devices', 'military devices for initiating explosives', 'military firing sets', 'air guns' (which can be easily converted) and 'weapons sights'. Sri Lanka's military budget for 2012 was $2.1 billion, 'a nearly 7 per cent increase from 2011', the ICG reported. 'While defence spending has remained at around 3 per cent of gross domestic product it makes up 20 per cent of total expenditures, dwarfing those on education and health'. Regarding the evidence that the government of Sri Lanka committed war crimes, UK Foreign Office Minister, Alistair Burt, said: 'It is not for me to judge where this evidence should lead'. When it came to atrocities committed a few years later in Syria by Assad, Burt had a different opinion.[28]

The mass slaughter and militarization of the countryside laid the basis for investment opportunities. The Sri Lanka High Commission (London) and the Sri Lanka Export Development Board (Colombo) held a joint-Business and Networking Event in September 2011 as part of Expo 2012, 'to engage British Business and Industry on a UK Trade & Investment Mission'. Titled 'Partnering with the Hub of Asia', and attended by 'a wide representation from the UK trade, industry, government, banking sector, media, leisure industry etc.', the event was inaugurated by Chris Nonis, High Commissioner for Sri Lanka, 'who focused on the plethora of commercial and economic opportunities that have emerged in the wake of the restoration of peace and political stability in the island' – the ethnic cleansing of 40,000 Tamils and the militarization of society defining 'peace' and 'political stability'.[29]

Chapter 9

Colombia – 'The best business environment'

Here, we investigate Britain's complicity in widespread human rights abuses in Colombia, ranging from intimidation of unions and protestors to the 'extinction' of indigenous communities. The chapter gives a brief history of the country before arguing that Britain's primary role is to protect large corporations from the threat of activists. Britain does so by pretending that countering narcotics is the objective of the SAS. In conclusion, we argue that the 'fumigation' programme carried out under the pretext of countering drug cultivation amounts to chemical warfare.

Since 1989, British special forces, including the SAS, the Special Boat Service and MI6 have been operating in civil war-torn Colombia under the cover of a counter-narcotics programme.

With a landmine epidemic, an internal refugee crisis of 4 million, and a political assassination rate (of unionists, activists, students, etc.) of 60,000 in the last decade at the hands of paramilitaries, Colombia is one of the world's major crises. Colombian children mine coal, gold, and emeralds for British exports. They cut flowers (carnations) and, in a disturbing development noted by the US Department of Labor, are exploited in pornography.[1]

Hell in Colombia

In 2010, Amnesty International expressed 'concern' about 'the extrajudicial execution of hundreds of civilians by the [Colombian] security forces'. In that year, Justice for Colombia (JFC) published photographs of the men who train them. 'On the right' of one picture 'is a Major in the Parachute Regiment of the British Army, on the left a Colombian soldier. Other British soldiers, including a Colonel, can be seen in the background'. JFC published another photo, which, it alleges, shows the ex-British Ambassador to Colombia, 'speaking with an unidentified group of British soldiers at a military base in Bogota ... Francisco Ramirez, a former counterinsurgency specialist in the Colombian security forces, says that he was trained by British troops'.[2]

Noting the daily killing of students, unionists, activists, 'subversives' and others, ABColombia stated that 'this repression sends a clear message to ordinary people not to organise themselves in defence of their rights'. In 2010, the UK Foreign and Commonwealth Office reported that as 'Colombia is becoming more and more important for UK exporters ... we do remain open for business ... According to The World Bank Group's "Doing Business Report" Colombia has the best business environment amongst the main economies of Latin America'. A year later, the Foreign Office enthused that 'Colombia has a sustained record of sound economic policies, and has strong economic fundamentals' – based, we might add, on child labour, chemical warfare, death-squads, paramilitaries, and, according to Amnesty, indigenous 'extinction'.[3]

Since the country's independence from Spain in 1819, an intermittent war has been in operation, fought between Colombia's wealthy land- and business-owning elite and the peasants; the latter consist mainly of the descendants of the Spanish poor, Afrocolombians (the descendants of Spain's African slaves), and the remnants of the indigenous South Americans.

The above is a capsule history, of course, but essentially describes the situation. Since the 1960s, the US military has trained the Colombian Army to act as one of its many proxies. The Colombian Army in turn trains the paramilitaries, an extensive network of death-squads that force peasants from their land and murder, kidnap, torture and beat students, community leaders, peace activists, unionists, prostitutes, disabled people, the homeless and homosexuals as part of a 'social cleansing' operation, generically designed to spread terror throughout the nation. The paramilitaries' main rival is the Fuerzas Armadas Revolucionarias de Colombia (FARC), a corrupt, self-professed Marxist terrorist organization responsible for about a quarter of all Colombia's murders – compared with the paramilitaries and Colombian Army, which murder the overwhelming majority of civilians.[4]

FARC recruits children and tortures them for 'insubordination' (such as crying or refusing to kill): children whom, having no alternative but prostitution, begging, and street crime, flock to the organization, but cannot leave upon joining. The organization's middle-aged commanders rape young girls and force them to have abortions. Despite FARC's atrocious behaviour, it has some measure of support among the general population, who benefit from community projects, such as bridge and health centre construction.[5]

By the year 2000, 0.4% of landowners (10,000 people) owned 61.2% of the land. In 2009, an Amnesty International report 'suggest[ed] that between 4 and 6 million hectares of land owned by thousands of *campesinos*, or collectively owned by Indigenous People and Afro-descendant communities, have been stolen' by government-backed paramilitaries. Amnesty notes that, 'At particular risk of displacement [are blacks and natives] in areas which have been earmarked for large economic projects, such as mineral and oil exploration, agro-industrial developments or hydro-electric installations', many of which are linked to Britain.[6]

In 2010 Members of the British Parliament 'expresse[d] ... concern about the devastating environmental impacts that the proposed La Colosa opencast goldmine in Colombia' – owned by a British company – 'will have on a region of considerable biodiversity and importance for food production'. In 2011, Parliament noted that the deviation of the River Rancheria 'will threaten water security for the region' and mentioned the 'evicted community of Tabaco'.[7]

In November, Parliament confirmed that the communities displaced by the Cerrejon Coal mines had not been compensated, and expressed 'concern about the devastating social and environmental impacts of the . . . company's huge opencast coal mine in Colombia', owned by British firms.[8]

Mercenaries & paramilitaries

The company Defence Systems Limited was founded in 1981. It went on to become ArmorGroup. It was acquired in 2008 by G4S. Most of ArmorGroup's employees were former SAS operatives, though the group primarily utilizes US mercenaries for international operations. DSL and subsequently ArmorGroup 'protected BP oil property', writes Deborah Avant. BP's own records affirm that, 'In response to a series of threats against oil companies operating in the country, the Colombian government authorized permanent security support for our facilities from the Colombian military and police, and BP agreed to help fund this support through Colombia's national oil company and BP's state partner, Ecopetrol'.[9]

Scholar Grace Livingstone notes that 'oil union leader, Carlos Mesias Arrigui Cerquera, was murdered by military or paramilitary forces in 1995, after leading an anti-BP strike'. In 1995, BP 'donated' $11 million to the military. Livingstone alleges that the company's hired goons took photos of locals and handed them on to paramilitaries, a claim which BP denies. BP constructed the Ocensa pipeline in Segovia (Antioquia), dismembering the lands of 1,000 poor people. Eventually, BP was taken to a British court by Colombian farmers. DSL allegedly supplied military equipment to the 14th Army Brigade to protect the pipeline. Forty-three people were murdered by the Brigade in Segovia in 1998. These are some examples of what Colombian environmental activists, union leaders, and so on, face on a daily basis.[10]

In 1994, the British Parliament professed concern over 'the level of political assassinations in Colombia, amounting to an average of eleven per day and the fact that the state security forces are implicated in at least 75 per cent of those killings'. The Parliament 'deplores the British Government policy of giving aid to the Colombian military forces'. Despite these professions of concern, the UK's military aid continues to flow.[11]

BP noted that in 1995 the company 'found two new major oil and gas accumulations overlying the recently-discovered Volcanera field'. The *Independent* noted in the same year that the Metropolitan Police and a Hereford-based SAS unit had been 'working closely' with the Colombian military. Human Rights Watch issued a report stating that at the time, paramilitary atrocities increased markedly. One group even named itself the Chainsaws. Another called itself Death to Communists and Guerrillas.[12]

The leaked Order 200-05/91 (1991) proved to Americas Watch (now part of HRW) the extent of the collusion between the paramilitaries and the UK-trained and armed military. 'In April 1989, President Virgilio Barco (1986–1990) spoke out against paramilitaries, calling them "terrorist organizations"', even though it was Barco who accepted SAS counter-narcotics training, which the press tacitly acknowledged means anti-FARC operations. 'In reality', said Barco, 'the majority of [the paramilitaries'] victims are not guerrillas. They are men, women, and even children, who have not taken up arms against institutions. They are peaceful Colombians'. Many paramilitaries even have offices and computers.[13]

A classified document leaked to HRW and signed by Maj. Gen. Manuel José Bonett Locarno (then-Commander of the Army's Second Division) 'suggest[ed] that any project that benefits the local population is suspicious and potentially subversive'. HRW commented that the Fourth Brigade's *Weekly Intelligence Summary* listed 'traditional political parties', 'leftist political parties', and 'trade unions' as military targets, with 'impunity that is nothing short of breathtaking'.[14]

HRW further alleges that President Samper 'appeared increasingly hostile to human rights and measures that would end the military-paramilitary partnership'. Autodefensas Campesinas de

Córdoba y Urabá (ACCU) was an umbrella of paramilitaries formed in the 1980s. A few years later, under President César Gaviria (1990-1994), the Colombian military – and, by definition, the ACCU – sought advice on intelligence gathering from MI6, further blurring the distinctions between oil, cocaine and counter-FARC activities. HRW added that the Army delegated to the ACCU lists of union leaders and human rights workers to be murdered.[15]

Britain's role deepens

A report backed by the National Union of Journalists, Connect, Unite, Unison and others notes that 'there are no conditions of any sort attached to UK military assistance to Colombia ... This is in direct contrast to US military assistance to Colombia which involves, for a large segment of the aid, regular, and public, human rights reviews and certifications by the US State Department' – which are as worthless as the paper on which they are printed.

The report notes that the British government 'says that some of the assistance provided to the Colombian military is for human rights training. However, HMG has refused to reveal what proportion of UK assistance is for this type of training nor to which units/personnel of the Colombian Army it is provided'. The report shows that the more 'human rights training' was provided, the worse the human rights violations become – as is also the case in Bangladesh and Somalia.[16]

By 1998, FARC controlled 60% of Colombia. The Anglo-American business-military elite devised a strategy to counter FARC's advances. General Peter Pace, Commander in Chief of the Southern Command (the Pentagon agency charged with ruling Latin America), explained that the motive of the Clinton-era Plan Colombia (2000) was 'to end the insurgency through negotiated settlement and defeat the illicit drug industry'. More importantly, it was to achieve 'unhindered access to strategic natural resources'.[17]

A US Congress report explains that Plan Colombia 'made significant progress in re-establishing government control over much of its territory'. In 2000, 317,000 Colombians were forced from their homes in a military-paramilitary push against the FARC and other guerrilla groups. This brought the number of internally displaced to 4 million: the biggest internal refugee crisis in the world. A year later, the British Parliament condemned 'a United States-led campaign to destroy the peace process between Andres Pastrana's Government and Colombia's guerrilla movements' and 'fabricate a myth that guerrillas and drugs traffickers are "one dangerous network" and legitimise an all-out counter-insurgency war'.[18]

Parliament noted that it is the military-sponsored paramilitaries that are responsible for 80% of the drugs trade. Parliament stated: 'the United States in its push for a military solution will waive Plan Colombia's human rights preconditions for military aid to the army for the second time when the Plan is reviewed in February [2001], effectively sanctioning more massacres, displacements, assassinations, torture and disappearances of the unarmed population'. Despite these warnings, Britain's support for the Colombian military continued.[19]

In February 2002, the Colombian military began a massive bombing campaign in the south of the country, followed by an effort to recapture FARC-held territory (Plan Patriota). The oil company-sponsored International Crisis Group conceded that, 'An unusually frank document ... concluded the 10 July 2003 London Meeting on International Support for Colombia organised by the British government for some 24 government, international financial institutions, UN and other international organisation delegations, was strongly supportive of the Uribe government'.[20]

Omitting much of the above, the *Guardian* reported that Uribe once governed Antioquia and had previously lectured in Latin American studies at St Antony's College, Oxford. The US Congress notes that 'Uribe is credited with restoring public security and creating a stable environment for investment'. In 2003, the *Guardian* reported that Britain supplied 'equipment and advice' to Bogota, becoming 'increasingly tangled' in the insurgency against 'leftwing guerrillas ... Whitehall refuses to disclose the extent of British military involvement on the grounds of national security'. A spokeswoman for the UK Foreign Office said: 'We provide some military aid but we don't talk about the details'.[21]

The *Guardian* revealed that the support included 'SAS training of the narcotics police, the Fuerza Jungla', and that New Labour greatly expanded its Colombia operations, 'sending ministers, retired generals and security advisers to Bogota. When Mo Mowlam was in the Cabinet Office in charge of drugs policy she went three times'. The report alleges that Mowlam arranged meetings with the Colombian military and 'Sir John Steele, head of security at the Northern Ireland Office, General Sir Michael Rose, a former SAS commander, and General Sir Roger Wheeler, former chief of the army general staff'. Britain's support also includes: 'Military advice to the army's ... counter-guerrilla mountain units. A surge in the supply of military hardware and intelligence equipment. Assistance in setting up an intelligence centre and a joint intelligence committee'.[22]

In the same year, the British Parliament noted that 'the subversive tactics of the paramilitaries are undermining democracy in Colombia by illegally targeting political activists such as students, trade unionists and intellectuals; and calls for international observers to be located in Colombia during elections'.[23]

The white stuff

Cocaine is a huge industry, worth some $60 billion per annum. Coke is mainly a middle-class drug, used by politicians, models, film stars, and people in music, media and other industries. More importantly, cocaine and other drug monies are untraceable and can be used for military black ops.[24]

A great deal is known about the US Central Intelligence Agency's role in drug running. Alfred McCoy's *The Politics of Heroin*, Gary Webb's *Dark Alliance* and Douglas Valentine's *The Strength of the Wolf* are vital exposés. Much less is known about MI6's role.

According to Grace Livingstone, throughout the 1980s drug barons, paramilitaries and members of the Colombia government began a heavy drug-money laundering campaign via land purchases, acquiring 10% of the country.[25]

The connections between drugs and politics are such that the Medellin and Cali cocaine cartels funded President Ernesto Samper's 1998 election campaign. Pablo Escobar's Medellin cartel attempted to get farmers to cultivate coca, which, initially, the FARC opposed. According to Livingstone, Escobar's money-laundering greatly aided the poor (undercutting FARC's campaign advantage) to the extent that churches praised his urban regeneration initiatives.[26]

Initially, Britain backed Escobar, until, it would seem, his poverty relief efforts got out of hand and ended up undermining big business. The Ford-sponsored Women's Commission commented on the 'narcotrade-financed paramilitary forces', adding that they 'often [work] with the support or acquiescence of [UK trained- and armed] Colombian police and military forces'.[27]

The standard propaganda is that UK Special Air Service assassins were sent by Prime Minister Thatcher in 1989 at the behest of President Barco, 'to fight the drug cartels'. In the real world, they were sent to fight the *FARC* cartels, specifically. By 1985, the wealthy Asociación Campesina de Agricultores y Ganaderos del Magdalena Medio (ACDEGAM) 'had powerful new members: drug traffickers who bought land in the Middle Magdalena', Human Rights Watch reported, adding that, 'In 1987 and 1988, the [ACDEGAM] even sponsored training centers with foreign instructors from Israel and Great Britain'.[28]

A 1990 inquiry led by Louis Blom-Cooper QC revealed that 'British mercenaries had been training the [Medellin] cartel's death squads', and that successive British governments 'turned a blind eye to the sale of weapons to the Medellin cartel'. The *Financial Times* reported that in 1988, ex-SAS mercenaries worked with the former Israeli Colonel Yair Gal Klein's Spearhead company to arm and train the Medellin cartel, and, again, 'the British government ha[d] turned a blind eye'. Mercenary firms cannot operate without the approval of the Foreign Office.[29]

Britain's active support for the drugs trade continues: 'In May 2006 troops of a High Mountain Battalion (whose members receive UK military assistance) were ordered by their commanding officer to ambush and kill ten counter-narcotics police officers near the town of Jamundi in the region of Valle del Cauca', according to a detailed account by the Justice for Colombia group. 'Small teams of SAS specialists rotate routinely through Bogota, and work with General Serrano's main unit, La Jungla', reports David Smith. The *Independent* notes that 'Colombian presidential candidate Luis Carlos Galán, a fierce opponent of the drug trade, was assassinated, some Colombian government sources say, by British mercenaries'.[30]

Former SAS mercenary David Tomkins was 'due to appear before US District Judge Adalberto Jordan' for his alleged role in the attempted murder of Escobar, whom, as noted, appeared to have fallen out of favour with Britain and America after diverting coke money to the poor. 'US officials [say Tomkins] will avoid trial and have time off his sentence', indicating that he is still a secret ally. Tomkins 'planned an attack on the drug lord's stronghold at the Hacienda Napoles, east of Medellin', the paper reported, but the 'helicopter flew into a mountainside, killing the pilot. Tomkins and his associate Peter McAleese, a former SAS officer, were forced to walk three days to safety through the Colombian jungle'.[31]

More recently, the International Crisis Group noted that Colombian police 'seized [a] USB memory stick of a key alleged associate of Daniel Barrera (alias "Loco Barrera"), a drug lord . . . , that reportedly contained a detailed monthly payroll of over $1.5 million for 890 politicians, military and justice officers and informants', indicating the levels of politico-drug interconnections throughout the country. In 2003, the late Pedro Juan Moreno, Chief of Staff in Antioquia, was accused of drug-running by US Customs, which seized shipments of potassium permanganate.[32]

The *London Progressive* writes: '[that] the British government is unconcerned as to who it is working with was [demonstrated] in December 2007', when then-Foreign Office Minister Kim Howells 'was photographed with soldiers of the High Mountain Battalions'. The paper adds that 'Howells also posed for the camera alongside [. . .] a general [who] has a 30 year history of involvement with right wing paramilitaries, death squads and drug traffickers'.[33]

The Guardian reports: 'Surrounding the smiling face of the Foreign Office minister Kim Howells in a picture taken in the Colombian region of Sumapaz are a general linked to paramilitary death squads and soldiers of a notorious unit of the Colombian army accused, including by Amnesty International, of torturing and killing trade unionists'. It also quotes the Foreign Office's response: 'The minister [Howells] is not under any illusions, but to effect change and get our points of view across, we have to engage. We make no secret of our military assistance to the Colombian armed forces, including in relation to human rights training'. Actually, the details of the training are kept secret, as this book has shown.

Colombia's coke is mainly channelled to Europe via the Caribbean, and to the US through Mexico. In July 2012, a US Congress report into HSBC's involvement in drug laundering found that 'the Mexican affiliate of HSBC transported $7 billion in physical US dollars to HSBC US from 2007 to 2008, outstripping other Mexican banks, even one twice its size, raising red flags that the volume of dollars included proceeds from illegal drug sales in US'. *Forbes* alleges that 'HSBC actively circumvented rules designed to "block transactions involving terrorists, drug lords, and rogue regimes"' – the latter referring to Iran and Syria.[34]

The *Daily Mail* reports: 'Concerns over the bank's links to Mexican drug dealers included £1.3 billion stashed in accounts in the Cayman Islands. One HSBC compliance officer admitted the accounts were misused by "organised crime"'. The *Daily Mail* also notes that David Cameron's Trade Minister, Lord Green of Hurstpierpoint, 'chaired HSBC during the period covered by the allegations'. Labour MP John Mann said of Lord Green: 'Someone whose bank has been assisting murdering drug cartels and corrupt regimes across the world should not be in charge of a government portfolio'.[35]

Chemical warfare

As the SAS and MI6 ran drugs by proxy and the Western media spun stories about chemical attacks in Syria, Britain was participating in America's anti-coca fumigation operations in Colombia. The anti-coca 'fumigation' is a massive chemical warfare campaign designed to destroy legal crops and free land for huge agribusiness.

In the first place, the Colombian peasants who grow cocaine do so because IMF adjustments and undercutting by multinationals have rendered their legal food production unprofitable. Because of the chemical spraying, hundreds of thousands of farmers in Putumayo have been prevented from growing bananas, plantains, yucca, fruit and cocoa. Carlos Castano Uribe, head of the National Department for Nature Reserves, called Colombia's protected parks, which host one third of the country's biodiversity, 'the gene bank of the nation'.[36]

The Sierra Navada de Santa Marta UNESCO-protected park, partially owned by the Kougi indigenous people, was allegedly sprayed by America's DynCorp (now owned by Computer Science Corporation), even though no coca was grown there. Congress reported that America's DFID-equivalent, the US Agency for International Development (USAID), 'funds alternative development programs to assist farmers of illicit crops in the switch from illicit to licit crops, and provides assistance with infrastructure and marketing. The approach includes job creation for rural families in coca-growing and conflict-prone areas with economic development potential', noting that USAID funded over 1,000 'alternative' crop projects.[37]

The primary ingredient of the chemical used by DynCorp to destroy coca and other crops is Monsanto's Roundup Ready.

Shortly after the operations began, Monsanto developed Roundup Ready-resistant GM crops. The *Washington Post* reported that the DynCorp Aerospace Technology branch involved in the operations was subcontracted to Eagle Aviation Service and Technology, which, in the 1980s, was hired by Oliver North to run weapons to the contras in Nicaragua during the Iran-Contra Affair. Britain's involvement in the spraying is extensive:[38]

Omitting the devastating effectives of the chemical warfare, and the real reasons for its use, the *Guardian* reported that the Colombian government 'allows the American technicians and pilots involved to be employed through a British-registered company, DynCorp Aerospace Operations (UK) Ltd, a subsidiary of DynCorp International ... It has a two-storey office block in Aldershot, the home of the British army'.[39]

DynCorp's chemical warfare programme intensified in 2000, and often resulted in shoot-outs between the ground-based guerrillas and the military helicopters guarding the spray planes. Grace Livingstone noted that there were 60 shootouts in the year 2000 alone.[40]

DynCorp mercenaries were allegedly caught running and taking drugs, Livingstone noted, adding that 'Documents relating to these cases have mysteriously disappeared'. The chemicals sprayed on plants, animals, women and children in Putumayo and elsewhere include Monsanto's Roundup Ready and the British company ICI's Cosmo-Flux. (Since the story broke, ICI has stopped supplying DynCorp with the chemical.) Monsanto's Roundup weed-killer warns commercial users to remove animals from the area prior to application and to wait six to eight *weeks* before harvesting because 'severe destruction' to trees, shoots, roots and foliage can occur.[41]

Glyphosate chemicals were mixed at a concentration twenty-times greater than recommended by the manufacturer. Soon after the operations began, Ecuadorian farmers complained of illness and dead crops as a result of 'herbicide drift'. The spraying has driven thousands of people from their homes into slums and shantytowns, where some of their children have died from starvation and respiratory problems and many have developed chronic skin and lung conditions.[42]

Chapter 10

Papua – 'Starve the bastards out'

It is well-known in Europe that Israel has been occupying Palestine illegally since 1967. Less known is Indonesia's occupation of West Papua for approximately the same amount of time. Indonesia invaded the island and continues to privilege western investors, particularly in the energy sector. Business policy has been so brutal that the British government has sought to distance itself by allowing businesses to employ mercenaries in the country.

Papua New Guinea (PNG) is comprised of islands near Australia and Indonesia. The population consists of over 6 million, most of whom are ethnic Melanesians that have inhabited the islands for 40,000 years. With 800 or so unique cultures, 85% of the population is rural. Many grow their own food and survive largely independent of the State. There has been a concerted effort, through 'education', construction projects and (as we shall see) violence, to force the rural population into towns.[1]

PNG was a Dutch possession until the British and Germans captured the southeast and northeast parts of the islands, respectively, in order to undermine their rival's empire. The colonial missionaries ensured that the country's religious base is broadly Christian, with much of the animist culture remaining intact. The other main ethnic groups are Malay and Javanese, many of whom colonized the islands as a result of Indonesian occupation. In the 1960s, Britain supported a coup bringing the fascist Suharto regime to power in Indonesia, a country which then annexed West Papua and continues the occupation.[2]

In 1975, PNG gained independence from Australia, but, in doing so, became a British colony. Despite popular myths that we live in a postcolonial age, the Head of State is the British Monarch and PNG is a member of the Commonwealth. PNG and West Papua suffer the curse of resource wealth. Both are rich in copper, gold, liquefied natural gas (LNG), oil, timber and fish. State-repression, including the sexual torture of children and the pollution of rivers and land by corporate waste contributes to the country's appalling health indicators.[3]

According to the World Health Organization, life expectancy at birth is 62 years for men and 65 for women. Infant mortality is 52 deaths per 1,000 live births – one of the worst in the world. Child mortality is even worse: 68 deaths per 1,000 live births. The maternal mortality rate is comparable to that of Bangladesh, with 250 women and child-mothers per 100,000 dying. The country's GDP is largely based on its resource wealth, making the people vulnerable to gold, oil and other international price fluctuations. The government of PNG's total annual health expenditure is 3.12% of GDP. Much of the same is true in West Papua.[4]

The Indonesian human-rights group TAPOL submitted the following evidence to the British Parliament in 2005:

> The widespread exploitation of West Papua's abundant natural resources by foreign companies and interests associated with the TNI [the Indonesian military] – including the illegal logging of the territory's extensive tropical forests – perpetuates the economic subjugation of the Papuan people. It is also a cause of tension and conflict. Extractive operations have involved the denial of land rights and severe environmental degradation. Some of the worst human rights violations have been committed in the vicinity of major enterprises, such as the Freeport copper-and-gold mine (in which Britain's Rio Tinto has an interest). There are concerns that BP's US$5 billion liquid natural gas project, Tangguh, will attract similar problems.[5]

Papua New Guinea

A European Community report notes PNG's Westminster-model democracy, and thus its 'male-dominated ... flawed electoral system functioning in a highly fragmented society'. In 2008, the Government of Papua New Guinea and the heads of the European Community agreed to an investment package of €130 million out to 2013. The loan was a hostile takeover of Papuan services, including 'energy, environment, transport, justice and home affairs'.[6]

The government 'will ensure fiscal and monetary stability is attained, land is sufficiently unlocked for development, law and order problems are normalised, and quality infrastructure connectivity are established to connect rural populations to markets and services', PNG's internal 'development' plan acknowledges. 'The Government will safeguard investors by enforcing contract and property rights law. In all its endeavor, the objective will be to promote a private sector led growth for the economy', emphasizing, 'Unlocking land for development'.[7]

A recent British Commonwealth delegation noted 'the cultural dimension of land ownership in PNG and how it impacted upon economic development opportunities'. In other words, indigenous peoples have to be forcibly removed in the name of progress. 'One of the explanations discussed with the delegation was that while PNG had witnessed the disappearance of indigenous culture around the Pacific, notably through the extortion of ancestral lands, Papua New Guineans were not keen to follow suit', thus the population has to be brutalized into silence.[8]

Police Brutality

Between April and July 2009, the PNG police's Mobile Squad burned down 130 buildings, including homes, in the Porgera Joint Venture region. 'Those who lost their homes included families with young children, pregnant women, elderly people and employees', Amnesty reported in 2009.[9]

The above follows a familiar pattern of brutality. In 2005, Human Rights Watch reported the torture of children by Her Majesty's Royal Papua New Guinea Constabulary:

> Brutal beatings, rape, and torture of children, as well as confinement in sordid police lockup[s], are widespread police practices ... Girls told us that they had been forced to chew and swallow condoms. Many of those we interviewed showed us fresh wounds and scars on their heads, faces, arms, legs, and torsos that they said were from police. Serious injuries to the face, particularly around the eyes, were common ... Girls often are subjected by police to sexual abuse, including rape – frequently pack rape (gang rape, also described as 'lineup sex') ... Some described seeing police rape girls vaginally and orally, sometimes using objects such as beer bottles ... Boys and men also reported sexual abuse by police, including oral and anal rape and attempts to force them to have sex with other detainees. More commonly, we heard accounts from boys in which they described instances of sexual humiliation, such as being forced to run or fight naked, ordered to expose themselves to female police officers, or stripped during interrogation ... [W]e interviewed children whom police had burned, cut, whipped while naked, and humiliated during their interrogations in order to coerce them to confess to a crime.[10]

The above are State-backed efforts to render the population pacified to accept the takeover of their lands ('Unlocking land for development') and other resources: hence, in that year, Britain exported 'incendiary hand grenades, military devices for initiating explosives, missile control equipment, exploding simulation devices, components for exploding simulation devices, anti-riot guns, components for anti-riot guns, crowd control ammunition, tear gas/irritant ammunition, training tear gas/irritant ammunition, CS hand grenades', and other weapons, to PNG.[11]

A few years after HRW's report, Britain's Commonwealth Parliamentary Association convened to discuss business in PNG. The delegation – who appear to be unfamiliar with the report – consisted of Baroness Taylor of Bolton (Labour), Lorely Burt (Liberal), Baroness Eccles of Moulton (Tory) and Kevan Jones (Labour). They enthused over 'one of the largest sites in the world of Liquefied Natural Gas (LNG) extraction, the PNG LNG project, which is scheduled to start production in 2014', whilst acknowledging conditions in the 'Autonomous' Region of Bougainville, where 'an eight year conflict ... ended in 1997 and accounted for the death of an estimated 20,000 people'.[12]

Mercenary Wars

The latter quote refers to a period of armed resistance by the Bougainville Revolutionary Army (BRA). In 1989, the BRA supported the Landowner Uprising, and succeeded in closing Rio Tinto's Panguna gold and copper mine.

In 1997, the government of PNG hired Lieutenant Colonel Tim Spicer's Sandline company to '[t]rain the State's Special Forces Unit (SFU) in tactical skills specific to the objective' of winning back the mine, and to 'gather intelligence to support effective deployment and operations; conduct offensive operations in Bougainville in conjunction with PNG defence forces to render the BRA military ineffective ... and provide follow-up operational support', in the words of the original Sandline-government contract.[13]

A Falklands War veteran, Spicer was a Royal Scots Guard officer under whose command an 18-year-old Irishman, Peter McBride of Belfast, was shot in the back. Spicer was awarded an OBE by Her Majesty for his part in Britain's occupation of Ireland. The two soldiers convicted of McBride's murder were later released after Spicer lobbied the authorities. They went on to fight in Iraq during the 2003–present occupation.[14]

Journalist and Pacific Media Watch convener Peter Cronau reports on the South Africa mercenary company Executive Outcomes (EO)'s 1996 efforts to rescue hostages. 'Those present in West Papua for the planning of the operation ... included the British Defence Attaché from Jakarta, a three member team from the Hostage Negotiation Unit of New Scotland Yard, several suspected members of the British SAS, and representatives of the Dutch military forces', says Cronau. 'The operation utilized Israeli surveillance equipment supplied by the Singapore government'. EO

UK's Senior Director was Spicer's friend, Simon Mann, later arrested in relation to an attempted coup in Equatorial Guinea.[15]

Covert Action Quarterly alleges that Spicer 'had met with two senior government officials about buying a copper mine owned by Rio Tinto'. *The Contemporary Pacific* journal notes that PNG's Defence Minister, Mathias Ijape, sought 'private sources of military hardware in early 1996. A foreign business associate, with whom he had worked on an earlier plan to establish an elite police unit, put him in touch with [Spicer]'. Sandline's efforts, in collusion with EO, resulted in disaster for the mercenaries. The PNG army essentially mutinied over their poor conditions, Spicer was arrested, and the incumbent government were eventually deposed.[16]

Despite this, the situation did not improve for Bougainville Papuans. A British Parliamentary Early Day Motion from 2000 states:

> the London-based Rio Tinto ... has been accused in a USA Class Action of War Crimes against the indigenous people of Bougainville Island, Papua New Guinea, that in order to force the re-opening of its Panguna Copper Mine, Rio Tinto encouraged or pressurised the PNG Government to take military action and to mount a naval blockade against its own people, that Rio Tinto provided vehicles and helicopters for military use, that Rio Tinto exhorted the PNG to 'Starve the Bastards out', that such actions were in breach of the Geneva Convention, the ensuing war crimes leading to the deaths of an estimated 15,000 civilians.[17]

Another from 2000 paraphrases a US lawsuit, alleging that Rio Tinto:

> treated the indigenous people as inferior and expendable, through apartheid, racial discrimination and cruel, inhuman and degrading treatment, constituting gross violation of their human rights, that Rio Tinto destroyed Bougainville's forests, fauna and river systems, generating billions of tons of toxic waste, killing animal and plant life, turning vast, fertile areas into a toxic, barren wasteland, that Rio

> Tinto chemically defoliated, bulldozed and sluiced of an entire mountainside of rainforest and that Rio Tinto caused serious illness and death to the people.[18]

Benny Wenda, the Chairman of the Koteka Tribal Assembly and the leader of the West Papua Independence Movement, stated:

> [Y]ou started to rip open and destroy our Land. We call our Land our Mother because she gives us everything we need to live. You sold our Mother to British, American & Australian companies like Rio Tinto & BP. You got rich whilst we West Papuans got poorer, not because we want your kind of riches, but because without our Mother we die.[19]

West Papua

The US Congress reports that 'in 1962 the United States pressured the Dutch to turn over control of West Papua to the United Nations'. This became the New York Agreement. Today, the UN is facilitating the corporate takeover of PNG (mentioned above), as its own publications concede: 'The result [of the Medium Term Plan] is a comprehensive development assistance framework that will form the basis of the work of the UN System in PNG'.[20]

'That fraudulent [New York Agreement] was endorsed by the General Assembly with the approval of the UK', Lord Avebury informed Parliament in 2007. The UK Foreign Office's Permanent Secretary 'recommended not entering into correspondence about self-determination, and in the UN we firmly supported the betrayal of the West Papuans, not on grounds of principle but out of solidarity with the Dutch and as a means of improving our relations with the military dictator General Suharto', Avebury continued. Suharto, he said, 'had done a splendid job exterminating half a million communists [sic – a million peasants] and was therefore a man to be encouraged'. Indonesia's Suharto was brought to power by an MI6-CIA coup.[21]

Indonesia formally conquered and colonised West Papua in

1969. In 2007, Lord Harries said: 'The so-called Act of Free Choice', which ceded West Papua to Indonesia, 'consisted of 1,026 people', about 1% of the West Papuan population, 'forced at gunpoint to vote for integration with Suharto's Indonesia, and this being taken as the voice of the people'. Lord Griffiths said: 'It was a United Nations set-up body that in New York allowed Indonesia to annex West Papua'. Lord Archer acknowledged that 'unlawful usurpation should evoke condemnation if international law is not to be brought into disrepute, but here there has been persecution, murder, evictions and burning of the villages of innocent human beings, while the world has looked on'. Britain, however, did much more than 'look on'.[22]

In 1969, the Foreign Office publicly endorsed the Indonesian occupation and claimed that the majority of West Papuans supported it. 'Privately ... we recognise that the people of West Irian (West Papua) have no desire to be ruled by the Indonesians who are of an alien (Javanese) race ... [T]he process of consultation did not allow a genuinely free choice to be made'. Indonesia's occupation is, and continues to be, a violation of the UN Charter and the Geneva Conventions, making Britain's trade with Indonesia – particularly in West Papua and its arms flows and training to Indonesia, which enforce the occupation – war crimes.[23]

Evidence submitted to Parliament cited 'strong evidence of genocide in West Papua since the Act of Free Choice in 1969 and found that the [Indonesian] security forces have engaged in "widespread violence and extrajudicial killings"'. The Indonesians, it said, have 'subjected Papuan men and women to acts of torture, disappearance, rapes and sexual violence, thus causing serious bodily and mental harm ... The sale of military equipment to Indonesia remains hugely contentious. British-made Hawk jets have been used in West Papua'.[24]

Evidence submitted to Parliament in 2004 suggests that 'The United Kingdom has always recognised that under international law, the people of West Papua are entitled to the fundamental human right of self-determination'. In 2007, Lord Avebury said: 'the UK does not support the independence of West Papua and we were accomplices in its unlawful annexation by Indonesia'. In the same hearing, Baroness Royall of Blaisdon said: 'the UK does not support independence for Papua. Like the vast majority of other international players, we respect Indonesia's territorial integrity and have never supported Papuan independence'.[25]

Baroness Rawlings said: 'We are not calling for the independence of Papua [sic – West Papua]', adding that 'DfID is closely involved in formulating the governor's development strategy, which will focus on the millennium development goals'. As noted, this is a violation of international law. DFID is the UK's tax-funded privatization corporation, erroneously called the Department for International Development. 'DfID is looking to align its own funding for Papua with the governor's vision', said the Baroness. The 'vision' is the corporate takeover noted above. 'The DfID-funded multi-stakeholder forestry programme has been working to improve land use in Papua, by supporting detailed mapping and informed policy change'.[26]

DFID, meaning UK taxpayers, also finances the Indonesian Police, which have a history of brutality in West Papua and in Indonesia proper – not to mention Indonesia's invasion of East Timor, which left 200,000 dead.

DFID's predecessor, the Overseas Development Administration, financed and facilitated Indonesian Police Force training. 'The UK-funded Indonesia National Police Management Training Project provided management training and other support to the Indonesian National Police (INP) between 1983 and 1996', a DFID report confirms. 'Project activities in the first phase consisted of training of trainers (ToT) courses at Bramshill Police Training College in the UK (until 1986) and in Indonesia (after 1986) to develop the capacity to deliver a new management training package in INP police training institutions, and study visits by senior INP officers to the UK to familiarise themselves with British police management methods and approaches to training'. Sheffield Hallam, Salford, and Manchester Universities, and the Police Forces of Surrey, Hertfordshire and Gloucestershire were involved.

The report acknowledges that 'the police are accused of torture and ill-treatment of prisoners', and admits that the INP 'is accountable to the Minister of Defence and the Commander of the armed forces', meaning that it is a paramilitary organization. 'For administrative purposes', the report continues, 'the INP has command and organisational structures similar to those of the navy, army and air force but is largely independent in respect of operational issues. The chief of police is a four star general and is a full member of the military council'.[27]

Britain's training has been put to use very efficiently. In 2008, to cite just one of daily examples of abuse, intimidation and brutality, Human Rights Watch condemned the Indonesian police for arresting 46 peaceful West Papuan demonstrators protesting occupation by raising their Morning Star flag in the city of Fakfak. 'According to local human rights workers, during the arrests the police beat and kicked almost all of the men. They also allege that the police subjected the Papuans to humiliating treatment'. They did this 'by forcing the men to strip to their underwear on the street before taking them by truck to the Fakfak police station. An eyewitness at the police station said detainees had bruises on their faces and bodies. Two detainees showed bleeding inside their right eyes'.[28]

The British government were so concerned about these abuses that they continued the training and, in 2009, exported nearly £7 million-worth of weapons to Indonesia, including 'assault rifles, 'small arms ammunition', 'submachine guns' and 'weapon sights'. We have seen that PNG is a Crown Colony and that Tim Spicer was made an Order of the British Empire. Indonesia's President Susilo Bambang Yudhoyono was made a Knight Grand Cross of the Order of Bath by her Majesty for his services to the Commonwealth.[29]

In 2012, TAPOL reported that Britain was training Indonesia's counterterrorism squad, Special Detachment 88. Under the counterterrorism banner, SD 88 'is reportedly being deployed to tackle other issues, such as alleged separatism in Indonesia's conflict-affected provinces' and 'to crack down on the Papuan independence movement'. TAPOL notes that 'the unit has been implicated in the assassination of [independence] leaders, such as Mako Tabuni who was shot dead in June'.[30]

SD 88 receives training at Jakarta's Centre for Law Enforcement Cooperation (JCLEC), 'which received a minimum of £400,000 in funding from Britain in the financial year 2011/12, as well as training provided by British officers'.[31]

In 2010, Amnesty reported that 'Police Mobile Brigade (Brimob) and military from the 1709 District Military Command (Kodim) led by the Yapen District Police Chief blocked hundreds of peaceful protesters as they marched on the morning of 9 August 2012 in Serui, Yapen Island'. TAPOL noted that British-made Tactica vehicles are used by Brimob. 'Amnesty International continues to receive credible reports of human rights violations committed by the security forces in the provinces of Papua and West Papua, including torture and other ill-treatment, unnecessary and excessive use of force and firearms by the security forces and possible unlawful killings'. Lord Avebury noted 'the suffering now being endured by West Papuans, unseen by human rights organisations, foreign journalists, the UNHCR and MPs, all of whom ... have been refused permission to enter the territory'.[32]

Britain's weapon exports to Indonesia continued into 2012, and included 'components for civil riot control agent[s]', 'explosives' and 'military communications equipment'.[33]

All of the above is a boon for British industry, as Early Day Motions have noted for 15 years or more.

'The UK has substantial economic and strategic ties with Indonesia and provides significant support for the major UK-based multinationals – Rio Tinto and BP – which operate in West Papua', evidence to Parliament affirmed in 2005. 'As a result FCO [UK Foreign and Commonwealth Office] policy on West Papua is determined primarily by economic and strategic considerations to the detriment of human rights', the authors continue.[34]

'BP's main operation in Indonesia is the Tangguh LNG plant in the Papua Barat province. Tangguh LNG is the first fully-vertically integrated LNG operation in the country, producing gas from Papua Barat offshore and delivering LNG to customers around Asia and the US', according to the company's website.[35]

'Tangguh started up in 2009 and is operating at design capacity; with work now ongoing to expand the plant through addition of a third LNG train', BP continues. In one of their internal reports, BP and the government of Indonesia note '[t]he annual joint training exercise required by the agreement with the police', which, they say, 'should be held every year. If a full exercise cannot be conducted, BP should work with the police and TNI [military] to schedule a more limited exercise'. As we have seen, the UK-armed and trained Indonesian police, financed by unquestioning UK taxpayers, fell under the military's command.[36]

'BP has a legal right to obtain a licence from Indonesia to operate in West Papua', writes George Monbiot. Monbiot's assertion may come as a surprise to scholars of international law. Monbiot quotes BP's licence, 'granted to [BP] by the Indonesian Government which is internationally recognised as the sovereign government of Papua, including by the UK and the United Nations', in what appears to be one of only two documents recognizing Indonesia's occupation as legitimate – the other being the Act of Free Choice of 1969.[37]

Chapter 11

Somalia – 'Now I'm a real killer'

Aid agencies estimate that nearly 260,000 Somalis died in the 2011 famine. This happened because the country's fragile socioeconomic system was destroyed in late-2006, when UK-armed and trained rebels overthrew the socialist government, Islamic Courts Union (ICU). In response, the non-extremist, armed youth wing of the ICU, al-Shabaab, was transformed into a terrorist organization. In this chapter we provide a background to the crisis and show how MI5-MI6 affiliates are connected to the 'al-Qaeda' elements of al-Shabaab.

Somalia, in East Africa, opposite Yemen (on the coast of the Gulf of Aden), shares at least two major characteristics with Aden (now Yemen): one, it is a former British colony; two, its strategic position makes it an important country for businesses and thus war planners.

A report by the US Department of Transportation states: 'Over 80 percent of international maritime trade moving through the Gulf of Aden is with Europe ... [R]outing from Europe to the Far East via the Cape of Good Hope, rather than through the Suez Canal [in order to avoid pirates] would incur an estimated additional $89 million annually, which includes $74.4 million in fuel and $14.6 million in charter expenses'. Thus, the Gulf of Aden has to remain open for trade. A UK MoD projection out to 2040 mentions 'the Horn of Africa and the global supply routes through the Red Sea and the Strait of Hormuz'.[1]

Commenting on the UK's *Strategic Defence and Security Review* (2010), Lord Sterling informed Parliament that 'the waters of the Middle East, including the Red Sea, the Gulf of Aden, the Gulf of

Oman and the Arabian Gulf are of vital strategic importance to the United Kingdom'. Roger Middleton, Britain's leading Somalia specialist, informed Chatham House that '[s]ome 16,000 ships a year pass through the Gulf of Aden, carrying oil from the Middle East and goods from Asia to Europe and North America'. The Gulf of Aden, he said, is 'one of the most important trade routes in the world'.[2]

Of secondary importance is the country's oil reserves. An area of Somalia called Puntland 'is believed to have *all the geological requirements to become a commercial oil-producing region*. Somalia, and in particular Puntland remains one of the last under-explored countries that has a *high potential for considerable reserves of hydrocarbons*', writes Range Resources Ltd.'s chief, Mike Povey (emphases in original). 'This view was further reinforced in the mid-1980s following the successful exploration efforts of Hunt Oil Corp across the Gulf of Aden in Yemen', he continues. 'Several major oil companies obtained exploration concessions and conducted considerable exploration and drilling over large parts of the State both onshore and offshore during the late 1980s and early 90s. These companies included AGIP, Shell (Pecten), Conoco, Phillips and Amoco'.[3]

'BP and Shell insist that their [Somalia] exploration contracts from the 1980s are still valid. Conoco, Chevron and ENI declined to comment, but industry sources said they also probably had similar claims', says Reuters. 'Although the contracts typically spanned only a few years, BP and Shell say the civil war forced them to declare "force majeure", a term that effectively stops the clock on the contract but keeps it intact'.[4]

In 2012, a British House of Commons Library Note affirmed that, 'Over the last year or so, ordinary Somalis have found themselves in even more of a life-and-death struggle to survive than before. During the second half of 2011', the Note continues, 'famine struck six regions in southern Somalia. An estimated four million people, or 53% of the Somalia population, were affected. The UN has declared that the famine has ended; however', the report concludes, 'the situation remains extremely fragile and could regress unless international humanitarian support is maintained'. Despite this, we mostly hear nothing about Somalia in the mainstream media but 'piracy, piracy, piracy', and, to a lesser extent, 'terrorism'.[5]

Roger Middleton writes in a Chatham House report: 'The only period during which piracy virtually vanished around Somalia was during the six months of rule by the Islamic Courts Union in the second half of 2006. This indicates that a functioning government in Somalia is capable of controlling piracy'. What, then, happened to the Islamic Courts Union? And why is a country so rich in resources so poor? Before looking into that, let us examine the historical context.[6]

Operation Restore Hopelessness

After Italy, West Germany and America rejected a settlement in the 1960s, Somalia's elite looked to the Soviet Union for assistance. The USSR provided 10,000 troops, an air force and weapons in an effort to establish a military base in the Indian Ocean region. The 1969 coup established Mohamed Siyad Barre as the new Marxist leader. During the Somalia-Ethiopia War (1977), the USSR double-crossed the regime, siding with the Ethiopian Marxist fascist, Mengistu Haile Mariam. The Somali National Movement (primarily based in Somaliland) challenged Barre's regime throughout the 1980s, until the United Somalia Congress overthrew it.

Most Westerners know Somalia from the alleged humanitarian intervention of late-1992, Operation Restore Hope – famous for the Black Hawk Down episode. 'If the Americans really wanted just to feed hungry people', writes Royal Africa Society Director Richard Dowden, 'they would have come six months earlier when the famine was at its height'.[7]

Africa specialist, Alex de Waal, writes: 'The humanitarian garb of Operation Restore Hope was superficial from the start'. It was 'launched in December 1992 just as the famine was waning' and had 'more to do with testing the newly emerging doctrine of "humanitarian intervention" than saving Somalis'.[8]

De Waal concludes that '[a]n independent review by the US Refugee Policy Group concluded that the operation saved between 10,000 and 25,000 lives rather than the two million initially advertised'. This is a generous estimate considering that the CIA guessed that 7,000 to 10,000 Somalis were killed by US forces, mainly women and children. Commanding General Anthony Zinni said: 'I'm not counting bodies ... I'm not interested'. The deaths resulted from the mission shift from 'humanitarian intervention' to capturing an alleged 'warlord', Farrah Adeed.[9]

The real purpose of the 1992 invasion appears to have been to wreck any chance of a stabilizing government and to secure Somalia's oil resources, specifically by discouraging Chinese and Russian exploration. The Senlis Council reports that 'it is argued – though the US denied allegations – that the AMOCO, CONOCO and CHEVRON contracts in Somalia were a major consideration in the US intervention'. During his reporting from Somalia, Dowden noted the presence of Chevron-owned villas. Since early-2008, 'China and Russia have been attempting to make deals with the Somali government for exploration purposes'.[10]

Between 1992 and 1994, 'the Americans intervened, but clashed with the [Somali] warlords. Then, after 9/11, they decided to hire some of them as bounty-hunters', reports journalist Aidan Hartley. The civil war (1992–2001) claimed 500,000 Somali lives. Somalia is largely a Sufi-based intergenerational, pastoralist clan culture. Al-Qaeda is a Salafist caliphate. Ergo, it is absurd to image that al-Qaeda could establish a strong, permanent presence in Somalia as a political ideology. Even the biased *9/11 Commission Report* confirms that Somalia was not wiring money to terrorists. Despite this, British Telecom and Barclays froze Somali bank accounts – in a country where many depend on aid from relatives abroad.[11]

Out of this mess emerged the Islamic Courts Union, which, despite the name, was a socialist, non-extremist, organization.

Somalia's capital Mogadishu 'became relatively peaceful, and the Islamic Courts [sic] received support from the population in areas it controlled', confirms a US Congressional report. '[T]he group had constituencies from multiple sub-clans and had broad support among Somali women', waylaying media allegations of misogyny. The report continues: 'There is no evidence to support the allegation that women were prohibited from working . . . [T]he assessment of the Islamic Courts by US officials was that less than 5 percent of the Islamic Courts leadership can be considered extremist, according to a senior State Department official'.[12]

Amnesty International reports: 'there were some functioning schools in cities, supported by civil society, diaspora groups and business actors and there was some scope to negotiate one's way through the dangers posed by warlords and clan militias'. The Islamic Courts Union (ICU) did, however, commit a grave sin: that of exercising an autonomy antithetical to Anglo-American interests.[13]

The TFG

In 2004, it was reported that British special forces would be training African Union troops to assist the latter's occupation, primarily designed to bolster the ICU's rival, the Transitional Federal Government (TFG). The TFG was a ragtag band of thugs comprised of Ethiopian and Somalia gangsters.[14]

Failing to achieve the objective, Ethiopia invaded Somalia in December 2006, triggering humanitarian crises that resulted in tens of thousands of deaths, hundreds of thousands of refugees, and major reversals of the ICU's achievements. Amnesty International reported that, 'The intensification of armed conflict since the end of 2006 has shattered any semblance of normalcy that the Somali people had managed to build, against enormous odds . . . The entry of Ethiopian troops into Somalia, to help the [TFG] to oust the Islamic Courts Union, commenced a new phase of conflict, with indiscriminate attacks and targeted killings and human rights abuses becoming part of daily life for the civilian population'. Amnesty adds that, 'The ICU was at the time in control of the capital Mogadishu and other parts of southern and central Somalia and was credited by some among the civilian population with restoring some security against violent crimes by warlords' militia'.[15]

The Senlis Council calls the TFG 'an incoherent body characterised by a "zero sum game" mentality ... It is failing to deliver any government services, security or aid, prompting the worst humanitarian crisis since early 1990s', adding that, 'Efforts to establish a government of national unity have been faced with strong resistance by those TFG members who believe that a genuine reconciliation process is not in their interest'. TFG techniques included scorched-earth campaigns, torture and indiscriminate civilian killings. HRW reports that '[s]ince January 2007 at least 870,000 civilians have fled the chaos in Mogadishu alone – two-thirds of the city's population. Across south-central Somalia, 1.1 million Somalis are displaced from their homes. Hundreds of thousands of displaced people are living in squalid camps along the Mogadishu-Afgooye road that have themselves become theaters of brutal fighting'.[16]

Lord Malloch-Brown authored a book in 2011 titled *The Unfinished Global Revolution*, a sequel to the Club of Rome's 1991 report, *The First Global Revolution*. The latter predicted the uprisings we have seen over the last few years, and offered ways to hijack them and turn them to elite interests. In 2006, when the atrocities in Somalia were taking place, Malloch-Brown was Minister of State for Africa. He told journalist Aidan Hartley that he fully backed the TFG.[17]

In *The Unfinished Global Revolution*, Malloch-Brown writes: 'The Indochinese who had collaborated with the Americans' during the US decimation of the region in the 1960s and 1970s, 'were marked men. They and their families had little choice but to flee. The result was a massive exodus by boat and land. At its peak in 1978 and 1979, up to sixty thousand were boarding boats from Vietnam in desperate search of asylum'. Malloch-Brown does not write that from December 2006 to the present, *hundreds of thousands* of Somalis, including thousands of Ethiopians, have fled by boat from Somalia to Yemen across the Gulf of Aden. This began under Malloch-Brown's watch as Africa Minister. Not a word of it is mentioned in his book, barring a reference to Somalia as 'a failed state' and a 'home to networks of terrorists'.[18]

HRW writes: 'The number of people making this journey' of hundreds of miles by sea in rickety boats to Yemen, 'has increased dramatically in recent years. In 2008 a record 50,000 asylum seekers and migrants arrived on Yemen's beaches, up from less than 27,000 the year before. That record had already been broken by the end of September 2009, with 50,486 recorded new arrivals in just nine months – a 50 percent increase over the number of arrivals during the same period in 2008'. In addition to the Somali and Ethiopian boat people, around 325,000 Somali refugees are trying to survive in Kenyan camps, where UK-trained and armed security forces extort the refugees and rape the women, according to HRW.[19]

Al-Shabaab (The Youth) is simply the armed wing of the non-violent ICU. When the ICU disintegrated, Al-Shabaab took over, and, unlike its predecessor, became a violent resistance movement that has committed grave human rights violations – though nothing on the scale of the TFG. As we shall see, British terrorist proxies infiltrated the group and turned it into an 'al-Qaeda' affiliate, thus giving the SAS an excuse to expand their operations in Somalia.

Where your taxes go

Despite being found guilty of murdering a political opponent by Britain's own High Court, which also found him guilty of 'carr[ying] out retaliations, including executions', Abdullahi Yusuf – then-leader of the TFG – was given a liver-transplant on Britain's National Health Service, as well as housing in the UK under New Labour during the Blair and Brown years. Richard Dowden quotes

Yusuf: 'They gave me the liver of an IRA terrorist. Now I'm a real killer'.[20]

'British taxpayers' money is helping to bankroll one side of this vicious conflict', Aidan Hartley reported a few years ago, writing as perhaps the only journalist to uncover the UK's complicity in the atrocities. '[S]everal Somali leaders who have been linked to allegations of war crimes against countless civilians are living double lives in Britain ... [having] been given British citizenship, state benefits and a subsidised home in [Britain]'. Under Yusuf, 'up to a million civilians ... fled the bombardments in Mogadishu'. By 2008, they were living 'in tents made of plastic and twigs ... This is a famine caused by men, not global warming'.[21]

One such warlord was Mohamed Darwiish, head of Somalia's National Security Agency, who used to work at Tesco in England. According to Hartley, the British Police were paying his salary through a UN programme. As for worsening the famine, examples include the former Interior Minister and later ephemeral Prime Minister, Guled Ga'amadheere, another British ally, regularly halting aid deliveries, many of which are pirated. In 2008, *The Times* (London) reported that the police in Mogadishu were responsible for crimes against humanity, including torture, and that they were being funded through the UN's Development Programme with British tax money. 'More than £10 million, including £2.5 million of British money, is being used to refurbish government buildings, cover running costs and provide technical assistance', the paper reported.[22]

'Members of the Somali parliament, many of whom earned their seats through military muscle, receive a monthly stipend of £600. But the biggest chunk of donor cash – some £15 million, including £3.2 million from the DfID [Department for International Development] – is being spent on ... police as salaries and to buy radios and vehicles', *The Times* concluded. It was also revealed in a Select Committee hearing in 2011, during the height of another famine, in which a child was dying every 20 minutes, that British aid to

Somalia is being funnelled to the Somaliland Police Force, which governs the most stable area of the country.[23]

The latter was let slip during the Select Committee hearing on the role of Britain's unelected, cross-party National Security Council, which James Arbuthnot MP enthusiastically described as 'the war cabinet'. Then-Development Secretary, Andrew Mitchell, told the Select Committee: 'We will be training 3,000 police in Somaliland', at which point the Chairman, Arbuthnot, interrupted, saying: 'I am sure that we will be doing some very good things'.[24]

Several months before, the *Telegraph* revealed that not all of the aid money would be going to the Somaliland Police Force, but to former UK Special Boat Service mercenaries to train Somalis in anti-piracy operations. 'The decision to call in ex-special forces soldiers earning up to £1,500-a-day is highly controversial'.[25]

HRW also confirmed that aid was being funnelled to the TFG via the World Food Programme (WFP). These reports were affirmed in a House of Commons Library Note: 'much international assistance to the TFG is being channelled through the UN Development Programme (UNDP) . . . The EU has supported training for the Somali National Police, which has been heavily involved in fighting [and complicit in torture]. There were reports of an internal discussion within the European Commission in 2007 about whether it might find itself implicated in war crimes charges against members of the TFG'. No such chance with victor's justice.[26]

In other words, both sides are being played off against each other in the old divide and conquer technique. 'DFID has pledged over £20 million in new commitments for Somalia, including £12 million to the WFP. No money goes directly to the TFG. *It is channelled through the UNDP and other donors* to build budgetary and financial management capacity' (emphasis added).[27]

The MI6–Al-Shabaab Axis

As documented in Stephen Dorril's *MI6*, Robert Dreyfuss's *Devil's Game*, John K. Cooley's *Unholy Wars*, Mark Curtis's *Secret Affairs* and elsewhere, MI6 and the SAS created an extensive global terrorist network in order to 'draw the Russians into the Afghan trap' (Brzezinski) in 1979, and that 'al-Qaeda' simply means 'the database', or 'computer file', of British-trained *mujahideen* (former New Labour Foreign Secretary, Robin Cook).[28]

In June 2011, the head of UK Counterterrorism Campbell McCafferty testified to a Committee that: 'There has not been any evidence of a link between the [Somali] pirates and al-Shabab'. However, such a 'link to terrorism would change entirely the international community's view . . . I think people are looking hard for those links'. The inference being that if terrorism doesn't exist, it has to be invented. MI5 chief, Jonathan Evans, said: 'Somalia has become the next destination after Pakistan for terrorist training due to the presence of al-Shabaab, an extremist group with links to al-Qa'ida'. As noted, Al-Shabaab was merely the armed wing of the non-extremist ICU. If the links with 'al-Qaeda' are genuine, how and when did they come about?[29]

Andrew Dismore MP confirmed that, in 1993, one Omar Bakri Mohammed 'was given indefinite leave to remain in the UK'. British Parliamentary documents reveal that MI6 'mobilised' a terrorist group called Al-Muhajiroun, led by Bakri, in the 1990s in order to fight in Serbia and inspire Kosovar nationalism. An MI5 agent once told Pulitzer Prize-winning journalist, Ron Suskind, that Bakri 'helped MI5 on several of its investigations'. In 1999, Bakri himself said: 'the British Government knows who we are. MI5 has interrogated us many times. I think now we have something called public immunity'. FBI agent and former prosecutor John Loftus, speaking on behalf of the FBI, alleged that the British extremist, Haroon Rashid Aswat (linked to the 7 July 2005 bombings), is an MI6 double-agent, and that through Al-Muhajiroun had recruited fighters for Somalia from the UK.[30]

Al-Muhajiroun cropped up again in 2013, after one of its former members, Michael Adebolajo, was convicted for murdering the British soldier, Lee Rigby. It was reported that Bakri 'radicalised'

Adebolajo and that the latter had been arrested in Kenya in 2011 for trying to recruit for Al-Shabaab. Despite this, Adebolajo was not only released by the Kenyan authorities, but left alone by British police.[31]

Abu Qatada, whom the *Daily Mail* described as 'Bin Laden's right-hand man in Britain', is alleged to be another MI5-MI6 agent, which explains the reason for his and Aswat's slow extraditions. According to a *Time* magazine article from 2002, 'senior European intelligence officials tell *Time* that Abu Qatada is tucked away in a safe house in the north of England, where he and his family are being lodged, fed and clothed by British intelligence services'. MI5 double-agent, Reda Hassaine, said: 'I saw Qatada brainwash young Muslims living in Britain from Africa, Somalia, Sudan, Morocco and my own country of Algeria'.[32]

On Al-Shabaab, the *Guardian* reported that 'Britons are believed to make up about a quarter of the 200 or so of its foreign fighters, according to the Royal United Services Institute'. Drawing on the mystical, Gnostic, individualistic Sufi Islam tradition, which is totally at odds with 'al-Qaeda's' Salafism, Somalia has rarely been a place of Islamic extremism. Since MI6's proxies have been pouring into the country, however, that has changed. After Somalia's first mosque bombing in 2010, many Somalis suspected foreign involvement. It was later revealed that SAS killers had been in Somalia for many years assisting the TFG and the Puntland Police Force.[33]

One of Al-Shabaab's leaders, Ahmed Abdi Godane (also known as Abu Zubair), joined Al-Ittihad al Islamiya (AIAI) in the 1990s – the only Islamic extremist organization known to have existed in Somalia. According to the US State Department, AIAI 'was an Islamist militant group founded by Somali Salafis in the 1980s. Many of its fighters trained with al Qaeda in Afghanistan during the Soviet occupation, and returned to Somalia after the war'. This was at a time when MI6, the SAS and US special forces were training 'al-Qaeda'.[34]

The MI5–MI6–Al-Shabaab links appear to cross virtual barriers. Al-Shabaab's website, alqimmah.net, reaches Somalis from its registered base in Sweden. It has posted anti-negotiation statements, written under religious pretexts, in order to encourage Al-Shabaab members to dismiss peace settlements, such as the Djibouti Round (2009). The website also schools young recruits in bomb-making and even attempts to incite Kenyan Muslims.

The website is run by Musa Said Yusuf Godir, whom, in 2008, was arrested in London with his colleague Ahmed Said Mohamed Faarax-Deeq, who runs other Al-Shabaab-affiliated websites. They were charged with terrorism offences. However, 'Both men were subsequently cleared of the charges and released', the UN reported. 'On the night of 28 July 2009, participants in an Al-Shabaab online forum celebrated the release of Faarax-Deeq', the agency added, concluding that: 'On 9 August 2009, a group of Somalis . . . hosted a reception for Faarax-Deeq and Godir in Leicester [UK]', all apparently under the nose of MI5.[35]

The above has given the SAS a pretext to enhance operations in Somalia, leading to untold numbers of civilian deaths and the escalation of atrocities. Up to 60 SAS commandos invaded Somalia in 2012, the *Daily Star* reported, with the usual provisos about counterterrorism. In violation of the UN Charter, Britain's then-Attorney General Dominic Grieve authorized the invasion with the professed aims of quelling the Shabaab militia.[36]

The press reported that SAS collaborate with the Kenyan military – which Britain also trains and arms – on the Somali-Kenya border. Daniel Bekele, Africa Director at Human Rights Watch, said: 'Kenya's Somalia operation has resulted in apparent attacks on a camp for displaced people and a fishing boat'. On 30 October, 2011, the Kenyan Air Force, using British weapons and tactical training, bombed an internally displaced persons' camp near Jilib (Somalia). Médecins Sans Frontières confirmed that it treated 45 wounded people, including 31 children, and confirmed that 5 civilians died as a result.[37]

Who are the pirates?

At a time of mass starvation in Somalia, media concerns focused on Somali piracy, not on the piracy of European fishing vessels in Somalia's waters. As Chatham House's Middleton revealed, the Islamic Courts Union, which Britain's proxies overthrew, 'virtually eliminated piracy'. Media headlines in a free system might include: 'European corporate pirates steal fish from 4 million starving Somalis', or, 'European corporate pirates dump foetal-deforming, cancer-causing toxic waste on Somali beaches', all of which is acknowledged in internal records, such as Parliamentary and Lords discussions, but kept from the public.[38]

Referring to the European fishing vessels that are depleting the Indian Ocean and coasts of the Horn of Africa, Britain's former Defence Minister Bob Ainsworth (who supported the invasion of Iraq, expanded the occupation of Afghanistan and voted for the destruction of Libya) acknowledged on behalf of Somalis during a Committee hearing, 'a moral argument that "You took our fish and therefore this is what we are doing"'. Likewise, Chatham House specialist Sally Healy said that 'the kind of issues that matter [to Somalis] would include some sort of recognition that there has been a plunder of Somali resources' by the EU. Since pirate activities began, Healy added, 'there is a visible difference to the amount of fish that have recovered in the ocean', which is crucial for a country starving to death, giving Somalis 'fish to eat'.[39]

Dr Lee Willett, a specialist of maritime studies at the Royal United Services Institute, was asked during a House of Lords hearing in 2010 whether the over-fishing of Somali waters by the European Union – which is heading the anti-piracy Operation Atalanta from UK bases in Northwood – was a serious issue for Somalis. 'Very much so', he replied, adding that many said 'because Western ships were coming illegally into their waters and taking their fish, they had no other choice'. In January 2012, Brunel University's Dr Anja Shortland published a Chatham House study, using 'satellite technology' to determine where the pirates' money goes. Dr Shortland 'conclud[ed] that there is significant evidence of shared, if unequal, economic benefits across different sections of local society'.[40]

Shortland herself wrote that 'conspicuous consumption appears to be limited by social norms dictating resource-sharing. Around a third of pirate ransoms are converted into Somali shillings, benefiting casual labour and pastoralists in Puntland ... Pirates', she added, 'probably make a significant contribution to economic development in the provincial capitals Garowe and Bosasso ... A military crack-down on [pirates] would deprive one of the world's poorest nations of an important source of income and aggravate poverty'.[41]

Dave Watts of the Foreign Affairs Committee revealed that 94% of pirates are released after capture, affording insurance companies the opportunity to make more money by offering piracy insurance policies. The piracy debacle is totally overblown and used as a pretext to militarize the strategically important region. A paper published by the UK's Defence Academy states that 'even a massive hike in insurance costs only adds around 2 percent to the cost. Even taking into account the costs of maritime operations, the total cost of piracy is estimated at somewhere between $7 and $12 billion annually – a large number, for sure, but dwarfed by worldwide maritime commerce of around $12.2 trillion in 2010'.[42]

Furthermore, Britain has *links* with Somali pirates. Middleton wrote: 'As one expert said, "money will go to Yusuf [the TFG warlord housed by the Blair government] as a gesture of goodwill to a regional leader" – so even if the higher echelons of Somali government and clan structure are not directly involved in organizing piracy, they probably do benefit ... Puntland', he added, 'is one of the poorest areas of Somalia, so the financial attraction of piracy is strong. Somalia's fishing industry has collapsed in the last fifteen years and its waters are being heavily fished by European, Asian and African ships'.[43]

The plight of 4 million people on the verge of starvation, the one million dependent upon the Red Cross, the tens of thousands killed by Britain's TFG proxies, the MI6 terrorist proxies that infiltrated Al-Shabaab and are exacerbating the war, the estimated 2.5 million internal and external refugees, the robbing of Somali fish and the dumping of toxic waste on the country's shores all appear to be of no interest to Western academics or those in mainstream media – unlike Somali piracy.

Chapter 12

Bangladesh – 'Survival of the fittest'

As the British government hyped-up claims that Libya's President Gaddafi was preparing to 'ethnically cleanse' rebels in Benghazi (a claim utilized to justify NATO's ruination of Libya), Amnesty International brought to public attention what had been in the public record for a number of years: that Britain was arming and training a death-squad, the Rapid Action Battalion, which targets unionists, students, political opponents and other groups that might bring justice to the exploited peoples of a former British colony. In this chapter we argue that Bangladesh is a model for the 'free-trade' agenda examined in the Introduction.

One in four Bangladeshi children are malnourished; sixty million live on the equivalent of one dollar a day; fifteen million live on the equivalent of twenty British pence a day; and extreme poverty reinforces an abusive patriarchal culture, in which sixty percent of women (compared with twenty-five percent in Britain) experience physical domestic abuse. The country ranks 108 out of 109 on the United Nations Gender Empowerment Index, and has one of the highest rates of maternal mortality in the world, with tens of thousands dying in childbirth.[1]

The one in four acutely malnourished Bangladeshis constitute part of the 'bottom billion', mentioned by the UK MoD in one of its reports, who are 'too preoccupied simply with survival' to rebel in the 'Darwinian "survival of the fittest"' system. As we shall see, those who do rebel – union leaders, entrepreneurs, communists groups, etc. – are tortured and/or killed by a UK-trained death-squad, the Rapid Action Battalion. The Bangladesh High Commission in London explains that '[t]he economy's biggest asset is its plentiful supply of very cheap labour, a major attraction for foreign investors ... The country's other endowments include its vast skilled and semi-skilled human resource base, fertile agricultural land, and substantial reserves of natural gas and coal ... Bangladesh's regulation of inward investment is recognised as the most liberal in South Asia'.[2]

It was reported that WikiLeaks revealed the UK's involvement with the Rapid Action Battalion, but in reality the UK-RAB ties were hinted at by Human Rights Watch in 2006 and confirmed in 2009 in the UK Foreign Office's *Annual Human Rights Report*.[3]

Under the cover of an aid programme, the UK's tax-funded Department for International Development (DFID) 'expressed its interest to develop a Special Economic Zone in Bangladesh that may be [an] ideal place for investment', reports the High Commission. 'The primary objective of EPZs' – Export Processing Zones, factories in which women (often girls) slave for up to 36-hour shifts under strip-lights to produce cheap clothes and other goods for the West – 'is to provide special area and physical facilities including land, building and utility services to the potential investors and a conducive investment climate'. DFID, meaning UK taxpayers, will invest around £200 million in the scheme.[4]

The Rapid Action Battalion

In 2002, as leader of the Bangladeshi National Party, Prime Minister Khaleda Zia initiated Operation Clean Heart under the pretext of reducing crime. Clean Heart was in fact a military operation aimed at attacking the poor, who are increasingly unwilling to be subjected to exploitation. According to Human Rights Watch, 40,000 military personnel were employed, arresting 10,000 civilians, killing at least 50 in custody. As the atrocities took place, Britain's arms sales to Bangladesh increased to £9 million and included: 'aircraft military communications equipment, assault rifles (40)', 'grenade launchers', 'semi-automatic pistols (50)', 'small arms ammunition', 'submachine guns (12)', and 'tear gas/irritant ammunition'.[5]

MI6 appears to have provided training to RAB, which boasted on its website in 2006 that RAB is expert in 'the most modern weapons, gadgets and law enforcement training in the world at par with the US FBI [sic] and UK's MI6 or Scotland Yard'. In 2011, as the media beat the drums for war against oil-rich Libya under the pretext that Gaddafi was a monster, Amnesty International confirmed that 'the UK police have been training the Rapid Action Battalion'. The FCO announced in 2009 that '[i]n Bangladesh the [UK] government has agreed to provide human rights training to the Rapid Action Battalion . . . whose chequered human rights record has been identified as a driver of radicalisation'.[6]

As noted with Somalia and Colombia, the phrase 'human rights training' is cynical PR. The more 'human rights training' these death-squads receive(d), the worse their abuses: RAB was no exception. Like Operation Clean Heart, the real goal of RAB is not 'crime prevention' and 'instant justice', as claimed by the successive Bangladeshi governments (all of which are supported by the UK), but instilling fear and punishing political and economic activism.

In 2011, after two years of 'human rights training', HRW reported that the '[p]eople taken into police custody [by RAB include] labor union leaders, journalists, [and] even politicians'. This is a clear indication that criminalizing dissent, and often punishing it with death and torture, is RAB's primary objective.[7]

In 2006, Prime Minister Khaleda Zia's Parliamentary Affairs Adviser, Salahuddin Quader Chowdhury, 'warned opposition members to follow the "right path" (*siratul mustakim*) because they are on RAB's "crossfire" list.' 'Crossfire', HRW confirms, is a euphemism for execution. Chowdhury later became a RAB victim himself (see below). The succeeding Awami League Government 'has admitted that torture continues', notes HRW.[8]

RAB was established in 2004 under Khalida's Government,

indicating that whichever government is in power, the same agenda is promoted. 'Torture methods attributed to RAB include beatings with batons on the soles of the feet (*falanga*) and other parts of the body, boring holes with electric drills on the legs and feet, and applying electric shock to open wounds', reports HRW. By 2006, RAB admitted killing at least 600 people, indicating that many more have perished in the following years.[9]

The youngest reported victim was Ashiqul Islam Raju (14), who was killed in September 2006. The oldest was Mohamed Ali (65). In a typical case, 'RAB arrested a 16-year-old boy [Samsul Haq] accused of theft and apparently shot him on a Dhaka street'. He was shot twice in the head and once in the chest with his hands tied behind his back. According to HRW, the 12 RAB battalions, consisting of 8,500 militia men and women, wear black shirts and sunglasses, and leave their victims out in the street for the public and media to see, sometimes tying them to carts in rows and leaving them outside police stations to rot in the heat.[10]

'RAB members tortured to death a witness to the murder of a prominent opposition member of parliament', HRW continues. In another case, RAB murdered 'a political activist for the Awami League who had been working on behalf of poor villagers engaged in a land dispute with a cousin of the state minister for home affairs... Some victims were reportedly activists of a banned communist group, the Purba Banglar Communist Party'.[11]

On 16 December, 2010, as MI6 trained Libyan terrorists to overthrow Gaddafi, Awami League back-bencher Salauddin Quader Chowdhury 'was severely tortured' by RAB, 'despite a serious heart condition'. According to Public Interest Lawyers (PIL), 'His torture included slitting the right side of his stomach with a knife, pulling out his toenails, tying him to a chair and repeatedly kicking him to the body and face, beating him with bats, pouring cold water into his nose so as to induce vomit and repeated standing on his chest. Thereafter', PIL continues, 'Chowdhury was taken into custody, he continued to be subjected to serious torture, including the electrocution of his genitals.... [H]e was not able to stand without assistance'.[12]

According to PIL, RAB admitted to having been trained by the British as late as December 2010.

'Detainees have been subjected to electric shocks, rape, severe kicking, and beating with objects that include iron rods, belts or sticks', HRW continues, adding: 'Soldiers and Rapid Action Battalion officers are protected from the civilian criminal justice system under laws that ensure that they can only be prosecuted [internally]', which they are not.[13]

Democracy promotion

The UK House of Commons Library notes that 'surges in local and global prices have the capacity to impoverish large swathes of the population. High food prices have in the past (2007–08) been linked to social unrest' – normal in the age of globalization. Elections were due to take place in Bangladesh in January 2007, but instead a Caretaker Government bolstered by the military declared a State of Emergency. According to Maryland University Professor Devin T. Hagerty, the real power lay with Fakhruddin Ahmed, 'a former World Bank official who once headed Bangladesh's central bank, and the army led by Chief of Army Staff General Moeen U. Ahmed'. Members of the Caretaker Government 'were drawn primarily from the private sector', and rapidly imposed privatization reforms.[14]

GDP grew by 6.7%, roughly the same as inflation, providing a good climate for investment and a bad one for per capita income. A senior Merrill Lynch adviser described the transition as 'probably the best reform story in Asia'. J.P. Morgan, the company for which Britain's ex-Prime Minister Tony Blair worked as an adviser, described Bangladesh as 'one of the "Five Frontier" markets'.[15]

Under Martial Law, an 'election' was held (and monitored by British delegates), in which the Awami League's old favourite Sheikh Hasina Wazed won a landslide victory, claiming 75% of the

Parliament. The transition to the Caretaker Government was characterized by 'mass arrests, illegal detention, torture, and at least 100 murders', says Peter Lloyd.[16]

In 2007, Britain exported £3 million-worth of weapons to Bangladesh, including: 'components for combat aircraft', 'components for military training aircraft', 'military aircraft ground equipment' and 'components for combat helicopters'. The British delegates declared the election 'free and fair'. Then-Foreign Secretary and European Council on Foreign Relations member, David Miliband, declared: 'The people of Bangladesh have spoken in huge numbers and they can be proud of the manner in which the elections were conducted'.[17]

The Foreign Office also funded pro-British, pro-regime propaganda: 'a one-hour TV special featuring British delegates reached an audience of 100 million people' – over a third of the population – the UK Foreign Office boasted. The BBC Media Action Group operates a Bangladeshi branch in association with the British Business Group (Bangladesh), which includes Thomson Reuters news agency. Reuters has uncritically repeated anti-opposition stories.[18]

The British Business Group (Bangladesh) also includes delegates from HSBC, Standard Charter Bank, W.F. Home Fashions, Marks and Spencer, George Clothing-ASDA (owned by WalMart), Unilever, Eurocross Frozen Food, Sainsbury, Tesco and GlaxoSmithKline pharmaceuticals. DFID will also 'support the BBC World Trust to hold a "Question Time equivalent programme" with politicians'. (Anyone familiar with Britain's TV programme *Question Time* will cringe.) A Sussex University Institute of Development Studies specialist informed a Select Committee that 'DFID support to civil society [in Bangladesh] has, with considerable success, supported raising the profile of governance issues within the public debate'.[19]

In 2008, Britain exported over £600,000 of weapons to Bangladesh, including 'military devices for initiating explosives' and 25 'combat shotguns'. Sheikh Hasina was hardly an exemplary modern democrat, hanging via kangaroo courts five people alleged to have been involved in the murder of her father, Sheikh Mujibur Rahman, in 1975. Sheikh Hasina was awarded the Indira Gandhi Prize for Peace and Disarmament in 2009, after she made rapprochement with India – a country imprisoning Bangladesh with a fence modelled on Israel's illegal annexation wall in Jerusalem.[20]

The neo-liberal future

In recent years, the UK-backed Awami Government began a privatization bonanza, liberalizing access to micro-credits. The credits are 'micro-managed' by NGOs, subcontracted by the government and often funded by UK taxpayers through Britain's DFID – as the Club of Rome proposed in 1991. Save the Children, an NGO working in the country, comments: '. . . the famous Bangladesh credit programmes typically do not benefit the poorest strata of society, and although they are targeted at women, may tend to exploit or burden women further', hence DFID's drive to get women into work. Christian Aid states: 'We are concerned by how little information about DFID's projects in Bangladesh is publicly available'.[21]

By 1998, over a thousand NGOs, many of them subcontracted by the government, were registered in Bangladesh. The majority were subsidised by foreign governments (mainly Britain's) and only one (MCC) had a code of conduct, such as rules for working hours. 'The likelihood of NGOs facilitating the empowerment of poor people seems to have diminished during their expansion' because, 'their clientele appear to have become increasingly credit-oriented', explains NGO worker and scholar, Mokbul Morshed Ahmad.[22]

Gender empowerment initiatives, such as the Activists of the All-India Democratic Women's Association, who protested in opposition to microfinance in December 2009 in Hyderabad (India), outside the country's central Reserve Bank, receive little to no media coverage in the West.[23]

A Chatham House report on the 'empowerment' of women notes

that '[m]icrofinance schemes focus disproportionately on women as their client base'. Jessica Schicks's Université Libre de Bruxelles study notes that 'over-indebtedness is currently one of the most serious risks of microfinance, endangering both social impact and industry stability. It has the potential to push customers further into poverty, accompanied by the material, psychological and sociological consequences of debt'. Schicks adds that 'anthropological research ... in Bangladesh reveals that loans are in many cases used by husbands and channelling them through female borrowers simply increases repayment pressures in the local cultural setting'.[24]

In a study for Brandeis University, Lamia Karim writes:

> ... over the past three decades microfinance has become inextricably linked to women's empowerment in developing countries. Yet in research I conducted in Bangladesh in 1998–99 and 2007, I discovered a soft, ugly underbelly to microfinance, particularly as it affects poor women. If you replace the word 'loan' with 'debt,' it's easy to see how microfinance can create a power imbalance between a lender and a financially strapped borrower, especially if that borrower is a woman ... In 1997, Grameen and Telenor Norway, one of the world's major mobile-telecommunications operators, jointly created a venture called Grameen Polli Phone (or 'Village Phone'), which offered rural Bangladeshis easy access to phone services ... Initially, many of the Grameen phone ladies made money. But soon other cell phone companies moved into their areas and effortlessly undersold them. With their customers gone, many of these women were still stuck with huge debts to repay. The phone ladies had little or no understanding of how competition works in an open market. But Grameen Polli Phone did. At the end of the day, the corporation used these women to usher in new corporate market forces and corner new markets. And the women were left as poor – or poorer – than they were before they got their loan.[25]

These and other schemes have forced women to sell their organs in order to meet loan repayments. *Christian Science Monitor* reports on '[t]he desperation caused by debt in Bangladesh', noting the case of

Selina Akter from Berendy village, whom, in a typical example, borrowed in order to start a vegetable farming business. 'When her business went through a bad streak, Ms Akter was unable to meet the required payments and had to take additional loans from another microfinance nongovernmental organization. All told, she amassed 400,000 taka ($5,280) in debt'. The reporter found that, 'Experts estimate that the Akter family is just one of the many in Bangladesh who get caught up in a "web of loans," with 250–300 people selling their organs each year for quick cash'. Naturally, the country's poor nutrition and sanitation mean that women, overworked as labourers, end up getting extremely ill with only one kidney, leading to more borrowing/debt to meet health costs.[26]

Rama, a bidi roller who makes $1 a day, lives with the agony of her daughter's suicide by 'self-burning'. 'Rama says her daughter was driven to despair by [her mother's] microloan debt' because debt-collectors 'harassed the family for payment'. Mounika was just 17. It took two days for her to die from her injuries. Angered, the economist Kurapati Venkat Narayana said: 'If the people who borrow die, the microfinance companies get the insurance amount', perversely incentivizing bullying tactics. In the UK, bullying tactics employed by debt collection agencies are also leading to record rates of suicide. Cottage industries supported by microloans can hardly compete in a federally-subsidized export economy.[27]

DFID, meaning UK taxpayers, 'is spending £15.5 million on Growth and Private Sector Development in 2009–10 and this will nearly double to £30.2 million in 2010–11', says Parliament. 'The increase is primarily to fund its work on creating an enabling business environment' – all under the cover of an aid programme. Parliament explains that concern for women's rights is because, 'women form an increasing proportion of the labour market', which the MoD notes will be 'subject to the ruthless laws of supply and demand', echoing Save the Children's observation that micro-credits often force women to work longer for less.[28]

A US National Intelligence Council projection, co-sponsored by

Shell, PFC Energy, the Evian Group and the Global Business Network, states: 'A flagrant characteristic of this world is that while there is economic growth, it is non-inclusive. World leaders (political as well as business) are effectively writing off the "human cost" of growth'. The projection further notes: 'Concerns for the suffering of the bottom 4 billion people on the planet are not addressed in a serious and sustained way, that is simply not one of the top priorities of most government and corporate leaders'. The report notes that '[c]orporate profits and a short-term focus (e.g., quarterly shareholder reports) fuel a climate in which the companies are the winners in this world ... CEOs have refused to recognize that for greater equity and distribution they should be the first ones to relinquish the ridiculously high (some would say obscene) and generally perceived as unjustified levels of remuneration'.[29]

Similarly, a UK MoD projection out to 2036, co-sponsored by the Eurasia Group and Morgan Aquila Ltd., states: 'there *will* continue to be winners and losers in a global economy led by market forces, especially so in the field of labour, which *will* be subject to particularly ruthless laws of supply and demand' (emphases in original). That means most of the world's workforce.[30]

Conclusion

Peaceniks – 'terrorist sympathisers'

This book is an indictment of Britain's war crimes and crimes against humanity. It has provided documentary evidence of widespread abuse in an attempt to bring some of Britain's secret wars to light. The purpose has been to inform general readers, activists, academics and journalists about the significant role Britain continues to play in the world.

Chapter 1 documented Anglo-American-French complicity in training, arming and directing terrorists to overthrow the government of Syria with the aim of privatizing the country's nationalized resources. Chapter 2 noted the near-identical strategy in Libya, with the exception of NATO involvement in the latter case. Chapter 3 exposed how these elements came together in Iraq to spawn ISIS. Chapter 4 exposed the Anglo-American-Israeli efforts in Iran to destabilize the Shia regime by supporting both Sunni and Shia anti-government terrorists. Chapter 5 provided a background to the current Saudi-Yemen war and documented Britain's complicity. Chapter 6 laid out the illegality of drone attacks.

In the Introduction, we documented the so-called free trade agenda that Euro-American policymakers are attempting to implement worldwide, which is based on a nineteenth century model. The Middle East and North Africa region is being radically altered by design in an effort to implement a widespread economic programme called the Broader Middle East and North Africa Initiative (BMENAI), a similar trade and investment project to that of the European Union after World War II. The BMENAI appears to be the regional component of the global 'free trade' agenda.

Part II looked at Britain's dangerous role in destabilizing Ukraine

(Chapter 7), exposed the hidden role of the UK in Sri Lanka's ethnic cleansing (Chapter 8), and documented genocide in Colombia (Chapter 9), support for Indonesia's occupation of Papua (Chapter 10), the instigation of a coup in Somalia (Chapter 11), and the training and arming of a death squad in Bangladesh (Chapter 12). When it comes to protecting human rights in other countries, there is a blatant disregard, unless doing so can serve as humanitarian propaganda.

Not only do internal documents acknowledge that supporting terrorists may lead to blowback, thereby putting civilians in danger, but other, more chilling, documents put a higher priority on supporting America's commitment to world domination – 'Full Spectrum Dominance' – than on safeguarding the general public against nuclear annihilation. This policy is being pursued in an effort to prevent China, Russia and emerging powers (including India) from taking independent economic paths. This is a global example of how force and the threat of force – even if it means nuclear war – is being employed to secure a 'free trade' agenda which will, at least in theory, centralize US hegemony.

In August 2015, Reyaad Khan and Abdul Raqib Amin were killed by RAF drone operators while travelling in a vehicle in Raqqa, Syria. According to Prime Minister Cameron, speaking in Parliament, Khan was the target (murder). Amin was killed alongside him (manslaughter). A third unidentified, alleged Islamic State fighter was killed with them, though the third person was not 'identified as a UK national', so his or her life is not significant, hence no details (name, age, nationality, etc.) emerged.[1]

The justification given by Cameron was that the killings were 'an act of self-defence', because Khan was 'involved in actively recruiting ISIL sympathisers and seeking to orchestrate specific and barbaric attacks against the west, including directing a number of planned terrorist attacks right here in Britain, such as plots to attack high profile public commemorations'. Surprisingly, evidence was provided, namely that Khan was *not* a threat to the UK. To quote

Cameron: 'there was nothing to suggest that Reyaad Khan would ever leave Syria'.[2]

It's okay to murder suspects

Cameron's statement raises all sorts of questions about how a Syrian-based alleged terrorist could pose a threat to Britons. Presumably, Khan was issuing instructions to terror cells in the UK, if Cameron is to be believed. But this becomes a matter for the British police, either national or regional. Contrary to popular belief, the British government does possess the proverbial licence to kill, a 'license' that it grants itself and one certainly not grounded in international law. Until the Khan case, targeted killings (murder) depended on the authorization of the Secretary of State. As journalist and author Ian Cobain discovered, the Intelligence Services Act 1994, Section 7(1), frees intelligence operatives from liability in acts abroad, 'if the act is one which is authorised to be done by virtue of an authorisation given by the Secretary of State'. In the case of Khan, the killings were not carried out by MI6, which is covered by the Intelligence Services Act 1994, but by the Royal Air Force.[3]

The pretext for the murder was later changed by the UK's Permanent Representative to the UN, Matthew Rycroft, who wrote that the killings were somehow justified in the 'collective self-defence' of Iraq.[4]

Inverting international legal norms, Secretary of State for Defence Michael Fallon, 'who authorised the lethal drone strike' (*Press and Journal*), appealed to Article 51 of the UN Charter, the right of collective and/or individual self-defence. Interestingly, the advice of the Attorney General, Jeremy Wright, has not been published by the government, indicating that the killings are violations of domestic and international law.[5]

Also inverting convention, former Attorney General Dominic Grieve opined that Article 51 does apply to the Khan case. The Cameron coalition government refused to publish Grieve's 2011 letter on Libya in full, implying that the bombing of Libya was illegal. Grieve himself advised that it was legal to illegally invade Somalia in 2012 with SAS troops (as noted in Chapter 11). However, as Fallon, Wright and Grieve surely know, Article 51 applies to imminent or actual attacks from states, not individuals – hence the appearance of the legally dubious Rycroft letter.[6]

Until the majority of MPs voted to bomb in December 2015, the common media line was that 'Britain is not at war with Syria'. Since 2010, and materially since at least 2011, Britain, France and the USA have been at war with Syria, by proxy. If Article 51 applied, the case could be argued that President Bashar al-Assad could have launched pre-emptive attacks on military targets in the UK. The Khan case is a criminal one, given that it involved the alleged planning of terrorism. Under a genuine self-defence doctrine, the UK had a legal obligation to apprehend Khan, and more realistically his inferred and alleged terror cells in the UK, whom the Prime Minister implied were preparing to carry out terrorist attacks. If the 'targeted killing' of Khan has a legal basis, it would have also been lawful for Muammar Gaddafi to launch 'targeted strikes' against civilians in London and Manchester, including Anas al-Liby, who was allegedly linked to the deaths of at least six Libyan civilians in 1996, when he was protected by the British government.[7]

Khan's case is not the first in which the state has slaughtered its own citizens. In the 1970s, the Ministry of Defence waged a dirty war in Northern Ireland, in which units from the Military Reaction Force murdered Protestants and Catholics as a part of strategy of tension. Northern Irish murdered by the MRF in the early-1970s include: Patrick McVeigh (shot in the back), John and Gerry Conway (travelling to a fruit stall), Aiden McAloon and Eugene Devlin (travelling in a taxi), Joe Smith, Hugh Kenny, Patrick Murray and Tommy Shaw (killed in drive-by shootings), and Daniel Rooney and Brendan Brennan (walking along a road). Thanks to a free media, the events were brought to public attention: 40 years after they happened.[8]

The answer to war is war

On Friday 13 November, 2015, Parisians paid the price for their government's secret foreign policy – the training and arming of the Free Syrian Army (FSA), a terrorist proxy group organized to remove President Assad – when gunmen and suicide bombers murdered over 100 people. In this book we have documented how the FSA and other terrorists created by the West morphed into ISIS, a regime as horrible as Britain's allies, the Saudi monarchy and Colombia gangs and paramilitaries. (The latter operate 'chop-up' houses in which political opponents are hacked to death.[9])

ISIS did not exist until Iraq was invaded by the US and Britain. ISIS barely existed until US-British-French special forces covertly created the FSA to oust Assad. War created ISIS and the kneejerk reaction among politicians and a large number of European citizens to the events in Paris is more war. A few weeks later, 'following a request from the French government' (BBC), Prime Minister Cameron held a second vote on a motion to openly bomb Syria (as opposed to secretly bomb Syria, as Britain had been doing for years).[10]

This time, the majority of MPs voted affirmatively, many having been briefed and/or pressured by the intelligence services. David Lammy (Labour MP), for instance, said: 'I sat with spooks [intelligence officers] last week [late-November] trying to persuade me'. Lammy bravely and sensibly voted against bombing, writing: 'Air strikes will harm civilians and could serve as a key recruitment tool for ISIS. We cannot fall into the trap set by terrorists; the attacks in Paris were not just a horrendous terrorist act, but also a provocation'. He added: 'I am worried that we are, in effect, taking the bait and performing the acts that ISIS have told their followers around the world would follow'.[11]

As an indication of how the often warped world view of MPs is shaped, Caroline Flint (Labour MP), who voted for the bombing, said: 'I had a[n intelligence] briefing on Monday [30 November] as a privy councillor with the National Security Advisor', Mark Lyall-

Grant, former UN Permanent Representative whom, in that capacity, attempted to justify the bombing of Libya in 2011 by saying that it was legal. As Ambassador for the UK Mission to the UN, Lyall-Grant also endorsed the sanctions imposed on Iran in 2012 – which, according to the UN, put millions of lives at risk – as what he called a 'peaceful incentive'.[12]

David Cameron was told by the Joint Intelligence Committee that 70,000 anti-ISIS fighters were in Syria and could act as a ground force in place of British troops. The fabricated figure was never intended for public scrutiny, but it seems that Cameron misunderstood this desired discretion and mentioned it in his pro-war speech to Parliament. The intelligence fabrication was immediately compared by the media to former PM Tony Blair's 'dodgy dossier', which Blair invoked in an effort to panic the public into supporting the very invasion of Iraq which created ISIS. During a meeting with ministers, Cameron referred to anti-war MPs as 'a bunch of terrorist sympathisers'.[13]

The importance of being active

As noted in Chapter 7, the government was advised that the severity of terrorism pales in comparison with the ever-present threat of terminal nuclear war resulting from state-on-state confrontation.

In November 2015, after the Paris attacks, the Turkish Air Force shot down a Russian jet which, it claims, had invaded Turkey's airspace. Moscow took this as a 'planned provocation' and reacted by sailing a warship past Istanbul. Ankara in turn described the alleged presence of a Russian sailor brandishing a rocket launcher as a 'provocation'. Turkey's Foreign Minister, Mevlüt Çavuşoğlu, said: 'If we perceive a threatening situation, we will give the necessary response'. Any response will in theory be supported by US, British and French nuclear forces because those countries and Turkey are members of NATO, whose charter commits members to collective self-defence.[14]

The events follow a potential nuclear confrontation which

occurred on 6 September, 2007, when Syria's radars were blinded during an air attack by Israel. Operation Orchard involved Israeli bombers destroying a facility in Dayr al-Zawr, Syria, said to be a nuclear reactor. The only mainstream publication to report on the seriousness of the operation was *The Spectator*. '[A] very senior British ministerial source' informed the investigators: 'If people had known how close we came to world war three that day there'd have been mass panic'. Involved parties are holding their silence. 'The only certainty in the fog of cover-up is that something big happened on 6 September – something very big'.[15]

In the absence of further information, we can only speculate that prior to the attack, the US raised its nuclear alert to DEFCON-3, a high warning, in an effort to caution Russia against coming to the aid of Syria and shooting down the Israeli jets.

The year 2007 was not the first in which we came close to annihilation. In September 1983, the Soviets shot down a Korean airliner, believing it to be an American spy plane. At that point, the Soviets and Americans had put their nuclear missiles on hair-trigger alert, in which state many hundreds remain today. Peter Burt discovered that in November, at the height of tensions, the US and NATO ran a war game entitled Operation Able Archer.

The Operation envisaged a Soviet invasion of Yugoslavia in collaboration with Warsaw Pact countries (Orange Forces). In response to such a move, a mass troop movement of 40,000 NATO ground troops (Blue Forces) across Western Europe, then already under Soviet occupation, was envisaged. The mass movement would be guided by a highly encrypted communications system. In the war game, Orange Forces would advance on Finland and Norway, eventually taking Greece. The escalation of hostilities would culminate in the use of chemical weapons before triggering the use of nukes. The exact details remain classified, but researchers have found that British bases RAF Brize Norton, Greenham Common and Mildenhall were involved in the game.

In response (in the real world), the Soviets secretly fitted a dozen aircraft based in East Germany with nuclear weapons. In addition, 70 SS-20 nukes were put on heightened alert. Nuclear-armed Soviet submarines were then sent to the Artic. NATO claimed that Soviet moves were part of a Russian war game. However, a British Joint Intelligence Committee report says: 'at least some Soviet officials/officers may have misinterpreted Able Archer 83 and possibly other nuclear CPXs [command post exercises] as posing a real threat'. Cabinet Secretary Sir Robert Armstrong noted, 'the concern of the Soviet Union over a possible Nato surprise attack mounted under cover of exercises'.[16]

Peter Dibb, former Director of the Australian Joint Intelligence Organization, said: 'Able Archer could have triggered the ultimate unintended catastrophe, and with prompt nuclear strike capacities on both the US and Soviet sides, [on] orders of magnitude greater than in 1962', referring to the Cuban Missile Crisis, which was only averted because a single Russian Commander, Vasili Arkhipov, countermanded an order to retaliate against the US Navy. In *Probable Nuclear Targets In The United Kingdom*, the Joint Intelligence Committee estimated that Soviet nuclear attack plans would involve an attack on London, in which eight hydrogen bombs and two atomic bombs would be detonated. Edinburgh would be destroyed by two hydrogen bombs and two atomic bombs; 'Glasgow by four hydrogen bombs and one atomic bomb', and submarine bases in Scotland 'by four hydrogen bombs and four atomic bombs. All in all, the JIC expected that during a war with the Soviet Union, the UK would be struck by about 300 nuclear weapons'.[17]

We have a choice. We can either sit back and allow our self-proclaimed leaders to push the world ever-closer to what they call Full Spectrum Dominance, thereby increasing the likelihood of 'doomsday' (Ministry of Defence), or we can educate ourselves, our friends and colleagues about what is really happening in the world. The challenge is big, but no bigger than winning the right to vote (as the British working classes finally did at the turn of the 20th century), ending Apartheid, or raising concerns about environmental destruction.

The steps toward a better world are within our reach and involve simple actions:

1) Commit to at least one cause, be it keeping the National Health Service public, stopping fracking, or the Campaign for Nuclear Disarmament. If a group dedicated to a cause you believe in doesn't exist, form it.
2) Stick with it – nothing happens in five minutes. None of us can change the world alone, but together anything is possible.

Notes

Introduction

1. Liam Fox in House of Commons Defence Committee, 'Operations in Libya', Ninth report of session 2012–12, Volume 1, HC 950, 8 February, 2012, p. EV 8, http://www.publications.parliament.uk/pa/cm201012/cmselect/cmdfence/950/950.pdf
2. On libel, see E.M. Barendt, 1997, *Libel and the Media: The Chilling Effect*, Clarendon. The UK has in fact been condemned by the United Nations Committee on Human Rights for its censorship laws. Writing in 2008, the Committee says that the Defamation Act 1952 'discourage[s] critical media reporting on matters of serious public interest, adversely affecting the ability of scholars and journalists to publish their work, including through the phenomenon known as libel tourism', where claimants are able to easily sue authors on frivolous grounds (Duncan Campbell, 'British libel laws violate human rights, says UN', *Guardian*, 14 August, 2008, http://www.theguardian.com/uk/2008/aug/14/law.unitednations).
   The author of the article was himself arrested under the Thatcher government for obtaining details about the Zircon satellite. The updated Defamation Act 2013 was alleged to protect free speech but in fact imposes the curious law that stating a fact may be libellous, but stating an opinion may not be.

   On the government's use of D-Notices (after 1993 DA-Notices and now DSMA-Notices), see The DSMA-Notice System, 'Agenda', no date, http://www.dsma.uk/. For critiques, see Nicholas Wilkinson, *Secrecy and the Media: The Official History of the United Kingdom's D-notice System*, 2009, Routledge and Pauline Sadler, 2001, *National Security and the D-Notice System*, Ashgate. In 'Appendix 7, Government actions against press and broadcasting leaks 1979–87', Michael Clarke (1992, *British External Policy-making in the 1990s*, Macmillan and the Royal Institute of International Affairs) provides a shocking chronology of arrests and raids (pp. 317–8). John K. Cooley provides a history of the US-British role in creating what is now 'al-Qaeda', writing: 'Because of the secretive nature of the British political establishment and the practice of sending warning "D notices" to editors or media executives contemplating a breach of security ... very little about this

British effort ever leaked out during the 1980s' (2002 (2nd), *Unholy Wars*, Pluto Press, p. 75).

For the 'hackles' quote, see Laurence Martin and John Garnett, 1997, *British Foreign Policy: Challenges and Choices for the 21st Century*, Pinter, p. 80.

3. Stuart Laycock, 2012, *All the Countries We've Ever Invaded*, The History Press (eBook), p. 1. Mike Davis, 2002 (2nd), *Late Victorian Holocausts*, Verso. John Newsinger, 2006, *The Blood Never Dried*, Bookmarks, p. 1.
4. Quoted in Carroll Quigley, 1981 [1949], *The Anglo-American Establishment From Rhodes to Cliveden*, GSG and Associates, pp. 254–5.
5. Sir Laurence Martin, 'Chatham House at 75: The Past and the Future', *International Affairs*, Vol. 71, No. 4, October, 1995, pp. 697–703.
6. Vincent Cable, 'The New Trade Agenda: Universal Rules Amid Cultural Diversity', *International Affairs*, Vol. 72, No. 2, April, 1996, pp. 227–246.
7. Ibid.
8. E.A. Benians, Sir James Butler and C.E. Carrington (eds.), *The Cambridge History of the British Empire, Vol. III, The Empire-Commonwealth, 1870–1919*, Cambridge University Press, p. 224.
9. Ratcliffe, 'The origins of the Anglo-French commercial treaty' in William Otto Henderson and Barrie M. Ratcliffe (eds.), 1975, *Great Britain and Her World, 1750–1914*, Manchester University Press, pp. 125–52.
10. Davis, op. cit. and Robert Renny, 1807, *A Demonstration of the necessity and advantages of a free trade to the East Indies*, C. Chapple, pp. 1–31.
11. John Gallagher and Ronald Robinson, 'The Imperialism of Free Trade', *Economic History Review*, Vol. 6, No. 1., 1953, pp. 1–15.
12. James Lawrence, 1998, *The Rise and Fall of the British Empire*, Abacus, pp. 170–2. Peter Harnetty, 1972, *Imperialism and Free Trade*, Manchester University Press, p. 2.
13. Andrew Thompson and Gary Magee, 'A soft touch? British industry, empire markets, and the self-governing dominions, c.1870–1914', *The Economic History Review*, Volume 56, Issue 4, November, 2003, pp. 689–717.
14. Harnetty, op. cit., p. 9 and Ratcliffe, op. cit.
15. *Daily Mail*, 'Star Wars 2010?', 23 April, 2010, http://www.dailymail.co.uk/news/article-1268138/X-37B-unmanned-space-shuttle-launched-tonight.html Gary Payton, Air Force Deputy Under-secretary for Space Systems, said of the X-37B: 'We, the Air Force, have a suite of military missions in space and this new vehicle could potentially help us do those missions better'. On US bases, see David Vine, 2015, *Base Nation*, Macmillan. On Total Information Awareness and its scope, see Laura K. Donohue, 2008, *The Cost of Counterterrorism*,

Cambridge University Press and Newton Lee, 2012, *Facebook Nation*, Springer. On the US military's encirclement of Russia, see my *Voices for Peace*, 2015, The Plymouth Institute for Peace Research, www.pipr.co.uk

16. US Space Command, 'Vision for 2020', February, 1997, archived at www.pipr.co.uk/archive
17. Sandra Polaski, 'US living standards in an era of globalization', Carnegie Endowment for International Peace, July, 2007, Policy Brief 53, http://carnegieendowment.org/files/pb_53_polaski__us_living_standards_final.pdf
18. US Department of State, 'US relations with France', Bureau of European and Eurasian Affairs, 20 March, 2015, http://www.state.gov/r/pa/ei/bgn/3842.htm and Council on Foreign Relations, 'US-France relations (1763–present)', no date, http://www.cfr.org/france/us–france-relations-1763–present/p17682
19. US Department of State, 'US relations with United Kingdom', Bureau of European and Eurasian Affairs, 30 April, 2015, http://www.state.gov/r/pa/ei/bgn/3846.htm
20. MoD and Defence Equipment and Support, '£120 million Anglo-French defence contract', Gov.uk, 5 November, 2014, https://www.gov.uk/government/news/120-million-anglo-french-defence-contract
21. Sir Laurence Martin and John Garnett, op. cit., pp. 76–80.
22. On Britain's training and arms to Turkey, see Secretary of State for Defence Nicholas Soames: 'Training has been provided in the UK to members of the Turkish armed forces during the past 12 months [from 1994–5], as is normal practice between NATO nations . . . [I]t is not normally our practice to disclose the precise details of military training given to any particular country as such details are regarded as being confidential between Governments' ('Turkish Forces', House of Commons Debate, 28 April, 1995, vol. 258 c772W, http://hansard.millbanksystems.com/written_answers/1995/apr/28/turkish-forces). This was followed by a Human Rights Watch report on Turkey's repression of Kurds: 'Some 2,685 villages and hamlets in Turkey's southeastern provinces have been completely or partially depopulated [of Kurds] since fighting broke out in the region in August 1984 between government forces and the [Kurdish PKK]' (Human Rights Watch, 'Turkey: Turkey's Failed Policy to Aid the Forcibly Displaced in the Southeast', June, 1996, Vol. 8, No. 9, (D), http://www.hrw.org/reports/1996/Turkey2.htm). Campaign Against the Arms Trade reports: 'During [Britain's John] Major Government (1990–7), the UK sold Turkey around £42 million of weapons per annum' (Nicholas Gilby, 'Turkey and the Arms Trade 1998–2002: A

Precis: Nurturing Turkey's War Machine', March, 2003, Campaign Against the Arms Trade, pp. 1–3).

23. Martin and Garnett, op. cit.
24. Secretary of State for Defence, 'Strategic Defence Review', July, 1998, MoD, archived at http://fissilematerials.org/library/mod98.pdf
25. Ministry of Defence, 'Delivering security in a changing world', Defence white paper, December, 2003, pp. 6, 10, archived at http://archives.livreblancdefenseetsecurite.gouv.fr/2008/IMG/pdf/whitepaper2003.pdf
26. Ministry of Defence, 'Adaptability and partnership: Issues for the Strategic Defence Review', February, 2010, Cm 7794, p. 12, https://www.gov.uk/government/uploads/system/uploads/attachment_data/file/35927/defence_green_paper_cm7794.pdf
27. Developments, Concepts and Doctrine Centre, 'Strategic Trends Programme: Future Character of Conflict', Ministry of Defence, February, 2010, pp. 4, 5, A2, https://www.gov.uk/government/uploads/system/uploads/attachment_data/file/33685/FCOCReadactedFinalWeb.pdf
28. David Blagden, 'Written Evidence to the Parliamentary Joint Committee on the National Security Strategy: Priorities for the 2015 NSS', Joint Committee on the National Security Strategy, *The Next National Security Strategy*, December, 2014, p. 4, http://www.parliament.uk/documents/joint-committees/national-security-strategy/The%20next%20security%20strategy%20(forth%20review)/ThenextNationalSecurityStrategyEvidence18122014.pdf
    For an account of the Mali bombing and Britain's role, see my 'AFRICOM, NATO & the EU', *Lobster*, Issue 67, summer, 2014, pp. 20–4, http://www.lobster-magazine.co.uk/free/lobster67/lob67-africom-nato-eu.pdf
29. Development, Concepts and Doctrine Centre, 'Strategic Trends Programme: Global Strategic Trends – Out to 2040', Ministry of Defence, February 2010 (2nd), Ministry of Defence, https://www.gov.uk/government/uploads/system/uploads/attachment_data/file/33717/GST4_v9_Feb10.pdf
    Alex Evans and David Stern, 'Organizing for influence: UK foreign policy in an age of uncertainty', Chatham House, June, 2010, p. vi, https://www.chathamhouse.org/sites/files/chathamhouse/public/Research/Europe/r0610_stevens_evans.pdf
30. Joel Faulkner Rogers, 'Report on British attitudes to defence, security and the armed forces', YouGov, 25 October, 2014, https://yougov.co.uk/news/2014/10/25/report-british-attitudes-defence-security-and-arme/
    On Sweden and Switzerland, see Michael Clarke, 1992, *British External*

Policy-making in the 1990s, Macmillan and the Royal Institute of International Affairs, p. 332.

31. The Institute for Democracy and Conflict Resolution note that, after 9/11, 'Polls ... suggested that approximately 65 per cent of Britons were willing to send troops to Afghanistan', to find the alleged suspect Osama bin Laden and oust his sponsors the Taliban. By 2009, only 22% of the public 'approved' (including 'strongly' and 'simply') of British involvement (Scotto et al., 'Attitudes towards British engagement in Afghanistan', Briefing Paper, March, 2011, http://www.idcr.org.uk/wp-content/uploads/2010/09/03_11.pdf). On Iraq, see Ipsos MORI, 'Iraq, the last pre-war polls', 21 March, 2003, https://www.ipsos-mori.com/newsevents/ca/287/Iraq-The-Last-PreWar-Polls.aspx. On Serbia and Libya, see, respectively, House of Commons Defence Committee, 'A new chapter to the Strategic Defence Review', Sixth Rep. of Sess. 2002–03, Vol. 1, HC 93-1, 15 May, 2003, Stationary Office, pp. 35-6 and Peter Kellner, 'Libya: voters divided on military action', YouGov, 16 May, 2011, https://yougov.co.uk/news/2011/05/16/libya-voters-divided-military-action/
32. On the popularity of the Armed Forces as an institution, but not necessarily their deployment in war, see Lindsey A. Hines et al., 'Are the armed forces understood and supported by the public? A view from the United Kingdom', *Armed Forces and Society*, Vol. 1, No. 26, 2014, pp. 1–26, https://www.kcl.ac.uk/kcmhr/publications/assetfiles/2014/Hines2014.pdf. A 2014 Chatham House study finds that 61% of Britons consider NATO important to UK security, 'may be driven in part by real concern about Russia'. 67% of the public consider Russia to be a 'threat to the security of the EU', and a quarter think 'conflict with Russia to be one of the top threats facing the UK'. Public paranoia about Russia is largely driven by the media (see Chapter 7). However, the concern about war with Russia should reach 100% of the public: the fact that it doesn't is also a media responsibility (Robin Niblett, 'In Britain, NATO has popular support to reverse decline', Chatham House, 4 September, 2014, https://www.chathamhouse.org/expert/comment/15663).

    On fakery in Syria, see Ben Hubbard and Hwaida Saad, 'Images of death in Syria, but no proof of chemical attacks', *New York Times*, 21 August, 2013, http://www.nytimes.com/2013/08/22/world/middleeast/syria.html?pagewanted=all&_r=1 The report says: 'The videos, experts said, ... did not prove the use of chemical weapons, which interfere with the nervous system and can cause defecation, vomiting, intense salivation and tremors. Only some of those symptoms were visible in some patients. Gwyn

Winfield, editor of CBRNe World, a journal that covers unconventional weapons, said that the medics would most likely have been sickened by exposure to so many people dosed with chemical weapons – a phenomenon not seen in the videos'. Agence-France Presse quotes Paula Vanninen, director of the Finnish Institute for Verification of the Chemical Weapons Convention: 'I am not totally convinced because the people that are helping them are without any protective clothing and without any respirators ... In a real case, they would also be contaminated and would also be having symptoms'. Dr Jean Pascal Zanders says: 'I have not seen anybody applying nerve agent antidotes ... Nor do medical staff and other people appear to suffer from secondary exposure while carrying or treating victims'. Professor Alexander Kekule of the Institute for Medical Microbiology at Halle University, Germany, 'said the symptoms did not fit with typical chemical weapons use as the victims did not appear to be suffering pain or irritation to their eyes, nose and mouth' (all quoted in BBC News Online, Q&A: Syria 'toxic attacks' near Damascus, 25 August, 2013, http://www.bbc.co.uk/news/world-middle-east 23788674). Israel's leading newspaper, *Haaretz*, quotes Dan Kaszeta, a private consultant and former Officer of the US Army Chemical Corps: 'None of the people treating the casualties or photographing them are wearing any sort of chemical-warfare protective gear ... and despite that, none of them seem to be harmed ... [T]here are none of the other signs you would expect to see in the aftermath of a chemical attack, such as intermediate levels of casualties, severe visual problems, vomiting and loss of bowel control'. The newspaper also quotes UK Ministry of Defence consultant, Steve Johnson of Cranfield University: 'From the details we have seen so far, a large number of casualties over a wide area would mean quite a pervasive dispersal. With that level of chemical agent, you would expect to see a lot of contamination on the casualties coming in, and it would affect those treating them who are not properly protected. We are not seeing that here', quoted in Gili Cohen and Anshel Pfeffer, 'Defence minister: Assad used chemical weapons in Syria multiple times', *Haaretz*, 21 August, 2013,
http://www.haaretz.com/news/diplomacy-defense/.premium-1.542849

Chapter 1: Syria

1. BBC News Online, 'Syria crisis: Cameron loses Commons vote on Syria action', 30 August, 2013, http://www.bbc.co.uk/news/uk-politics-23892783 and Reprieve, 'UK pilots conducted strikes on Syria', 17 July, 2015, http://www.reprieve.org.uk/press/uk-pilots-conducted-strikes-in-syria/

2. See United Nations, 'Charter of the United Nations', 24 October, 1945, http://www.un.org/en/charter-united-nations/index.html and Theo Farrell, 'Are the US-led air strikes in Syria legal – and what does it mean if they are not?', *Telegraph*, 23 September, 2014, http://www.telegraph.co.uk/news/worldnews/middleeast/syria/11116792/Are-the-US-led-air-strikes-in-Syria-legal-and-what-does-it-mean-if-they-are-not.html
3. UN Security Council, 15 August, 2014, http://www.un.org/press/en/2014/sc11520.doc.htm and Richard Barrett quoted in Mehdi Hasan, 'Islamic State could attack west in response', *Huffington Post*, 19 August, 2014, http://www.huffingtonpost.co.uk/2014/08/18/richard-barrett_n_5688484.html
4. Quoted in Bryan Bender, 'US wants more from Saudis in fight against extremists', *Boston Globe*, 5 September, 2014, https://www.bostonglobe.com/news/nation/2014/09/04/amid-talk-more-military-force-confront-islamic-state-some-see-religious-retreat-theologians/7Y0JD78VbNf5a8RlctbmIK/story.html and Edward Delman, 'An anti-ISIS summit in Mecca', *The Atlantic*, 26 February 2015.
5. Vasudevan Sridharan, 'ISIS crisis: Obama authorizes surveillance flights over Syria', *International Business Times*, 26 August, 2014, www.ibtimes.co.uk/isis-crisis-obama-authorises-surveillance-flights-over-syria-1462553 and Metin Turcan, 'Don't expect Peshmerga fighters to beat the Islamic State', *Al-Monitor*, 2 September, 2014, http://www.usnews.com/news/articles/2014/09/02/dont-expect-peshmerga-fighters-to-beat-the-islamic-state
6. UN Refugee Agency, 'Total number of Syrian refugees exceeds four million for first time', 9 July, 2015, www.unhcr.org/559d67d46.html and Refugees International, 'Helpful facts & figures', 2014, www.refintl.org/get-involved/helpful-facts-%2526-figures. See also Reuters, 'Syria death toll now exceeds 210,000 – rights group', 7 February, 2015, http://uk.reuters.com/article/2015/02/07/uk-mideast-crisis-toll-idUKKBN0LB0DU20150207
7. John C. Buss, 'Democratization as a United States Strategy for Middle East Security', US Army War College, Strategy Research Project, 18 March, 2005, Pennsylvania: Carlisle Barracks, www.dtic.mil/cgi-bin/GetTRDoc?AD=ADA433675. The document predicting the date of the Arab Spring is Sherifa Zuhur, 'Egypt: Security, Political, and Islamist Challenges', Strategic Studies Institute, 1 October, 2007, http://www.strategicstudiesinstitute.army.mil/pubs/display.cfm?pubID=787. Zuhur writes: 'in 3 to 4 years, if not sooner, Egypt's political security and stability will be at risk. Widespread economic and political discontent might push that date forward' (pp. vii–i).

Referring to the likes of Ben Ali, Mubarak, Gaddafi and Assad, who would not agree to the reform demands, Leslie Campbell, Director of the Middle East Program at the National Democratic Institute for International Affairs, said that, 'the unspoken fact behind all of the discussions is that we are trying to work with a bunch of people who are going to be kicked out of office if democratic change moves forward'. Campbell said that, 'for now, it's easier to support free-trade agreements than political change' (Jeremy M. Sharp, 'The Broader Middle East and North Africa Initiative: An Overview', Congressional Research Service, Order Code RS22053, 15 February, 2005, http://www.fas.org/sgp/crs/mideast/RS22053.pdf).

Nadia Oweidat, Cheryl Benard, Dale Stahl, Walid Kildani, Edward O'Connell, Audra K. Grant, 2008, *The Kefaya Movement: A Case Study of a Grassroots Reform Initiative*, CA: The RAND Corporation, http://www.rand.org/content/dam/rand/pubs/monographs/2008/RAND_MG778.pdf

The RAND Corporation's 2008 report on a once-genuine, grassroots reform organization in Egypt, Kifaya (Enough!), notes that: 'Given the current negative popular standing of the United States in the region, U.S. support for reform initiatives is best carried out through nongovernmental and nonprofit institutions ... Many are alarmed that the United States appears to be addressing democratic reform as a security issue. It is therefore critical that the United States couch its support for democracy in the Middle East in terms likely to appeal to the local populations and work with its allies to build the infrastructure needed'.

8. The 'manufacturing democracy' quote is in Buss, op. cit. The Carnegie Endowment reference is Marina Ottaway and Amr Hamzawy, 'Political Reform in the Middle East: Can the United States and Europe Work Together?', Democracy and Rule of Law Project, December, 2004, Carnegie Endowment, www.carnegieendowment.org/2004/12/10/political-reform-in-middle-east-can-united-states-and-europe-work-together/3yd. Other documents include Mona Yacoubian, 'Promoting Middle East Democracy', Special Report 127, October 2004, United States Institute for Peace, www.usip.org/files/resources/sr127.pdf and Robert Looney, 'The Broader Middle East Initiative: Requirements for Success in the Gulf', *Strategic Insights*, Volume 3, Issue 8, August, 2004, pp. 1–9, www.dtic.mil/cgi-bin/GetTRDoc?AD=ADA521636
9. Quoted in Ben Smith, 'Unrest Spreads to Syria', House of Commons Library, SN/IA/5928, 11 June, 2011, http://researchbriefings.files.parliament.uk/documents/SN05928/SN05928.pdf On Gaddafi's 'cosmetic' changes, see International Crisis Group, 'Popular Protest in North Africa and the Middle

East (V): Making Sense of Libya', Crisis Group Middle East/North Africa Report No 107, 6 June 2011, http://www.crisisgroup.org/~/media/Files/Middle%20East%20North%20Africa/North%20Africa/107%20-%20Popular%20Protest%20in%20North%20Africa%20and%20the%20Middle%20East%20V%20-%20Making%20Sense%20of%20Libya.pdf

10. Development, Concepts and Doctrine Centre, 'Strategic Trends Programme: Global Strategic Trends – Out to 2040', Ministry of Defence, February 2010 (2nd), Ministry of Defence, pp. 11, 85, https://www.gov.uk/government/uploads/system/uploads/1attachment_data/file/33717/GST4_v9_Feb10.pdf
11. Ben Smith, 'Military forces in Syria and the rise of the jihadis', House of Commons Library, SNIA/6610, 29 April, 2013, http://researchbriefings.files.parliament.uk/documents/SN06610/SN06610.pdf and Deutsche Welle, 'Assad accuses Turkey of helping "terrorists" gain ground in Syria', 17 April, 2015, www.dw.com/en/assad-accuses-turkey-of-helping-terrorists-gain-ground-in-syria/a-18389840
12. Radio Free Europe Online, 'IS militant seeks Chechen wife for 15-year-old child fighter', 15 December, 2014, www.rferl.org/content/chechnya-wife-isis-fighter-syria/26745188.html and *Guardian*, 'Uighurs sent back from Thailand were on way to join jihad, says China', 12 July, 2015, www.theguardian.com/world/2015/jul/12/uighurs-sent-back-from-thailand-were-on-way-to-join-jihad-says-china. Malcolm W. Nance, 2015, *The Terrorists of Iraq: Inside the Strategy and Tactics of the Iraq Insurgency*, 2003–2014, CRC Press, pp. 322–5.
13. Christof Lehmann, 'Dumas, "Top British Officials Confessed to Syria War Plans Two Years before Arab Spring"', nsnbc International, 16 June, 2013, http://nsnbc.me/2013/06/16/dumas-top-british-officials-confessed-to-syria-war-plans-two-years-before-arab-spring/. Nick Hopkins, 'Syria conflict: UK planned to train and equip 100,000 rebels', BBC News Online, 3 July, 2014, http://www.bbc.co.uk/news/uk-28148943. Nafeez Ahmed, 'Syria intervention plan fueled by oil interests, not chemical weapon concern', *Guardian*, 30 August, 2013, www.theguardian.com/environment/earth-insight/2013/aug/30/syria-chemical-attack-war-intervention-oil-gas-energy-pipelines

    On Ahmed see Jonathan Cook, 'Why the Guardian axed Nafeez Ahmed's blog', Jonathan Cook: The Blog from Nazareth, 4 December, 2014, http://www.jonathan-cook.net/blog/2014-12-04/why-the-guardian-axed-nafeez-ahmeds-blog/
14. Barbara Jones, 'What was Our Man on the Libyan Farm really up to? Hard-working manager met with SAS troops before farcical operation to meet rebels', *Daily Mail*, 13 March 2011, www.dailymail.co.uk/news/article-

1365736/What-Our-Man-Libyan-Farm-really-Hard-working-manager-met-SAS-troops-farcical-operation-meet-rebels.html

15. Foreign and Commonwealth Office, 'Foreign Office Minister meets Syrian National Council members', 12 October, 2011, www.gov.uk/government/news/foreign-office-minister-meets-syrian-national-council-members
16. UK Elite Special Forces Website, 'British Special Forces Training Syrian Rebels?', 5 January, 2012, www.eliteukforces.info/uk-military-news/0501012-british-special-forces-syria.php
17. Haroon Siddique, 'Syria crisis: Opposition hold key meeting as car bomb hits Damascus – Sunday 4 November', *Guardian*, 4 November, 2012, http://www.theguardian.com/world/2012/nov/04/syria-crisis-opposition-key-meeting-doha and HRW, 'Syria: Armed opposition groups committing abuses', 20 March, 2012, https://www.hrw.org/news/2012/03/20/syria-armed-opposition-groups-committing-abuses
18. Smith, op. cit.
19. *Sunday World*, 'Tinker, raiders, soldier, spy', 7 November, 2011, www.sundayworld.com/news/tinker-raiders-soldier-spy
20. Ruth Sherlock, 'Libya's new rulers offer weapons to Syrian rebels', *Daily Telegraph*, 25 November, 2011, www.telegraph.co.uk/news/worldnews/middleeast/syria/8917265/Libyas-new-rulers-offer-weapons-to-Syrian-rebels.html
21. Seymour M. Hersh, 'The red line and the rat line', *London Review of Books*, Vol. 36, No. 8, 17 April, 2014, www.lrb.co.uk/v36/n08/seymour-m-hersh/the-red-line-and-the-rat-line
22. Julian Borger and Nick Hopkins, 'West training Syrian rebels in Jordan', *Guardian*, 8 March, 2013, www.theguardian.com/world/2013/mar/08/west-training-syrian-rebels-jordan and Duncan Gardham and Richard Spillett, 'Suspected terrorist stopped at Heathrow with a guide to jihad walks free after intelligence services "refuse to hand over evidence" ', *Daily Mail*, 1 June, 2015, www.dailymail.co.uk/news/article-3105884/Terror-suspect-Bherlin-Gildo-freed-intelligence-services-refuse-hand-evidence.html
23. Quoted in Christopher Hope and Tom Whitehead, 'Syria is now the biggest threat to Britain's security', *Telegraph*, 10 April, 2014, www.telegraph.co.uk/news/politics/10758623/Syria-is-now-the-biggest-threat-to-Britains-security.html

Chapter 2: Libya

1. Quoted in my 'AFRICOM, NATO & the EU', *Lobster*, Issue 67, summer, 2014, www.lobster-magazine.co.uk/free/lobster67/lob67-africom-nato-eu.pdf

2. Quoted in ibid.
3. For extensive details and sources, see my 'Libya One Year On (Part Four): Opened for Business', Axis of Logic, 6 May, 2012, http://axisoflogic.com/artman/publish/Article_64476.shtml. On the betrayal of former allies, see Ian Cobain, 2012, *Cruel Britannia*, Portobello.
4. For details and sources, see my Libya series, www.axisoflogic.com
5. Quoted in my 'Libya One Year On (Part One): The Propaganda and the Law', Axis of Logic, 23 April, 2012, http://axisoflogic.com/artman/publish/Article_64475.shtml
6. On Azzouz, see Sam Webb, 'Al-Qaeda leader in Libya was detained by British police on suspicion of terror offences – but later released and fled the UK to train bombers', *Daily Mail*, 28 September, 2014, http://www.dailymail.co.uk/news/article-2772495/Al-Qaeda-leader-Libya-detained-British-police-suspicion-terror-offences-later-released-fled-UK-train-bombers.html. See also Robert Mendick, Tom Whitehead and Raf Sanchez, 'Freed UK prisoner is al-Qaeda ringleader', *Telegraph*, 27 September, 2014, www.telegraph.co.uk/news/uknews/terrorism-in-the-uk/11125944/Freed-UK-prisoner-is-al-Qaeda-ringleader.html. For a transcript of the coup document, see Cryptome.org, 'The Qadahfi Assassination Plot', 16 February, 2000, http://cryptome.org/qadahfi-plot.htm
7. Cryptome.org, op. cit.
8. Martin Bright, 'MI6 "halted bid to arrest bin Laden"', *Guardian*, 10 November, 2002, www.theguardian.com/politics/2002/nov/10/uk.davidshayler. See also, Annie Machon, '"Spies, Lies and Whistleblowers" – The Gaddafi Plot Chapters', anniemachon.ch, http://anniemachon.ch/spies-lies-and-whistleblowers-the-gaddafi-plot-chapters. On al-Liby, see Mark Curtis, 2010, *Secret Affairs*, Serpent's Tail, pp. 229–30. See also, Library of Congress, 'Al-Qaeda in Libya: A Profile', August, 2012, http://fas.org/irp/world/para/aq-libya-loc.pdf
9. Quoted in Reuters, 'Rebel army chief is veteran Gaddafi foe: think-tank', 1 April, 2011, www.reuters.com/article/2011/04/01/us-libya-rebel-military-idUSTRE7304RC20110401 and Gordon Thomas and Marco Giannangeli, 'Libya defector Moussa Koussa was an MI6 double agent', *Express*, 3 April, 2011, www.express.co.uk/news/uk/238354/Libya-defector-Moussa-Koussa-was-an-MI6-double-agent and Democracy Now!, 'Gen. Wesley Clark Weighs Presidential Bid: "I Think About It Every Day"', 2 March, 2007, www.democracynow.org/2007/3/2/gen_wesley_clark_weighs_presidential_bid

10. Ian Birrell, 'MI6 role in Libyan rebels' rendition "helped to strengthen al-Qaida"', *Guardian*, 24 October, 2011, www.theguardian.com/world/2011/oct/24/mi6-libya-rebels-rendition-al-qaida
11. Library of Congress, op. cit., p. 11–2. Mendick, Whitehead and Sanchez, op. cit. and Alessandria Masi, 'Al Qaeda leader Abu Abd al-Baset Azzouz, accused of participation in Benghazi attack, reportedly awaiting trial in US', *International Business Times*, 4 December, 2014, www.ibtimes.com/al-qaeda-leader-abd-al-baset-azzouz-accused-participation-benghazi-attack-reportedly-1734429
12. Liam Fox in House of Commons Defence Committee, 'Operations in Libya', Ninth report of session 2012–12, Volume 1, HC 950, 8 February, 2012, p. 44, http://www.publications.parliament.uk/pa/cm201012/cmselect/cmdfence/950/950.pdf
13. Barbara Jones, 'What was Our Man on the Libyan Farm really up to? Hard-working manager met with SAS troops before farcical operation to meet rebels', *Daily Mail*, 13 March 2011, www.dailymail.co.uk/news/article-1365736/What-Our-Man-Libyan-Farm-really-Hard-working-manager-met-SAS-troops-farcical-operation-meet-rebels.html
14. Sidney Blumenthal, 'UK game playing; new rebel strategies; Egypt moves in', 8 April, 2011, email to Hillary Clinton, *New York Times*, https://assets.documentcloud.org/documents/2084634/emails.pdf
15. Ibid and Holly Watt, 'Secret MI6 plot to help Gaddafi escape Libya revealed', *Telegraph*, 27 September, 2013, www.telegraph.co.uk/news/uknews/defence/10339439/Secret-MI6-plot-to-help-Col-Gaddafi-escape-Libya-revealed.html
16. Blumenthal, op. cit.
17. Blumenthal, 'Bin Laden, AQ & Libya', email to Hillary Clinton, 2 May, 2011, *New York Times*, https://assets.documentcloud.org/documents/2084634/emails.pdf
18. Sean Rayment, 'How the special forces helped bring Gaddafi to his knees', *Telegraph*, 28 August, 2011, http://www.telegraph.co.uk/news/worldnews/africaandindianocean/libya/8727076/How-the-special-forces-helped-bring-Gaddafi-to-his-knees.html
19. Mark Hookham, 'MI6 warns Libyan arms dumps are "Tesco for world terrorists"', *Sunday Times*, 16 June, 2013, www.thesundaytimes.co.uk/sto/news/uk_news/National/article1274615.ece
20. Defense Intelligence Agency, 'Brigades of the Captive Omar Abdul Rahman Claim Responsibility for Attack on Benghazi, Libya', 16 September, 2012, 14-L-0552/DIA/394, www.judicialwatch.org/document-archive/pgs-394-398-396-from-jw-v-dod-and-state-14-812/

Chapter 3: Iraq

1. Charles Tripp, Evidence to Parliament, 'Report on the Future of Iraq', November, 2002, Appendix 11, www.publications.parliament.uk/pa/cm200203/cmselect/cmfaff/196/196ap13.htm
2. Foreign and Commonwealth Office, 'Iraq – a bright future or back to chaos?', 2010, news release, www.parliament.uk/business/publications/research/key-issues-for-the-new-parliament/britain-in-the-world/iraq–a-bright-future-or-back-to-chaos/
3. Harlan Ullman and James Wade, 'Shock and Awe: Achieving Rapid Dominance', National Defense University and Institute for National Strategic Studies, October, 1996, www.pipr.co.uk/wp-content/uploads/2014/07/Ullman_Shock.pdf. On the *Lancet* figures and the media's handling of them, see David Cromwell and David Edwards, 2008, *Newspeak in the 21st Century*, Pluto. ORB, 'Update on Iraqi Casualty Data', January, 2008, www.opinion.co.uk/Newsroom_details.aspx?NewsId=120. For the media's handling, see Cromwell and Edwards, op. cit. On polls, see Joe Emersberger, 'Poll shows that UK public drastically underestimates Iraqi War deaths', Spinwatch, 4 June, 2013, www.spinwatch.org/index.php/issues/war-and-foreign-policy/item/5499-poll-shows-that-uk-public-drastically-underestimates-iraqi-war-deaths
4. For details and sources, see my 'Remembering Iraq: The sanctions genocide', Axis of Logic, 3 August, 2013, http://axisoflogic.com/artman/publish/Article_65877.shtml
5. Chris Busby, Malak Hamdan and Entesar Ariabi, 'Cancer, Infant Mortality and Birth Sex-Ratio in Fallujah, Iraq 2005–2009', *The International Journal of Environmental Research and Public Health*, 2010, Vol. 7, Issue 7, pp. 2828–2837 and Patrick Cockburn, 'Toxic legacy of US assault on Fallujah "worse than Hiroshima" ', *Independent*, 24 July, 2010, www.independent.co.uk/news/world/middle-east/toxic-legacy-of-us-assault-on-fallujah-worse-than-hiroshima-2034065.html. On Vietnam, see Ash Anand, 'Vietnam's horrific legacy: The children of Agent Orange', 25 May, 2015, news.com.au, www.news.com.au/world/asia/vietnams-horrific-legacy-the-children-of-agent-orange/story-fnh81fz8-1227367090862 and Jason Grotto, 'Agent Orange: Birth defects plague Vietnam; U.S. slow to help', *Chicago Tribune*, 8 December, 2009, http://articles.chicagotribune.com/2009-12-08/health/chi-agent-orange3-dec08_1_defoliants-vietnam-war-agent-orange
6. Quoted in Thomas E. Ricks, 'Military plays up role of Zarqawi', *Washington*

Post, 10 April, 2006, www.washingtonpost.com/wp-dyn/content/article/2006/04/09/AR2006040900890.html

7. Christopher G. Pernin, Brian Nichiporuk, Dale Stahl, Justin Beck and Ricky Radaelli-Sanchez, 2008, *Unfolding the Future of the Long War*, RAND Corporation, www.rand.org/content/dam/rand/pubs/monographs/2008/RAND_MG738.pdf
8. Henry McDonald, 'UK agents "did have role in IRA bomb atrocities" ', *Guardian*, 10 September, 2006, www.theguardian.com/politics/2006/sep/10/uk.northernireland1 and Elite UK Forces, 'SAS – Basra Rescue', no date, www.eliteukforces.info/special-air-service/sas-operations/basra-raid/
9. Anderson quoted in my, *The New Atheism Hoax*, 2015, Plymouth Institute for Peace Research, www.pipr.co.uk/ebooks. Richard Oppel, 'Five years in – Iraq's insurgency runs on stolen oil profits', *NYT*, 16 March, 2008.
10. Quoted in Oppel, op. cit.
11. Michael Luo, 'Baghdad "disheartening," general says – Africa & Middle East – International Herald Tribune', *NYT*, 19 October, 2006, www.nytimes.com/2006/10/19/world/africa/19iht-iraq.3224123.html?pagewanted=all&_r=0
12. Fred W. Baker, 'Al Qaeda in Iraq Duped Into Following Foreigners, Captured Operative Says', US Department of Defense, *American Forces Press Service*, 18 July, 2007, http://archive.defense.gov/news/newsarticle.aspx?id=46764
13. Marc Santora, 'Two Americans killed in helicopter crash in Iraq', *NYT*, 2 February, 2007, www.nytimes.com/2007/02/02/world/middleeast/02cnd-iraq.html
14. Richard Oppel and Marc Santora, 'Seven Killed as U.S. Copter Crashes in Iraq', *NYT*, 7 February, 2007, www.nytimes.com/2007/02/07/world/middleeast/07cnd-iraq.html
15. See my *New Atheism Hoax*, 2015, Plymouth Institute for Peace Research, www.pipr.co.uk/ebooks
16. Sam Dagher and Atheer Kakan, 'Iraqi Premier Says Leader in Insurgency Is in Custody', *NYT*, 28 April, 2009, www.nytimes.com/2009/04/29/world/middleeast/29iraq.html
17. Timothy Williams, 'Nebulous Sunni insurgent urges attack', *NYT*, 8 July, 2009, www.nytimes.com/2009/07/09/world/middleeast/09iraq.html
18. Sam Dagher, 'Minorities trapped in northern Iraq's maelstrom', *NYT*, 15 August, 2009, www.nytimes.com/2009/08/16/world/middleeast/16khazna.html
19. Marc Santora, 'At least 20 dead in Iraqi bus bombings', *NYT*, 25 August, 2009,

http://query.nytimes.com/gst/fullpage.html?res=9F05E7D61F31F936A1575BC0A96F9C8B63 and Santora, 'Iraqis demand Syria turn over suspects', 25 August, 2009, www.nytimes.com/2009/08/26/world/middleeast/26iraq.html

20. Steven Lee Myers, 'Iraq suicide bomber strikes in Anbar', *NYT*, 18 February, 2010, www.nytimes.com/2010/02/19/world/middleeast/19iraq.html
21. Gianluca Mezzofiore, 'Isis leadership: Who's who in "fluid" Islamic State structure of power', *Business Insider*, 2 July, 2015, www.ibtimes.co.uk/isis-leadership-whos-who-fluid-islamic-state-structure-power-1509014
22. Thom Shanker, 'Qaeda leaders in Iraq neutralized, U.S. says', *NYT*, 4 June, 2010, www.nytimes.com/2010/06/05/world/middleeast/05military.html
23. Steven Lee Myers, 'Commander in Iraq assesses foe and friend', *NYT*, 13 November, 2010, http://atwar.blogs.nytimes.com/2010/11/13/senior-commander-in-iraq-assesses-foe-and-friend/
24. Defense Intelligence Agency, August, 2012, 14-L-0552/DIA/287, www.judicialwatch.org/document-archive/pgs-287-293-291-jw-v-dod-and-state-14-812-2/
25. Tim Arango and Duraid Adnan, 'For Iraqis, aid to rebels in Syria repays a debt', *NYT*, 12 February, 2012, www.nytimes.com/2012/02/13/world/middleeast/for-iraqis-aid-to-syrian-rebels-repays-a-war-debt.html
26. Anne Barnard and Hwaida Saad, 'Rebels gain control of government air base in Syria', *NYT*, 5 August, 2013, www.nytimes.com/2013/08/06/world/middleeast/rebels-gain-control-of-government-air-base-in-syria.html
27. Dan Lamothe, 'U.S. accidentally delivered weapons to the Islamic State by air drop, military says', *Washington Post*, 21 October, 2014, www.washingtonpost.com/news/checkpoint/wp/2014/10/21/u-s-accidentally-delivered-weapons-to-the-islamic-state-by-airdrop-militants-allege/
28. Anne Barnard and Eric Schmitt, 'As foreign fighters flood Syria, fears of a new extremist haven', *NYT*, 8 August, 2013, www.nytimes.com/2013/08/09/world/middleeast/as-foreign-fighters-flood-syria-fears-of-a-new-extremist-haven.html and Michael R. Gordon and Ben Hubbard, 'Qaeda-Linked Group Is Seen Complicating the Drive for Peace in Syria', *NYT*, 21 October, 2013, www.nytimes.com/2013/10/22/world/middleeast/qaeda-affiliate-in-syria-is-undermining-peace-efforts-us-official-says.html
29. *Fox News Insider*, 'Herridge: ISIS Has Turned Libya Into New Support Base, Safe Haven', 2 March, 2015, http://insider.foxnews.com/2015/03/02/catherine-herridge-isis-has-turned-libya-new-support-base-safe-haven
30. On Turkey, see my *The New Atheism Hoax*, 2015, Plymouth Institute for Peace

Research, www.pipr.co.uk/ebooks. On Turkish complicity with IS, see Natasha Bertrand, 'Senior Western official: Links between Turkey and ISIS are now "undeniable" ', *Business Insider*, 28 July, 2015, http://uk.businessinsider.com/links-between-turkey-and-isis-are-now-undeniable-2015-7?r=US&IR=T

31. On UK complicity, see Fran Abrams, 'British government supplied Saddam with Anthrax', *Independent*, 23 October, 2011, www.independent.co.uk/news/british-government-supplied-saddam-with-anthrax-1154032.html
32. For instance, UK MoD, 'Air strikes in Iraq', www.gov.uk/government/publications/british-forces-air-strikes-in-iraq-monthly-list/raf-air-strikes-in-iraq-january-2015. US Department of State, 'U.S. security cooperation with Iraq', Bureau of political-military affairs, 19 August, 2015, www.state.gov/t/pm/rls/fs/2015/246199.htm. Martin Chulov, Fazel Hawramy and Spencer Ackerman, 'Iraq army capitulates to Isis militants in four cities', *Guardian*, 12 June, 2014, www.theguardian.com/world/2014/jun/11/mosul-isis-gunmen-middle-east-states
33. F. Michael Maloof, 'Source: Besieged Iraq sees Obama as jihad "accomplice" ', *World Net Daily*, 16 June, 2014, www.wnd.com/2014/06/source-besieged-iraq-sees-obama-as-jihad-accomplice/ .
34. Barney Guiton, ' "ISIS sees Turkey as its ally": Former Islamic State member reveals', *Newsweek*, 7 November, 2014, http://europe.newsweek.com/isis-and-turkey-cooperate-destroy-kurds-former-isis-member-reveals-turkish-282920 and Bertrand, op. cit.
35. Aaron Klein, 'Turkey accused of training ISIS soldiers', *WND*, 10 October, 2014, www.wnd.com/2014/10/turkey-accused-of-training-isis-soldiers/
36. Mitchell Prothero, 'U.S. training helped mold top Islamic State military commander', *McClatchy*, 15 September, 2015, www.mcclatchydc.com/news/nation-world/world/middle-east/article35322882.html
37. Aaron Klein, 'Blowback! U.S. trained Islamists who joined ISIS', *WND*, 17 June, 2014, www.wnd.com/2014/06/officials-u-s-trained-isis-at-secret-base-in-jordan
38. Prothero, op. cit.
39. Ibid.
40. Ibid.
41. Andrew Dismore, House of Commons, 16 Oct. 2001, Column 1086, www.publications.parliament.uk/pa/cm200102/cmhansrd/vo011016/debtext/11016-15.htm. Ron Suskind, 2008, *The Way of the World: A Story of Truth and Hope in an Age of Extremism*, Pocket Books and Robin Cottle, 'Son of hate-preacher Omar Bakri joins Syria jihadis to fight for Islamic State', *Daily*

Star, 31 July, 2015, www.dailystar.co.uk/news/latest-news/456973/Omar-Bakri-Islamic-State-Syria-Jihadis

42. BBC News Online, '"Jihadi John" UK harassment claims revealed in emails', 26 February, 2015, www.bbc.co.uk/news/uk-31647271
43. ANI, 'Former British army officials now training ISIS militants in Iraq, Syria: CIA, MI6', 31 August, 2014, www.business-standard.com/article/news-ani/former-british-army-officials-now-training-isis-militants-in-iraq-syria-mi6-cia-114083100175_1.html
44. Henry Samuel, 'Up to ten former French soldiers "have defected to Islamic State"', *Telegraph*, 21 January, 2015, www.telegraph.co.uk/news/worldnews/europe/france/11361338/Up-to-ten-former-French-soldiers-have-defected-to-Islamic-State.html
45. Simon Tomlinson and Ted Thornhill, 'Agent "working for Canadian intelligence" has been arrested in Turkey for allegedly helping three British girls cross into Syria to join ISIS', *Daily Mail*, 12 March, 2015, www.dailymail.co.uk/news/article-2991628/Man-held-Turkish-authorities-helping-three-British-girls-cross-Syria-join-ISIS.html
46. Ed Adamczyk, 'Putin confirms Syria airstrikes serve to help Assad regime', United Press International, 12 October, 2015, www.upi.com/Top_News/World-News/2015/10/12/Putin-admits-Syria-airstrikes-serve-to-help-Assad-regime/5211444650476/

Chapter 4: Iran

1. *Telegraph*, 'MI6 chief Sir John Sawers: "We foiled Iranian nuclear weapons bid"', 12 July, 2012, http://www.telegraph.co.uk/news/uknews/terrorism-in-the-uk/9396360/MI6-chief-Sir-John-Sawers-We-foiled-Iranian-nuclear-weapons-bid.html
2. Robert Dreyfuss, 2006, *Devil's Game*, New York: Owl Books and William Engdahl, 2004, *A Century of War*, London: Pluto Press.
3. Ibid.
4. Stephen Kinzer, 'All the Shah's Men: An American Coup and the Roots of Middle East Terror Intelligence in Recent Public Literature', https://www.cia.gov/library/center-for-the-study-of-intelligence/csi-publications/csi-studies/studies/vol48no2/article10.html
5. Thatcher quote and details in Mark Curtis, 2010, *Secret Affairs*, London: Serpent's Tail. Engdahl, op. cit.
6. Engdahl, op. cit.
7. Engdahl and Curtis, op. cit.

8. Deborah Sherwood, 'Elite Troops Lead Fight to Protect Oil Route', *Daily Star*, 15 January, 2012, http://www.dailystar.co.uk/news/view/230215/Elite-troops-lead-fight-to-protect-oil-route-and-stop-petrol-prices-rocketing/, Yossi Melman, 'Mossad, MI6, the CIA and the case of the assassinated scientist', *Independent*, 30 November, 2010, http://www.independent.co.uk/news/world/middle-east/yossi-melman-mossad-mi6-the-cia and-the-case-of-the-assassinated-scientist-2146995.html and William Lowther and Colin Freeman, 'US funds terror groups to sow chaos in Iran', *Telegraph*, 25 February, 2007, http://www.telegraph.co.uk/news/worldnews/1543798/US-funds-terror-groups-to-sow-chaos-in-Iran.html
9. Burton quoted in Lowther and Freeman, ibid. Uzi Mahnaimi, 'MI6 chief visits Mossad for talks on Iran', *Sunday Times*, 5 May, 2008.
10. Laura Trevelyan, 'New MI6 boss is "excellent dancer"', BBC, 16 June, 2009, http://news.bbc.co.uk/1/hi/uk/8104141.stm. John Baron, House of Commons, 'Iran', 28 November, 2011, Column 639 and AFP, 'MI6 chief says spying crucial to stop Iran nuclear drive', 28 October, 2010, http://www.google.com/hostednews/afp/article/ALeqM5il08nLoJP61L4nq41YEGvu02h03A
11. Patrick Cockburn, 'Just who has been killing Iran's nuclear scientists', *Independent*, 6 October, 2013, www.independent.co.uk/voices/comment/just-who-has-been-killing-irans-nuclear-scientists-8861232.html
12. Holly Fletcher, 'Mujahadeen-e-Khalq (MEK) (aka People's Mujahedin of Iran or PMOI)', Council on Foreign Relations, 18 April, 2008, http://www.cfr.org/iran/mujahadeen-e-khalq-mek-aka-peoples-mujahedin-iran-pmoi/p9158
13. Jeremiah Goulka, Lydia Hansell, Elizabeth Wilke and Judith Larson, 'The Mujahedin-e Khalq in Iraq A Policy Conundrum', 2009, RAND.
14. Ibid.
15. Ibid.
16. Adam Price, 'Iraq', House of Commons, 21 November, 2005, Col. 1563W, http://www.publications.parliament.uk/pa/cm200506/cmhansrd/vo051121/text/51121w11.htm and Howells, 'Mujahedin-e Khalq', House of Commons, 28 March, 2006, Column 918W, http://www.publications.parliament.uk/pa/cm200506/cmhansrd/vo060328/text/60328w22.htm
17. Stephen Jones, 'People's Mujahiddin of Iran (PMOI) or Mujahiddin e Khalq (MEK): An update', House of Commons Library, 23 March, 2009, SN/IA/05020.
18. Foreign Affairs Committee, 'Press Notice', 2 March, 2008,

http://www.parliament.uk/business/committees/committees-archive/foreign-affairs-committee/fac-pn-19-07-08/

19. Robert Verkaik, 'MI6 warned Werrity [sic] that he was jeopardising British policy in Iran', *Daily Mail*, 22 October, 2011. See also: 'Adam Werritty "plotted with Israel" to topple Iran's President Ahmadinèjad' http://www.telegraph.co.uk/news/uknews/defence/8829922/Adam-Werritty-plotted-with-Israel-to-topple-Irans-President-Ahmadinejad.html, and: 'Revealed: Fox's best man and his ties to Iran's opposition' http://www.independent.co.uk/news/uk/politics/revealed-foxs-best-man-and-his-ties-to-irans-opposition -2371352.html
20. Robert Lowe and Claire Spencer (eds.), 'Iran, Its Neighbours and the Regional Crises', Chatham House, 2006.
21. Mark Perry, 'False Flag', *Foreign Policy*, 13 January, 2012, www.foreignpolicy.com/articles/2012/01/13/false_flag

Chapter 5: Yemen

1. Stephen Dorril, 2000, *MI6*, The Fourth Estate, pp. 677–98.
2. Quoted in Mark Curtis, 2004, *Unpeople*, Vintage.
3. Dorril and Curtis, op. cit.
4. John K. Cooley, 2002 (2nd), *Unholy Wars*, Pluto Press, pp. 301–3.
5. Human Rights Watch, 'In the Name of Unity', December, 2009, 1-56432-568-7.
6. Ibid.
7. Ibid.
8. Ibid.
9. Ibid.
10. Ibid.
11. Ministry of Defence (UK), *Annual Accounts 2006–07* and *Annual Accounts 2009–10*, The Stationery Office Ltd.
12. HRW, 'In the Name...', op. cit.
13. Ibid.
14. Ibid.
15. Ibid.
16. Ibid.
17. Ibid.
18. Ibid.
19. Ibid.
20. Ibid.

21. Human Rights Watch, 'All Quiet on the Northern Front?', March, 2010, 1-56432-607-1.
22. Ibid.
23. Foreign and Commonwealth Office (UK), 'United Kingdom Strategic Export Controls', 2006, The Stationery Office.
24. Human Rights Watch, 'Invisible Civilians', November, 2008, 1-56432-396-X.
25. Human Rights Watch, 'All Quiet . . .', op. cit.
26. Department for Business, Innovation, and Skills, 'Strategic Export Controls: Country Pivot Report', 2009, London.
27. Human Rights Watch, 'All Quiet . . .', op. cit.
28. Ibid.
29. Ibid.
30. Quoted in ibid. Department for Business, Innovation, and Skills, 'Strategic Export Controls: Country Pivot Report', 2010, Stationery Office.
31. HRW, op. cit. and Ministry of Defence (UK), *Annual Accounts 2009–10*, The Stationery Office.
32. Jamie Doward and Philippa Stewart, 'UK training Saudi forces used to crush Arab spring', *The Observer*, 28 May, 2011, http://www.guardian.co.uk/world/2011/may/28/uk-training-saudi-troops and HRW, 'In the Name . . .', op. cit.
33. Parliament, 'Defence – Thirteenth Report', 2 August, 2000, http://www.parliament.the-stationery-office.co.uk/pa/cm199900/cmselect/cmdfence/453/45308.htm#a27 and Amnesty International, 'Saudi Arabia: Assaulting Human Rights in the Name of Counter-terrorism', July, 2009, MDE 23/009/2009.
34. Department for Business Enterprise and Regulatory Reform, 'Strategic Export Controls: Country Pivot Report', 2008, London, and Department for Business, Innovation, and Skills, 'Strategic Export Controls: Country Pivot Report', 2010, Stationery Office.
35. Ministry of Defence (UK), 'Secretary of State for Defence visits Saudi Arabia', 27 September, 2010, http://www.mod.uk/DefenceInternet/DefenceNews/DefencePolicyAndBusiness/SecretaryOfStateForDefenceVisitsSaudiArabia.htm
36. Jerome Taylor, 'How Britain taught Arab police forces all they know: Campaigners raise questions about "cosy relationship" as death toll mounts', *Independent*, 19 February, 2011, http://www.independent.co.uk/news/world/politics/how-britain-taught-arab-police-forces-all-they-know-2219270.html and Her Majesty's Armed Forces, 'The Royal Military Academy

Sandhurst', http://www.hmforces.co.uk/education/articles/1615-the-royal-military-academy-sandhurst

37. Department for Business, Innovation, and Skills, 'Strategic Export Controls: Country Pivot Report', 2009, Stationery Office. Amnesty International, 'Bahrain: Protecting human rights after the protests', November, 2011, MDE 11/066/2011.
38. Amnesty International, 'Moment of truth for Yemen', April, 2011, MDE 31/007/2011.
39. House of Commons, 'Yemen: Military Aid', 30 November, 2011, Column 919W, http://www.publications.parliament.uk/pa/cm201011/cmhansrd/cm111130/text/111130w0004.htm
40. See my, 'How to create your very own terrorist State', *Yemen Times*, July, 2010, archived at http://www.aljazeerah.info/Opinion%20Editorials/2010/July/27%20o/How%20US-UK%20Create%20'Terrorist'%20States%20Yemen%20as%20a%20Case%20Study%20By%20Tim%20Coles.htm
41. Ratedesi, 'UPS Yemen Bomb Scare is a Hoax BBC Confirms No Explosives', 30 October, 2010, http://www.ratedesi.com/video/v/Ym4ywpzV23w/UPS-Yemen-Bomb-Scare-is-a-Hoax-BBC-Confirms-NO-Explosives

Chapter 6 Drones

1. Alice Ross and James Ball, 'GCHQ documents raise fresh questions over UK complicity in US drone strikes', *Guardian*, 24 June, 2015, www.theguardian.com/uk-news/2015/jun/24/gchq-documents-raise-fresh-questions-over-uk-complicity-in-us-drone-strikes. On Abdulmutallab and his father, see CNN, 'Source: CIA failed to circulate report about bombing suspect', 30 December, 2009, http://edition.cnn.com/2009/CRIME/12/29/airline.terror.cia/
2. Pew Research Center, 'Public Continues to Back U.S. Drone Attacks', 28 May, 2015, www.people-press.org/2015/05/28/public-continues-to-back-u-s-drone-attacks/
3. US Space Command, 'Vision for 2020', February, 1997, www.pipr.co.uk/archives. Project for the New American Century, 'Rebuilding America's Defenses', September 2000, pp. 5, 60, www.informationclearinghouse.info/pdf/RebuildingAmericasDefenses.pdf
4. Jack Serle, 'Almost 2,500 now killed by covert US drone strikes since Obama inauguration six years ago: The Bureau's report for January 2015', Bureau of Investigative Journalism, 2 February, 2015, www.thebureauinvestigates.com/2015/02/02/almost-2500-killed-covert-us-drone-strikes-obama-inauguration/
5. Philip Alston, 'Report of the Special Rapporteur on extrajudicial, summary or

arbitrary executions, Philip Alston', UN Human Rights Council, General Assembly, 28 May, 2010, A/HRC/14/24/Add.6, www2.ohchr.org/english/bodies/hrcouncil/docs/14session/A.HRC.14.24.Add6.pdf

6. Human Rights Watch, 'Letter to Obama on Targeted Killings and Drones', 7 December, 2010, www.hrw.org/news/2010/12/07/letter-obama-targeted-killings-and-drones
7. Spellar, 'ASTOR', House of Commons, 1 March, 1999, Col. 506, www.publications.parliament.uk/pa/cm199899/cmhansrd/vo990301/text/90301w03.htm
8. Ibid. On Britain's penetration of Serbia, see Tim Youngs, 'Kosovo: The diplomatic and military options', House of Commons Library, 27 October, 1998, Research Paper 98/93, http://researchbriefings.files.parliament.uk/documents/RP98-93/RP98-93.pdf. Young writes: 'A number of commentators believe that the British SAS and American Special Forces have been operating on the ground in Kosovo for some weeks' (p. 28). Note the chronology: special forces illegally invaded Serbia prior to the reported ethnic cleansing. The chronology is reversed in standard histories: that in reaction to Milošević's reported ethnic cleansing, US-British military elements (notably NATO) were put into operation.
9. Lord Kennet, 'Western European Union', House of Lords, 21 July, 1999, Col. 1049, www.publications.parliament.uk/pa/ld199899/ldhansrd/vo990721/text/90721-22.htm and Spellar, 'Phoenix UAV System', House of Commons, 3 November, 1999, Col. 218, www.publications.parliament.uk/pa/cm199899/cmhansrd/vo991103/text/91103w10.htm
10. Geoff Hoon, 'Strategic Defence Review', House of Commons, 18 July, 2002, Vol. 389, cc460-75, http://hansard.millbanksystems.com/commons/2002/jul/18/strategic-defence-review and Royal Air Force, 'Reaper MQ9A RPAS', no date, www.raf.mod.uk/equipment/reaper.cfm
11. Public Interest Lawyers, 'Written evidence from Public Interest Lawyers on behalf of Peacerights', House of Commons, 772 Defence Committee, www.publications.parliament.uk/pa/cm201314/cmselect/cmdfence/772/772vw17.htm and Tom Watson, 'Unmanned Air Vehicles [sic]', House of Commons, 4 March, 2013, Col. 848W, www.publications.parliament.uk/pa/cm201213/cmhansrd/cm130304/text/130304w0003.htm
12. Nick Hopkins, 'UK to double number of drones in Afghanistan', *Guardian*, 22 October, 2012, www.theguardian.com/world/2012/oct/22/uk-double-drones-afghanistan
13. Quoted in John F. Burns, 'A nation challenged', *New York Times*, 17 February, 2002, www.nytimes.com/2002/02/17/world/a-nation-challenged-the-

manhunt-us-leapt-before-looking-angry-villagers-say.html?pagewanted=all and Drones Team, 'Yemen: reported US covert actions 2001-2011', Bureau of Investigative Journalism, 29 March, 2012, www.thebureauinvestigates.com/2012/03/29/yemen-reported-us-covert-actions-since-2001/

14. BIJ, ibid.
15. Alice Ross and James Ball, 'GCHQ documents raise fresh questions over UK complicity in US drone strikes', *Guardian*, 24 June, 2015, www.theguardian.com/uk-news/2015/jun/24/gchq-documents-raise-fresh-questions-over-uk-complicity-in-us-drone-strikes
16. Ibid. On legal definitions of 'civilian', a House of Commons Library paper explains that Resolution 1973, invoked as a justification to bomb Libya, 'offers protection to a wide category of people in Libya, even if they are or have been fighting. In humanitarian law [sic]', the authors continue, 'A "civilian" is "any person not a combatant"; but the definition of combatant is narrow and does not cover rebel forces' (Ben Smith and Arabella Thorp, 'Interpretation of Security Council Resolution 1973 on Libya', House of Commons Library, SN/IA/5916, 6 April, 2011, http://researchbriefings.files.parliament.uk/documents/SN05916/SN05916.pdf).
17. Alice K. Ross, 'GCHQ intel sharing for drone strikes may be "accessory to murder"', BIJ, 25 October, 2012, www.thebureauinvestigates.com/2012/10/25/gchq-intel-sharing-for-drone-strikes-may-be-accessory-to-murder-court-hears/
18. Robert Verkaik, 'MPs to probe claims that the U.S. is operating a secret "drone war" from Britain's RAF bases', *Daily Mail*, 16 March, 2013, www.dailymail.co.uk/news/article-2294588/MPs-probe-claims-U-S-operating-secret-drone-war-Britains-RAF-bases.html and Damien McElroy, Chris Woods and Emma Slater, 'US drone strikes on Yemen escalate', *Telegraph*, 29 March, 2012, www.telegraph.co.uk/news/worldnews/al-qaeda/9171946/US-drone-strikes-on-Yemen-escalate.html
19. David Axe, 'Hidden history', *Wired*, 13 August, 2012, www.wired.com/2012/08/somalia-drones/. On the appalling story of Diego Garcia, see Mark Curtis, 2003, *Web of Deceit*, Vintage, pp. 414–31.
20. Quoted in Ross and Ball, op. cit. Paraphrased in Anna Thomas, 'Jemima Stratford QC's Advice', 29 January, 2014, http://appgdrones.org.uk/jemima-stratford-qcs-advice/

Chapter 7: Ukraine

1. The CIA puts the number of ethnic Russians in Ukraine at 17.3%, 'World Factbook: Europe: Ukraine', no date, www.cia.gov/library/publications/the-

world-factbook/geos/up.html and Permanent Mission of the Russian Federation to the European Union, 'Trade', no date, http://www.russianmission.eu/en/trade

2. NATO, 'NATO-Ukraine Relations', September, 2014, www.nato.int/nato_static_fl2014/assets/pdf/pdf_2014_09/20140901_140901-Backgrounder_NATO-Ukraine_en.pdf and Zbigniew Brzezinski, 1997, *The Grand Chessboard*, Basic Books.
3. Prime Minister's Office, 'Our 5 priorities for the NATO Summit Wales 2014', 1 September, 2014, www.gov.uk/government/publications/our-5-priorities-for-the-nato-summit-wales-2014/our-5-priorities-for-the-nato-summit-wales-2014 and Council on Foreign Relations (US), 'Budapest Memorandums on Security Assurances, 1994', 5 December, 1994, www.cfr.org/nonproliferation-arms-control-and-disarmament/budapest-memorandums-security-assurances-1994/p32484. European Union Committee, 'The European Union and Russia', Lords, 14th report of session 2007–08, 22 May, 2008, p. 66, www.publications.parliament.uk/pa/ld200708/ldselect/ldeucom/98/98.pdf
4. David Blagden, 'Written Evidence to the Parliamentary Joint Committee on the National Security Strategy: Priorities for the 2015 NSS', Joint Committee on the National Security Strategy, 'The next National Security Strategy', December, 2014, p. 7, http://www.parliament.uk/documents/joint-committees/national-security-strategy/The%20next%20security%20strategy%20(forth%20review)/ThenextNationalSecurityStrategyEvidence18122014.pdf
5. DCDC, 'Strategic Trends Programme: 2007–2036', Ministry of Defence, 21 January, 2007 (3rd), pp. 85, archived at http://www.cuttingthroughthematrix.com/articles/strat_trends_23jan07.pdf. Bulletin of the Atomic Scientists, 'Timeline: It is 3 minutes to minute', http://thebulletin.org/timeline
6. Martin Delgado, 'Spy chief's warning over Russia threat: Former head of MI6 says Vladimir Putin's regime poses "state to state threat"', *Daily Mail*, 28 February, 2015, www.dailymail.co.uk/news/article-2973912/Spy-chief-s-warning-Russia-threat-Former-head-M16-says-Vladimir-Putin-s-regime-poses-state-state-threat.html and Ben Smith and Claire Mills, 'Ukraine: towards a frozen conflict?', House of Commons Library, SNIA/6978, 9 September, 2014, http://researchbriefings.files.parliament.uk/documents/SN06978/SN06978.pdf and DCDC, op. cit., p. 72. On Russia's regular approaches to British airspace, see Levi Winchester, 'RAF deployed jets in response to Russian military aircraft EIGHT TIMES last year', *Express*, 21 February, 2015,

www.express.co.uk/news/uk/555757/RAF-scrambled-jets-Russian-military-aircrafts-eight-times-2014

7. Details and sources in my 'Introduction', *Voices for Peace*, 2015, Plymouth Institute for Peace Research, p. 4n1, www.pipr.co.uk/ebooks
8. Ibid.
9. Ibid.
10. Select Committee on the European Union, 'Memorandum by Dr Frank Umbach, German Council on Foreign Relations (DGAP)', 20 December, 2007, www.publications.parliament.uk/pa/ld200708/ldselect/ldeucom/98/98we13.htm and Pavel K. Baev, 'Russia's security relations with the United States: Futures planned and unplanned' in Stephen J. Blank (ed.), *Russian Nuclear Weapons: Past, Present, and Future*, November, 2011, p. 170, www.strategicstudiesinstitute.army.mil/pdffiles/PUB1087.pdf
11. Claire Mills, 'UK Military Assistance to Ukraine', House of Commons Library, Briefing Paper, No. SN07135, 20 May, 2015, http://researchbriefings.files.parliament.uk/documents/SN07135/SN07135.pdf
12. *The Wire: The Magazine of the Royal Corp of Signals*, 'News from squadrons', June, 2011, p. 70, www.army.mod.uk/documents/general/June_Wire.pdf and MoD, 'Annual Report and Accounts 2012–2013', 31 March, 2013, www.gov.uk/government/uploads/system/uploads/attachment_data/file/222874/MOD_AR13_clean.pdf
13. FCO, 'Human Rights and Democracy: The 2012 Foreign and Commonwealth Office Report', April, 2013, Stationery Office, p. 109 and Amnesty International, 'With or without EU agreement, Ukraine must eradicate torture', Press Release, 19 November, 2014, PRE01/612/2013
14. Ben Smith, 'Ukraine, the EU, Russia and Tymoshenko', House of Commons Library, SNIA/6117, 10 November, 2011, www.parliament.uk/briefing-papers/SN06117.pdf
15. British Council, 'Democratising Ukraine Small Project Scheme (DFID-funded)', 2005, www.britishcouncil.org/development-governance-experience-democratising-ukraine.pdf
16. WFD, 2010, *Annual Review*, WFD and UKAid (DFID) and WFD, *Annual Report: Strengthening Human Resources Development in Southern Parliaments*, 2009/10, GTF Number: 394 and *Annual Report 2010/11*.
17. Department of Information and Communication of the Secretariat of the CMU, 'British businessmen note improving the investment climate in Ukraine', 27 July, 2012, www.kmu.gov.ua/control/en/publish/article?art_id=245431142 and Nikki

Ikani, 'Yanukovych, Russia and the EU', Europe on the Strand, 22 February, 2014, http://europeonthestrand.ideasoneurope.eu/2014/02/22/yanukovych-russia-and-the-eu-why-we-saw-this-one-coming/

18. Olga Onuch, 'Who were the protestors?', *Journal of Democracy*, Volume 25, No. 3, July, 2014, pp. 44–51.
19. Amnesty International, 'Ukraine', *State of the World's Human Rights 2014/15*, pp. 383–7, www.amnesty.org/en/documents/pol10/0001/2015/en/. Department for Business Innovation and Skills, 'Strategic Export Controls: Country Pivot Report 1st January–31st December 2013', p. 584. FCO, 'Annual Report and Accounts 2013–2014', 1 July, 2014, www.gov.uk/government/publications/foreign-and-commonwealth-office-annual-report-and-accounts-2013-14–2
20. For instance, BBC News Online, 'Crimea referendum: Voters "back Russia union" ', 16 March, 2014, www.bbc.co.uk/news/world-europe-26606097
21. Amnesty, op. cit. and Damien Sharkov, 'Ukrainian Nationalist Volunteers Committing "ISIS-Style" War Crimes', *Newsweek Europe Online*, 10 November, 2014, http://europe.newsweek.com/evidence-war-crimes-committed-ukrainian-nationalist-volunteers-grows-269604
22. Ibid.
23. HRW, 'Ukraine: Rising Civilian Death Toll', 3 February, 2015, www.hrw.org/news/2015/02/03/ukraine-rising-civilian-death-toll
24. Sean Rayment, 'Military intervention in Ukraine risks spiralling into "all-out war" with Russia', *Mirror*, 20 April, 2014, www.mirror.co.uk/news/uk-news/ukraine-crisis-head-mi6-warns-3434167 and Kim Sengupta, 'Ukraine crisis', *Independent*, 5 May, 2014, http://www.independent.co.uk/news/world/europe/ukraine-crisis-mercenaries-m16-and-ready-meals–evidence-of-western-involvement-or-something-far-less-controversial-9322948.html
25. Amnesty, op. cit. and Mills, op. cit.
26. ITV News, 'UK to send 1,000 troops and Typhoon jets to Baltic states', 5 February, 2015, www.itv.com/news/update/2015-02-05/uk-to-send-1-000-troops-and-typhoon-jets-to-baltic-states/ and Lewis Dean, 'UK to send 1,000 troops and fighter jets to Baltics in Nato effort to reassure Russia neighbours', *International Business Times*, 5 February, 2015, www.ibtimes.co.uk/uk-send-1000-troops-4-fighter-jets-nato-effort-reassure-russia-neighbours-1486752

Chapter 8: Sri Lanka

1. Hugo Swire, 'UK welcomes UN Human Rights Council Resolution on Sri Lanka', Foreign and Commonwealth Office, 1 October, 2015, https://www.gov.uk/government/news/uk-welcomes-un-human-rights-council-

resolution-on-sri-lanka and Shihar Aneez, 'Sri Lanka war crimes resolution softened before U.N. debate', 29 September, 2015, http://uk.reuters.com/article/2015/09/29/uk-sri-lanka-warcrimes-idUKKCN0RT1SM20150929

2. See my, 'How Britain armed the Sri Lanka massacre', *Peace Review*, Vol. 23, Issue 1, 2011, pp. 77–85 and Phil Miller, 'Britain's dirty war against the Tamil people, 1979–2009', International Human Rights Association Bremen, June, 2014, http://ptsrilanka.org/images/documents/britains_dirty_war.pdf
3. Global Security, 'Sri Lanka Military Industry', website, no date, http://www.globalsecurity.org/military/world/sri-lanka/industry.htm and Jon Lunn, Claire Taylor and Ian Townsend, 'War and peace in Sri Lanka', House of Commons Library, Research Paper, 09/51 5 June, 2009.
4. Meera Shekar, Aparnaa Somanathan and Lidan Du, 'Sri Lanka Malnutrition in Sri Lanka: Scale, Scope, Causes, and Potential Response', World Bank, Human Development Unit (South Asia Region), Report No. 40906-LK, 24 September, 2007 and Jon Lunn and Gavin Thompson, 'Sri Lanka since the end of the civil war', House of Commons Library, SN06097, 24 October, 2011.
5. S. U. Kodikara, 'Major Trends in Sri Lanka's Non-Alignment Policy after 1956', *Asian Survey*, Vol. 13, No. 12, December, 1973, pp. 1121–1136 and Bruce Matthews, 'Sinhala Cultural and Buddhist Patriotic Organizations in Contemporary Sri Lanka', *Pacific Affairs*, Vol. 61, No. 4, Winter, 1988–1989, pp. 620–632.
6. Bryan Pfaffenberger, 'The Cultural Dimension of Tamil Separatism in Sri Lanka', *Asian Survey*, Vol. 21, No. 11, November, 1981, pp. 1145–1157.
7. Robert N. Kearney, 'Territorial Elements of Tamil Separatism in Sri Lanka', *Pacific Affairs*, Vol. 60, No. 4, Winter, 1987–1988, pp. 561–577.
8. Pfaffenberger, op. cit. and Kumar Rupesinghe, 'Ethnic Conflicts in South Asia: The Case of Sri Lanka and the Indian Peace-Keeping Force (IPKF)', *Journal of Peace Research*, Vol. 25, No. 4, December, 1988, pp. 337–350.
9. Special Forces, 'Sri Lanka – Special Task Force', website, no date, http://www.special-forces-adventure-training.co.uk/History_of_SAS_elite_british_special_forces_22_B_squadron_Special_Air_Service.htm and Global Security, op. cit.
10. Joseph Brewda, 'The SAS: Prince Philip's manager of terrorism', *Executive Intelligence Review*, 13 October, 1995, archived at http://www.larouchepub.com/other/1995/2241_sas.html
11. Margaret Thatcher, 'Press Conference in Sri Lanka', 12 April, 1985, http://www.margaretthatcher.org/document/106022 and K.T. Rajasingham, 'Sri Lanka: The Untold Story', *Asia Times*, 26 October, 2001, http://www.atimes.com/ind-pak/DC09Df04.html

12. Matthews, op. cit. and AP, 'British Official', 17 April, 1987, http://www.apnewsarchive.com/1987/British-Official/id-43f0a19875197b493dddae85d1d04e44
13. International Crisis Group, op. cit.
14. Lunn et al., op. cit., ICG ibid. and Liam Fox, 'Dr Fox statement on his defence responsibilities', Ministry of Defence, 10 October, 2011, http://www.mod.uk/DefenceInternet/DefenceNews/DefencePolicyAndBusiness/DrFoxStatementOnHisDefenceResponsibilities.htm
15. Pratap Chatterjee, 'Ex-SAS Men Cash in on Iraq Bonanza', CorpWatch, 9 June, 2004, http://www.corpwatch.org/article.php?id=11355 and Lunn et al., op. cit.
16. *Sunday Times* (Sri Lanka), 'Special Assignment: International dogs of war on security mission in Lanka', 2 November, 2003, http://sundaytimes.lk/021103/news/special.html
17. Ibid.
18. Ibid.
19. Foreign and Commonwealth Office (UK), 'Strategic Export Controls'.
20. Foreign and Commonwealth Office (UK), *Annual Human Rights Report 2004*, FCO and FCO, 'Strategic Export Controls', 2002.
21. Lunn et al., op. cit.
22. FCO, 'Strategic Export Controls', 2004.
23. LankanNewspapers.com, 'Sri Lanka's Special Task Force to handle SAARC security summit', 7 October, 2011, http://www.lankanewspapers.com/news/2011/10/71352_space.html
24. Lunn, et al., op. cit.
25. FCO, 'Strategic Export Controls', 2006.
26. Quoted in Lunn et al., op cit., FCO, *Annual Human Rights Report 2007*, and FCO, 'Strategic Export Controls', 2007.
27. UN quoted in ICG, op. cit.
28. Department for Business, Innovation and Skills, 'Strategic Export Controls', *Country Pivot Report*, 2010, BIS, International Crisis Group, 'Sri Lanka: Women's Insecurity in the North and East', Asia Report No. 217, 20 December, 2011 and Burt quoted in Lunn and Thompson, op. cit.
29. EDB, 'UK High Commission promotes Sri Lanka Expo 2012 in London', website, no date, http://www.srilankaexpo.com/index.php/expo-media/expo-news-summery/223-edb-uk-high-commission-promotes-sri-lanka-expo-2012-in-london and UKTI, 'What are the Opportunities?', 6 May, 2010, http://www.ukti.gov.uk/uktihome/item/106354.html

Chapter 9: Colombia

1. Amnesty International, 'The Struggle for Survival and Dignity', February, 2010, AMR 23/001/2010, Amnesty International, 'Leave Us in Peace!', 2008, AMR 23/023/2008, US Department of Labour, 'List of Goods produced by child labor or forced labour', September, 2011 and Grace Livingstone, 2003, *Inside Colombia: Drugs, Democracy and War*, Rutgers University Press. Child labour in coal mining is nothing new. See, for instance, Tony Lloyd MP's 'Early day motion 688', Session 1992–93, 28 October, 1992, http://www.parliament.uk/edm/1992-93/688
2. Amnesty, 'The Struggle...', ibid. and Justice for Colombia, 'British military involvement in Colombia', website, no date, http://www.justiceforcolombia.org/campaigns/military-aid/photos.php Tom Watson, 'Colombia (Human Rights)', Parliament, 27 January, 2010, Column 309WH, http://www.publications.parliament.uk/pa/cm200910/cmhansrd/cm100127/halltext/100127h0009.htm
3. ABColombia (with Christian Aid, Oxfam, and others), 'Fit for purpose: How to make UK policy on Colombia more effective', www.abcolombia.org.uk, no date, Jeremy Browne, 'Shared Responsibility: The Future of UK/Colombia Relations', Foreign and Commonwealth Office, 9 August, 2010, http://www.fco.gov.uk/en/news/latest-news/?view=Speech&id=22671704, FCO (UK), 'Colombia', 13 June, 2011, http://www.fco.gov.uk/en/travel-and-living-abroad/travel-advice-by-country/country-profile/south-america/colombia/?profile=economy. The reference to indigenous peoples facing 'extinction' can be found in Amnesty International, 'Everything left behind', AMR 23/015/2009, June, 2009.
4. Forrest Hylton, 2006, *Evil Hour in Colombia*, Verso and Hugh O'Shaughnessy and Sue Branford, 2005, *Chemical Warfare in Colombia: The Costs of Coca Fumigation*, London: The Latin America Bureau.
5. Human Rights Watch, 2003, *'You'll Learn Not to Cry'*, HRW and Livingstone, op. cit.
6. ABColombia, op. cit. and Amnesty, 'Everything...', op. cit.
7. Ian Lavery, 'La Colosa Gold Mine, Colombia', Early Day Motion, 13 July, 2011, http://www.parliament.uk/edm/2010-12/2076 and Jeremy Corbyn, 'Cerrejon Coal Company Mine', Early Day Motion, 8 November, 2011, http://www.parliament.uk/edm/2010-12/2396
8. Ibid.
9. Deborah Avant, 'The Evolution of a private military and security company: The example of ArmorGroup (formerly DSL, now part of G4S)' in Paul D. Wil-

liams, 2008, *Security Studies: An Introduction*, Routledge, Box 28.1 and BP, 'A security and human rights legacy in Colombia', website, no date, http://www.bp.com/sectiongenericarticle800.do?categoryId=9040580&contentId=7067679. See also Michael Gillard, Ignacio Gomez and Melissa Jones, 'BP sacks security chief: Inquiry into arms and spy scandal', *Guardian*, 17 October, 1998, http://www.theguardian.com/uk/1998/oct/17/1

10. Livingstone, op. cit. and Diane Taylor, 'Colombian farmers sue BP in British court', *Guardian*, 15 October, 2014, http://www.theguardian.com/global-development/2014/oct/15/colombian-farmers-sue-bp-british-court
11. Dennis Canavan, 'Human Rights in Colombia', Early Day Motion, 16 November, 1994, http://www.parliament.uk/edm/1994-95/13
12. BP, 'BP Makes Major New Oil and Gas Finds in Colombia', 27 July, 1995, http://www.bp.com/genericarticle.do?categoryId=2012968&contentId=2001694, Christopher Bellamy, 'SAS helps to free UK soldier in Colombia', *Independent*, 10 December, 1995, http://www.independent.co.uk/news/sas-helps-to-free-uk-soldier-in-colombia-1524984.html and Human Rights Watch, 1996, http://www.hrw.org/legacy/reports/1996/killertoc.htm
13. HRW, ibid.
14. Ibid.
15. Ibid.
16. Justice for Colombia (with Unite, Unison, National Union of Journalists, and others), 'UK Military Aid to Colombia Alternatives to a Flawed Policy', September, 2008, JFC.
17. O'Shaughnessy and Branford, op. cit.
18. June S. Beittel, 'Colombia: Issues for Congress', Congressional Research Service, 18 March, 2011, Livingstone, op. cit. and Rudi Vis, 'Plan Colombia, The Peace Process and Paramilitaries', Early Day Motion 214, 17 January, 2001, http://www.parliament.uk/edm/2000-01/214
19. Ibid.
20. International Crisis Group, 'Colombia: Negotiating with the Paramilitaries', Latin America Report No. 5, 16 September, 2003.
21. David Pallister, Sibylla Brodzinksy and Owen Bowcott, 'Secret aid poured into Colombian drug war', *Guardian*, 9 July, 2003, http://www.guardian.co.uk/world/2003/jul/09/colombia.davidpallister and Beittel, op. cit.
22. Pallister et al., ibid.
23. Adam Price, 'Elections in Colombia', Early Day Motion, 8 September, 2003, http://www.parliament.uk/edm/2002-03/1630

24. O'Shaughnessy and Branford, op. cit.
25. See, for instance, Alexander Cockburn and Jeffrey St. Clair, 1998, *Whiteout*, Verso, Alfred McCoy, 2003, *The Politics of Heroin*, Chicago Review Press, Douglas Valentine, 2004, *The Strength of the Wolf*, Verso, and Gary Webb, 1998, *Dark Alliance*, Seven Stories.
26. Livingstone, op. cit.
27. Women's Commission for Refugee Women and Children, 'Unseen Millions: The Catastrophe of Internal Displacement in Colombia', March 2002, New York.
28. Pallister et al., op. cit. and HRW, 1996, op. cit.
29. Livingstone, op. cit.
30. JFC, 'Military Aid...', op. cit., Smith quoted in Livingstone, op. cit. and Jonathan Brown, 'Basingstoke's medallion man goes on trial for attempt to assassinate Pablo Escobar', *Independent*, 26 June, 2004, http://www.independent.co.uk/news/world/americas/basingstokes-medallion-man-goes-on-trial-for-attempt-to-assassinate-pablo-escobar-6166635.html
31. Ibid and Sky News Online, 'Mercenary Hired To Bomb Drug Lord Escobar', 30 June, 2004, http://news.sky.com/story/278481/mercenary-hired-to-bomb-drug-lord-escobar
32. International Crisis Group, 'Dismantling Colombia's New Illegal Armed Groups', Latin America Report No. 41, 8 June, 2012 and Pallister et al., op. cit.
33. Daniel Read, 'Britain's Secret War in Colombia', *London Progressive Journal*, 3 July, 2009, http://londonprogressivejournal.com/article/view/473. See also, Seumas Milne, 'Anger at minister's photo with Colombian army unit linked to trade unionist killings', *Guardian*, 11 February, 2008, http://www.theguardian.com/world/2008/feb/11/colombia.humanrights
34. *Times of India*, 'HSBC exposed US, India to terror funding risk', 18 June, 2012, http://articles.timesofindia.indiatimes.com/2012-07-18/us/32729610_1_hsbc-affiliates-al-rajhi-bank-saudi-arabia and *Forbes*, 'HSBC Helped Terrorists, Iran, Mexican Drug Cartels Launder Money, Senate Report Says', 16 July, 2012, http://www.forbes.com/sites/afontevecchia/2012/07/16/hsbc-helped-terrorists-iran-mexican-drug-cartels-launder-money-senate-report-says/
35. Rob Davies and Tim Shipman, 'HSBC let drug gangs launder millions: First Barclays, now Britain's biggest bank is shamed – and faces a £640million fine', *Daily Mail*, 17 July, 2012, http://www.dailymail.co.uk/news/article-2174785/HSBC-scandal-Britains-biggest-bank-let-drug-gangs-launder-millions–faces-640million-fine.html

36. O'Shaughnessy and Branford, op. cit.
37. Ibid. and Beittel, op. cit.
38. O'Shaughnessy and Branford, op. cit. and Ken Guggenheim, 'Drug Fight in Colombia Questioned', *Washington Post*, 5 June, 2001, http://www.washingtonpost.com/wp-srv/aponline/20010605/aponline142615_000.htm
39. Pallister et al., op. cit.
40. Livingstone, op. cit.
41. Ibid., Permanent Peoples' Tribunal Session on Colombia Hearing on Biodiversity Humanitarian Zone, 'Accusation Against the Transnational DynCorp', February, 2007, www.prensarural.org/spip/IMG/doc/dyncorp_acus_eng.doc and O'Shaughnessy and Branford, op. cit.
42. O'Shaughnessy and Branford, ibid. and ABColombia, op. cit.

Chapter 10: Papua

1. European Community-Papua New Guinea, 'Country Strategy Paper and National Indicative Programme for the period 2008–2013', no date, circa 2007.
2. For instance, Matthew Jones, '"Maximum Disavowable Aid": Britain, the United States and the Indonesian Rebellion, 1957–58', *The English Historical Review*, Vol. 114, No. 459, November, 1999, pp. 1179–1216.
3. European Community, 'Country Strategy…', op. cit.
4. World Health Organization and National Department of Health (PNG), 'Papua New Guinea: Pharmaceutical Country Profile', January, 2012.
5. TAPOL, Select Committee on Foreign Affairs Written Evidence, http://www.publications.parliament.uk/pa/cm200506/cmselect/cmfaff/574/574we21.htm
6. European Community, op. cit.
7. Department of National Planning and Monitoring (PNG), 'Papua New Guinea Medium Term Development Plan 2011–2015', August, 2010.
8. Commonwealth Parliamentary Association (UK), 'CPA UK Branch Delegation to Papua New Guinea, Solomon Islands and the Autonomous Region Bougainville', 13–25 February, 2013, CPA UK.
9. Amnesty International, 'Undermining Rights', January 2011, ASA 34/001/2010 and Department for Business, Innovation and Skills, 'Strategic Export Controls: Country Pivot Report', 2009.
10. Human Rights Watch, *'Making Their Own Rules'*, September 2005, Vol. 17, No. 8 (C).

11. Foreign and Commonwealth Office, 'Strategic Export Controls', 2005.
12. Parliamentary Commonwealth Association, op. cit.
13. Sandline International and Government of PNG, 'Agreement for the Provision of Military Assistance', January, 1997, http://psm.du.edu/media/documents/industry_initiatives/contracts/industry_contract_sandline-papua-new-guinea.pdf
14. SourceWatch, 'Tim Spicer', no date, http://www.sourcewatch.org/index.php?title=Tim_Spicer
15. Peter Cronau, 'Mercenaries', *Bushfire Media*, 13 July, 1999, http://www.asiapac.org.fj/cafepacific/resources/aspac/cronau2.html
16. Pratap Chatterjee, 'Mercenary Armies and Mineral Wealth', *Covert Action Quarterly*, Fall, 1997, archived at http://www.thirdworldtraveler.com/New_World_Order/Mercenaries_Minerals.html and Terence Wesley-Smith, 'Papua New Guinea', *Contemporary Pacific*, Fall, 1998, pp. 446–455.
17. Michael Clapham, 'Rio Tinto PLC and War Crimes', Early day motion, 12 December, 2000, http://www.parliament.uk/edm/2000-01/88
18. Michael Clapham, 'Rio Tinto PLC: Racial Discrimination and Environmental Destruction', Early day motion, 12 December, 2000, http://www.parliament.uk/edm/2000-01/91
19. Quoted in Lord Judd, 8 January, 2007, Column 97, http://www.publications.parliament.uk/pa/ld200607/ldhansrd/text/70108-0014.htm
20. Bruce Vaughn, 'Indonesia: Domestic Politics, Strategic Dynamics, and U.S. Interests', Congressional Research Archive, 31 January, 2011 and United Nations, 'Papua New Guinea: United Nations Development Assistance Framework (UNDAF) 2012–2015', no date, UN.
21. Lord Avebury, House of Lords, 8 January, 2007, http://www.publications.parliament.uk/pa/ld200607/ldhansrd/text/70108-0014.htm
22. Harries, Archer, and Griffiths in House of Lords, ibid.
23. Quoted in Harries, op. cit.
24. West Papua Association UK, Written Evidence, Select Committee on Foreign Affairs, February, 2004, http://www.publications.parliament.uk/pa/cm200304/cmselect/cmfaff/389/389we20.htm
25. Oxford Papuan Rights Campaign, Written Evidence, Select Committee on Foreign Affairs Written Evidence, http://www.publications.parliament.uk/pa/cm200405/cmselect/cmfaff/109/109we58.htm, Lord Avebury, op. cit. and Baroness Royall, House of Lords, op. cit.

26. Baroness Rawlings, House of Lords, op. cit.
27. Phil Evans, Keith Biddle and John Morris, 'Evaluation of the Indonesia National Police Management Training Project, 1983–96', Evaluation Report EV6 12, Department for International Development (UK), DFID.
28. Human Rights Watch, 'Indonesia: Release Peaceful Demonstrators in Papua', 25 July, 2008, http://www.hrw.org/news/2008/07/23/indonesia-release-peaceful-demonstrators-papua
29. Department for Business, Innovation, and Skills, 'Strategic Export Controls: Country Pivot Report', 2009, London.
30. TAPOL, 'Britain and Indonesia – Too close for comfort?', 30 October, 2012, http://westpapuamedia.info/tag/uk-indonesia-relationship/
31. Ibid.
32. Amnesty International, 'Indonesia: Security forces block peaceful demonstration in Papua', 13 August, 2012 and Avebury, op. cit.
33. Department for Business, Innovation and Skills, 'Strategic Export Controls', Country Pivot Report, 2012, BIS.
34. West Papua Association UK, op. cit.
35. BP, 'BP in Indonesia', website, no date, www.bp.com/en/global/corporate/about-bp/bp-worldwide/bp-in-indonesia.html
36. Ibid. and Tangguh Independent Advisory Panel, 'Report on Operations of the Tangguh LNG Project', October, 2012.
37. George Monbiot, 'In Bed with the Killers', *Guardian*, 3 May, 2005, http://www.monbiot.com/2005/05/03/in-bed-with-the-killers/

Chapter 11: Somalia

1. Department of Transportation (US), 'Economic Impact of Piracy in the Gulf of Aden on Global Trade', undated, http://www.marad.dot.gov/documents/HOA_Economic%20Impact%20of%20Piracy.pdf and Ministry of Defence (UK), 'Strategic Trends Programme: Out to 2040', February, 2010, http://www.mod.uk/nr/rdonlyres/38651acb-d9a9-4494-98aa-1c86433bb673/0/gst4_update9_feb10.pdf
2. Lord Sterling, House of Lords, 'The Strategic Defence and Security Review', 12 November, 2010, Column 416, http://www.publications.parliament.uk/pa/ld201011/ldhansrd/text/101112-0001.htm and Roger Middleton, 'Piracy in Somalia: Threatening global trade, feeding local wars', Africa Programme, October, 2008, Chatham House Briefing Paper, AFP BP 08/02, http://www.chathamhouse.org/sites/default/files/public/Research/Africa/1008piracysomalia.pdf

3. Mike Povey (Executive Chairman), 'Letter to Manager of Company Announcements, Australian Stock Exchange Limited', 1 December 2005, Range Resources Limited, http://www.rangeresources.com.au/fileadmin/user_upload/asx/ASX_Announcement-_Puntland_Oil_and_Gas__01-12-05_.pdf
4. Tom Bergin, 'Somalia to struggle to tap Western oil investment', 21 August, 2007, Reuters, http://www.rangeresources.com.au/fileadmin/user_upload/In_the_News/Somalia_to_struggle_to_tap_Western_oil_investment__19-09-2007_.pdf. and BBC News Online, 'BP and Amoco in oil mega-merger', 11 August, 1998, http://news.bbc.co.uk/1/hi/149139.stm
5. Jon Lunn and Gavin Thompson, 'Somalia: recent political, security and humanitarian developments', House of Commons Library, SN06115, 28 February, 2012.
6. Middleton, op. cit.
7. Richard Dowden, 2009, *Africa: Altered States, Ordinary Miracles*, Portobello.
8. Alex de Waal, 'US War Crimes in Somalia', *New Left Review*, July–August, 1998, pp. 131–144.
9. Quoted in ibid.
10. Senlis Council, 'Chronic Failures in the War on Terror: From Afghanistan to Somalia', May, 2008, Senlis Council
11. See my, 'Somalia still suffers', *Z Magazine*, July–August, 2010.
12. Ted Dagne, 'Somalia: Current Conditions and Prospects for a Lasting Peace', Congressional Research Service, Order Code RL33911, 12 March, 2007.
13. Amnesty International, 'In the Line of Fire', July, 2011, AFR 52/001/2011.
14. Pana Press, 'UK to train Somali ground forces, disarm militias', 22 October, 2004, http://www.panapress.com/UK-to-train-Somali-ground-forces,-disarm-militias–12-556723-32-lang2-index.html
15. Amnesty International, 'In the Line . . .', op. cit.
16. Senlis Council, op. cit. and Human Rights Watch, 'Yemen: Asylum Seekers Run Gauntlet of Abuses Tens of Thousands Face Murderous Smugglers at Sea, Abusive Policies on Land', 20 December, 2009.
17. See my, 'Somalia still suffers', op. cit.
18. Mark Malloch-Brown, *The Unfinished Global Revolution*, Penguin, 2009.
19. Human Rights Watch, 'Hostile Shores', December, 2009 and Human Rights Watch, 'Welcome to Kenya: Police Abuse of Somali Refugees', June, 2010, HRW.
20. Duncan Campbell, 'Briton's widow seeks arrest of Somali president', *Guardian*, 27 May, 2005. Yusuf quoted in Dowden, op. cit.

21. Aidan Hartley, 'The Terror of Tesco's Finest...', *Daily Mail*, 23 May, 2008, http://www.dailymail.co.uk/home/moslive/article-1020934/The-terror-Tescos-finest–forklift-driver-Leicester-Somalias-feared-general.html
22. Ibid. and Rob Crilly, 'British taxpayer funds Somali police force for regime accused of war crimes', *The Times*, 2 June, 2008, http://www.timesonline.co.uk/tol/news/world/africa/article4046164.ece
23. Ibid.
24. Liam Fox, William Hague, Andrew Mitchell and Oliver Letwin, 'Strategic Defence and Security Review and the National Security Strategy', Uncorrected Transcript of Oral Evidence to be published as HC 761-ii, Select Committee Session 2010-11, House of Commons, 9 March, 2011.
25. *Telegraph*, 'Somaliland: UK Assistance to Police Special Protection Unit and Coast Guard', 4 February, 2011, http://www.telegraph.co.uk/news/wikileaks-files/london-wikileaks/8304903/SOMALILAND-UK-ASSISTANCE-TO-POLICE-SPECIAL-PROTECTION-UNIT-AND-COAST-GUARD.html
26. Jon Lunn, 'Interlocking crises in the Horn of Africa', House of Commons Library, Research Paper 08/86, 25 November, 2008.
27. Ibid.
28. Alexander Cockburn and Jeffrey St. Clair, 'Zbigniew Brzezinski: How Jimmy Carter and I Started the Mujahideen', *Counterpunch*, 15 January, 1998, http://www.counterpunch.org/1998/01/15/how-jimmy-carter-and-i-started-the-mujahideen/ and Robin Cook, 'The struggle against terrorism cannot be won by military means', *Guardian*, 8 July, 2005, http://www.guardian.co.uk/uk/2005/jul/08/july7.development
29. Campbell McCafferty, 'Piracy off the coast of Somalia', Foreign Affairs Committee, 29 June, 2011, http://www.publications.parliament.uk/pa/cm201012/cmselect/cmfaff/c1318-ii/c131801.htm and Kim Sengupta, 'Britain's new year resolution: intervene in Somalia', *Independent*, 22 December, 2011 http://www.independent.co.uk/news/world/africa/britains-new-year-resolution-intervene-in-somalia-6280391.html
30. Andrew Dismore MP, House of Commons, 16 October, 2001, Columns 1084–1086. MI5 agent and Bakri quoted in Nafeez Mosaddeq Ahmed, 'UK pays price for MI5 courting terror', *Asia Times*, 30 May, 2013. Loftus interviewed on Fox News, http://www.youtube.com/watch?v=oM0ff1NyMg8. Al-Muhajiroun-MI6 links, see 'Supplementary memorandum from Institute for Policy Research & Development (PVE 19A)', House of Commons, undated, http://www.publications.parliament.uk/pa/cm200809/cmselect/cmcomloc/memo/previoex/uc19a02.htm

31. In 'Hero's final hours' (*Daily Mirror*, 25 May, 2013), Andrew Gregory writes: 'Omar Bakri Mohammed ... claimed he converted Adebolajo when the terror suspect was in his early 20s'. Also see Nicolas Helen, Richard Kerbaj, Dipesh Gadher and David Leppard, 'Missed clues on terror suspects', *Sunday Times*, 26 May, 2013, which states that Adebolajo 'was arrested in Kenya more than two years ago and accused of leading a group of youths trying to join [al-Shabaab]'.
32. Sue Reid, 'The brave agent who exposed Hamza only to be betrayed by MI5', *Daily Mail*, 10 April, 2012, http://www.dailymail.co.uk/debate/article-2127942/Reda-Hassaine-The-brave-agent-exposed-Abu-Hamza-betrayed-MI5.html and Bruce Crumley, 'Sheltering a Puppet Master?', *Time*, 7 July, 2002, http://www.time.com/time/world/article/0,8599,300609,00.html
33. Sandra Laville, 'Unpredictable "lone wolves" pose biggest Olympic security threat', *Guardian*, 9 March, 2012, http://www.guardian.co.uk/uk/2012/mar/09/lone-wolves-olympic-security-threat. On the mosque bombing, see my 'Somalia still suffers', op. cit.
34. Nathaniel Horadam, 'Profile: Sheikh Hassan Dahir Aweys', *Critical Threats*, 14 November, 2011, http://www.criticalthreats.org/somalia/al-shabaab-leadership/hassan-dahir-aweys-november-14-2011, footnote 6 and Department of State (US), 'Background Information on Designated Foreign Terrorist Organizations Contents', Appendix B, no date, http://www.state.gov/documents/organization/10300.pdf
35. United Nations Security Council, 'Letter dated 10 March 2010 from the Chairman of the Security Council Committee pursuant to resolutions 751 (1992) and 1907 (2009) concerning Somalia and Eritrea addressed to the President of the Security Council', S/2010/91, 10 March, 2010.
36. Dominik Lemanski, 'SAS targets Somali terror forces', *Daily Star*, 11 March, 2012.
37. Human Rights Watch, 'Kenya: Respect law in Somali military operations', 19 November, 2011, http://www.hrw.org/news/2011/11/18/kenya-respect-law-somalia-military-operations
38. House of Lords, 'Combating Somali Piracy: the EU's Naval Operation Atalanta', European Union Committee, 12th Report of Session 2009–10, HL Paper 103, 14 April, 2010, Stationery Office Ltd.
39. Richard Ottaway, Bob Ainsworth, Menzies Campbell, Ann Clwyd, Rory Stewart, and Dave Watts, 'Piracy off the coast of Somalia', Uncorrected Transcript of Oral Evidence to be published as HC 1318-ii, Session 2010–12, House of Commons, 29 June, 2011, http://www.publications.parliament.uk/pa/cm201012/cmselect/cmfaff/uc1318-ii/uc131801.htm

40. Willett in House of Lords, 'Combating Somali…', op. cit. and Shortland quoted in Jon Lunn, 'Does Somali piracy have any "development effects"?', House of Commons Library, SN06238, 28 February, 2012.
41. Shortland quoted in Lunn, ibid.
42. Watts, 'Piracy off the coast…', op. cit. and Lt. Col. T.A.H. Kirkwook, Defence Academy of the United Kingdom, Defence Research Paper, '90 by Sea: Maritime Commerce and the Royal Navy', http://www.da.mod.uk/Research-Publications/category/62/90-percent-by-sea-maritime-commerce-and-the-royal-navy-19076
43. Middleton, op. cit.

Chapter 12: Bangladesh

1. UNICEF, 'UNICEF welcomes Kiwanis partnership to fight deadly maternal and neonatal tetanus worldwide', Press Release, 24 June, 2010, http://www.unicef.org/media/media_54057.html, Nurul Islam Hasib, 'Child malnutrition still high', bdnews24.com, 17 April, 2012, http://www.bdnews24.com/details.php?id=222639&cid=2 and House of Commons International Development Committee, 'DFID's Programme in Bangladesh', Third Report of Session 2009–10, Volume I, HC 95-I, 4 March, 2010, The Stationery Office, http://www.publications.parliament.uk/pa/cm200910/cmselect/cmintdev/95/95i.pdf
2. Ministry of Defence (UK), 'The Strategic Trends Programme: Out to 2040', MoD, http://www.mod.uk/nr/rdonlyres/38651acb-d9a9-4494-98aa-1c86433bb673/0/gst4_update9_feb10.pdf and Bangladesh High Commission (London), 'Trade and Investment Promotion', website, no date, http://www.bhclondon.org.uk/TradeN_Commerce.htm
3. Human Rights Watch, 'Judge, Jury, and Executioner', December, 2006, HRW, http://www.hrw.org/sites/default/files/reports/bangladesh1206webwcover.pdf and Foreign and Commonwealth Office (UK), 2009, *Annual Human Rights Report*, FCO, http://centralcontent.fco.gov.uk/resources/en/pdf/human-rights-reports/human-rights-report-2009
4. Bangladesh High Commission (London), 'Trade and Investment Promotion', website, no date, http://www.bhclondon.org.uk/TradeN_Commerce.htm
5. HRW, 'Judge, Jury…', op. cit. and Foreign and Commonwealth Office (UK), 'United Kingdom Strategic Export Controls', 2006, The Stationery Office Ltd.
6. HRW, 'Judge, Jury…', op. cit. , Amnesty International, 'Bangladesh: UK-trained security forces must stop extrajudicial executions', 27 January, 2011,

http://www.amnesty.org.uk/news_details.asp?NewsID=19210Amnesty, Foreign and Commonwealth Office, 2009, *Annual Human Rights Report*, http://centralcontent.fco.gov.uk/resources/en/pdf/human-rights-reports/human-rights-report-2009

7. Human Rights Watch, 'Bangladesh: Government Should Support Anti-Torture Bill No Law on the Books to Punish This Endemic Problem', 29 March, 2011, http://www.hrw.org/en/news/2011/03/29/bangladesh-government-should-support-anti-torture-bill
8. HRW, 'Judge, Jury . . .', op. cit.
9. Ibid.
10. Ibid.
11. Ibid.
12. Public Interest Lawyers, 'Lawyers challenge UK Government over Torture of Bangladeshi MP', no date, http://www.publicinterestlawyers.co.uk/news_details.php?id=45
13. Human Rights Watch, 'Bangladesh: Government Should Support Anti-Torture Bill No Law on the Books to Punish This Endemic Problem', 29 March, 2011, http://www.hrw.org/en/news/2011/03/29/bangladesh-government-should-support-anti-torture-bill
14. Jon Lunn and Gavin Thompson, 'Bangladesh: an update', House of Commons Library, Standard Note: SN06149, 5 December, 2011, http://www.parliament.uk/briefing-papers/SN06149 and Devin T. Hagerty, 'Bangladesh in 2007: Democracy Interrupted, Political and Environmental Challenges Ahead', *Asian Survey*, Vol. 48, No. 1, January–February 2008, pp. 177–183.
15. Quoted in ibid.
16. Quoted in ibid.
17. Foreign and Commonwealth Office (UK), 2007, *Annual Exports*, http://www.fco.gov.uk/resources/en/pdf/4103709/2007-strat-exp-cont-data and Foreign and Commonwealth Office (UK), 2008, *Annual Human Rights Report*, FCO, http://uk.sitestat.com/fcoweb/fcogov/s?fco.en.publications-and-documents.publications1.annual-reports.human-rights-report.p.pdf.human-rights-2008&ns_type=pdf&ns_url=http://www.fco.gov.uk/resources/en/pdf/pdf15/human-rights-2008
18. FCO, 2009, 'Annual Human Rights . . .', op. cit. and British Business Group, website, no date, http://www.bbg.org.bd/memList.php and http://www.bbg.org.bd/memprofile.php and http://www.bbg.org.bd/membership.php

19. Ibid. and House of Commons, 'DFID's programme ...', op. cit.
20. Department for Business Enterprise and Regulatory Reform, 'Strategic Export Controls: Country Pivot Report', 2008 and Lunn and Thompson, 'Bangladesh...', op. cit.
21. Quoted in Mokbul Morshed Ahmad, 'Distant Voices: The Views of the Field Workers of NGOs in Bangladesh on Microcredit', *The Geographical Journal*, Vol. 169, No. 1, March, 2003, pp. 65–74 and House of Commons, 'DFID's programmes...', op. cit.
22. Mokbul Morshed Ahmad, op. cit.
23. Judith Rodin, 'Speeches and Presentations', 19 June 19, 2006, http://www.rockefellerfoundation.org/news/speeches-presentations/remarks-by-dr-judith-rodin-president and Corey Flintoff, 'India's Poor Reel Under Microfinance Debt Burden', National Public Radio, 31 December, 2010, http://www.npr.org/2010/12/31/132497267/indias-poor-reel-under-microfinance-debt-burden
24. John Ward, Bernice Lee, Simon Baptist and Helen Jackson, 'Evidence for Action', Chatham House, September, 2010, Chatham House and Jessica Schicks, 'Microfinance Over-Indebtedness', Solvay Brussels School, CEB Working Paper No. 10/048, 2010.
25. Lamia Karim, 'The Hidden Ways Microfinance Hurts Women', *Brandeis Magazine*, Fall-Winter, 2012, http://www.brandeis.edu/magazine/2012/fall-winter/inquiry/karim.html
26. Vishnu Sridharan, 'Selling organs to pay off debt', *Christian Science Monitor*, 9 January, 2012, http://www.csmonitor.com/Commentary/Opinion/2012/0109/Selling-organs-to-pay-off-debt-Microfinance-needs-reforms
27. Flintoff, op. cit.
28. House of Commons, 'DFID's programmes...', op. cit.
29. National Intelligence Council, 2009, 'Global Scenarios to 2025', Government Printing Office.
30. Ministry of Defence (UK), 'Strategic Trends Programme: 2007-2036' (3rd ed.), 23 January, 2007, The Developments, Concepts and Doctrine Centre.

Conclusion

1. David Cameron, 'Syria: refugees and counterterrorism – Prime Minister's statement', 7 September, 2015, Gov.UK, https://www.gov.uk/government/speeches/syria-refugees-and-counter-terrorism-prime-ministers-statement
2. Ibid.
3. Ian Cobain, 'How secret renditions shed light on MI6's licence to kill and

torture', *Guardian*, 14 February, 2012, http://www.theguardian.com/world/2012/feb/14/mi6-licence-to-kill-and-torture. See also Intelligence Services Act 1994, http://www.legislation.gov.uk/ukpga/1994/13/contents

4. BBC News Online, 'Ambassador gives "Iraq defence" for UK's Syria drone strike', 11 September, 2015, http://www.bbc.co.uk/news/uk-34215799
5. Lindsay Watling, 'Family could sue over RAF drone kill', *Press and Journal*, 9 September, 2015, https://www.pressandjournal.co.uk/fp/news/politics/690143/questions-raised-over-legality-of-raf-drone-strike-as-fallon-insists-he-would-not-hesitate-to-do-it-again/. BBC Magazine Online, 'Who, what, why?: When is it legal to kill your own citizens?', 8 September, 2015, http://www.bbc.co.uk/news/magazine-34184856
6. Sky News Online, 'Was UK right to kill jihadis in drone strike?', 8 September, 2015, http://news.sky.com/story/1548754/was-uk-right-to-kill-jihadis-in-drone-strike. On the government's refusal to publish the letter on Libya, see my 'Libya one year on (part 3): The propaganda and the law', Axis of Logic, 23 April, 2012, http://axisoflogic.com/artman/publish/Article_64475.shtml
7. 'One of the world's most wanted terrorists captured in Libya by elite US troops was given political asylum in Britain ... Liby, who studied electronic and nuclear engineering in Tripoli, is thought to have been with bin Laden in Sudan in the early Nineties. He then turned up in the UK in 1995 where he was granted political asylum as an enemy of Gaddafi' (Ian Drury and Martin Robinson, 'Manchester link of al-Qaeda commander captured in daring US Delta Forces raid as it emerges Jihadist gave Scotland Yard the slip 13 years ago after being given asylum in the UK', *Daily Mail*, 7 October, 2013, http://www.dailymail.co.uk/news/article-2447532/Al-Qaeda-commander-Abu-Anas-al-Liby-snatched-Libya-US-Delta-Force.html#ixzz3tY5ZxoRH). See also: 'The Libyan al-Qaeda cell [funded by MI6] included Anas al-Liby ... The Observer has been restrained from printing details of the allegations during the course of the trial of David Shayler, who was last week sentenced to six months in prison for disclosing documents obtained during his time as an MI5 officer. He was not allowed to argue that he made the revelations in the public interest'. See Martin Bright, 'MI6 "halted bid to arrest bin Laden" ', *Observer*, 10 November, 2002, http://www.theguardian.com/politics/2002/nov/10/uk.davidshayler
8. BBC News Online, 'Undercover soldiers "killed unarmed civilians in Belfast" ', 21 November, 2013, http://www.bbc.co.uk/news/uk-24987465. On divide and rule tactics, see Martin Ingram and Greg Harkin, 2004, *Stakeknife*, O'Brien Press and Kevin Fulton, 2006, *Unsung Hero*, John Blake.

9. Human Rights Watch, 'Colombia: Disappearances plague major port', 20 March, 2014, https://www.hrw.org/news/2014/03/20/colombia-disappearances-plague-major-port
10. Jim Waterson, 'Week in Westminster', BBC Radio 4, 5 December, 2015, http://www.bbc.co.uk/programmes/b06qv3zn
11. Ibid. and David Lammy MP, 'Statement on Syrian Intervention', 1 December, 2015, http://www.davidlammy.co.uk/#!Statement-on-Syrian-Intervention/em4gf/565d83400cf2c000e9297752
12. Toby Helm and Peter Beaumont, 'UK warns Iran of more sanctions pain', *Guardian*, 7 October, 2012, http://www.theguardian.com/world/2012/oct/07/uk-warns-iran-more-sanctions. Then-Defence Secretary Philip Hammond explained: 'We can definitely make the pain much greater . . . The only thing that is likely to budge the regime is if they see or sense an existential threat. If the level of economic pressure starts to translate into potentially regime-threatening disruption and dissent on the streets of Tehran, then they may change course'. On Lyall-Grant and Libya, see David Fisher, 'Libya: A Last Hurrah or Model for the Future?' in David Whetham and Bradley J. Strawser (eds.), 2015, *Responsibilities to Protect: Perspectives in Theory and Practice*, Brill Nijhoff, p. 23. On Iran, see Mark Lyall-Grant, 'The UK is committed to finding a peaceful, negotiated solution with Iran on the nuclear issue', Foreign and Commonwealth Office, 20 March, 2014, https://www.gov.uk/goverment/speeches/the-uk-is-committed-to-finding-a-peaceful-negotiated-solution-with-iran-on-the-nuclear-issue
13. Nicholas Watt, 'David Cameron accuses Jeremy Corbyn of being "terrorist sympathiser"', *Guardian*, 2 December, 2015, http://www.theguardian.com/politics/2015/dec/01/cameron-accuses-corbyn-of-being-terrorist-sympathiser
14. Reuters, 'Turkey angered by rocket-brandishing on Russian naval ship passing Istanbul', 6 December, 2015, www.reuters.com/article/us-mideast-crisis-turkey-russia-idUSKBN0TP0JW20151206#z4FKmVtqCvqzE7bx.99
15. James Forsyth and Douglas Davis, 'We came so close to World War Three that day', *Spectator*, 3 October, 2007, http://new.spectator.co.uk/2007/10/we-came-so-close-to-world-war-three-that-day/
16. Jamie Doward, 'How a Nato war game took the world to brink of nuclear disaster', *Observer*, 2 November, 2013, http://www.theguardian.com/uk-news/2013/nov/02/nato-war-game-nuclear-disaster
17. Ibid. and Eric Schlosser, 'Nuclear weapons: An accident waiting to happen', *Guardian*, 14 September, 2013, http://www.theguardian.com/world/2013/sep/14/nuclear-weapons accident-waiting-to-happen

Index

7/7 (London bombings) 49
9/11 8, 73, 133, 168n31

Abdulmutallab, Umar Farouk 73
Abu Dhabi 70
Adebolajo, Michael 139
Adeed, Farrah 133
Afghanistan 2, 12, 22, 23, 29, 48, 61–62, 76, 168n31
Ahmad, Mokbul Morshed 151
Ahmadi-Roshan, Mostafa 55
Ahmed, Fakhruddin 149
Ahmed, Mohammed Younis al- 40
Ahmed, Moeen U. (Gen.) 149
Ahmed, Nafeez 23
Ainsworth, Bob 142
Akter, Selina 153
Al Sabah, Sheikh Saad al-Abdullah al-Salim (Emir of Kuwait) 70
Albania 23
Algeria 22, 23, 28, 140
Ali, Mohamed 148
Alimohammadi, Masoud 55
Al-Ittihad al-Islamiya 140
Al-Muhajiroun 49, 139
'Al-Qaeda' 13, 20, 60–62, 139
  as 'Al-Nusra Front' 22, 24
  in Iraq 36-38, 41–42, 48
  in Libya 30, 33, 204n7
  in Somalia 130
  in Yemen 61–62, 77–78
Al-Shabaab 130, 140
Al-Zarqawi, Abu Musab 36, 38
Alston, Philip 74–75
Amin, Abdul Raqib 156
Anderson, Jon Lee 37
Arab Spring 15, 21, 23, 24
  in Bahrain 69
  in Yemen 68–71
Arbuthnot, James 138
Archer, Peter (Lord) 125
Armenia 88
Assad, Bashar al- 12, 14, 21, 24, 40, 42, 44, 50, 158–59, 171n7
Aswat, Haroon Rashid 139
Atta, Qassim 41
Austin, Lloyd J. (Gen.) 42
Australia 23
  Entities in Syria 25
  and Indonesia 118
  and Operation Overhead 74, 78
Avant, Deborah 107
Axe, David 79
Azerbaijan 23
Azzouz, Abd al-Baset 29–31, 33, 44, 47

Baghdadi, Abu Omar al- 39–41,
Bahrain 69
Bakri, Omar 48–49, 149
Balochis (ethnic group) 52, 58–59
Bandaranaike, Sirimavo 96
Bangladesh 145–154, 8, 13, 15, 156
  health and wellbeing 145
  Rapid Action Battalion 8, 145–154

Barak, Ehud 55
Barco, Virgilio 112
Barre, Mohamed Siyad 132
Barrera, Daniel 113
Barrett, Richard 20
Bartlett, Richard 29
Batirashvili/al-Shishani, Tarkhan 47–48
Bekele, Daniel 141
Belgium 23
Ben Ali, Zine 21, 171n7
Bergner, Kevin (Brig. Gen.) 38
Bin Laden, Osama 29, 38, 168n31, 204n7
Blair, Tony 10, 136, 149, 160
Blom-Cooper, Louis (QC) 112
Blumenthal, Sidney 31
Bosnia-Herzegovina 23
Brazil 5
Brennan, Brendan 158
Brown, Gordon 136
Browne, Jeremy 88–89
Bruce, Malcolm 102
Brzezinski, Zbigniew 22, 60, 84, 139
Burden, Richard 71
Burt, Alistair 24, 103
Burt, Lorely 121
Burton, Fred 55
Bush, George W. 73–75

Cable, Vince 3–4
Cambodia 23
Cameron, David 19–20, 27, 33, 156–57, 159–60
Campbell, Leslie 171n7
Canada 50
Carter, Jimmy 22
Caslen, Robert L. (Maj. Gen.) 40
Çavusoglu, Mevlüt 50, 160
Central Intelligence Agency (CIA) 73
  and 'al-Qaeda' 61–62
  and drones 77
  in Indonesia 124
  in Iran 52–59
  and Islamic State 49
  in Libya 29–30
  in Syria 24–25
  in Ukraine (alleged) 92
Cerqueira, Carlos Mesias Arrigui 107
Chechnya 23, 47–48
China 4–5, 7, 22, 52, 84, 156
  and Somalia 133
  Uighurs (ethnic group) 23
  Turkmens (ethnic group) 23
Chirac, Jacques 8
Chowdhury, Salahuddin Quader 147
Churchill, Winston 54
Clark, Wesley 30
Clarke, Victoria 77
Clinton, Hillary 32
Cobain, Ian 157
Cohen, Gili 169n32
Colombia 104–17, 13, 15, 156, 159
  and chemical 'fumigation' 115–117
  and cocaine 111
  and corporations 106–108
  and paramilitaries 107–109
Congo 12
Conway, Gerry 158
Conway, John 158
Cook, Robin 61, 139
Cooley, John K. 138
Cronau, Peter 122
Cuba 5
Curtis, Mark 54, 60, 138
Czech Republic 87

Dabbagh, Ali 40
Dagan, Meir 55
Dagestan 28
Darwiish, Mohamed 137
Davis, David 80
Davis, Mike 2, 5
De Waal, Alex 132
Denmark 23
Devlin, Eugene 158
Dibb, Peter 162
Diego Garcia 79
Dismore, Andrew 49, 139
Disraeli, Benjamin 4
Ditmas, Harry 100
Djibouti 77, 79
D-Notices/DSMA-Notices 1, 164–65n2
Dorril, Stephen 60, 138
Douglas-Home, Alec 60
Dowden, Richard 132, 136
Dreyfuss, Robert 138
Drones/Unmanned Aerial Vehicles 73–82, 7, 9, 15, 155
  and 9/11 73
  and Yemen 72–73
Dumas, Roland 23, 31
Dunne, Philip 77
Dutch West Indies 5

Eccles, Diana (Baroness) 121
Egypt 11, 20, 22, 23, 46, 53, 91
  and the Arab Spring 170n7
  and *Kifaya* (Enough!) 20, 171n7
  and Libya 32
Emwazi, Mohammed 49
Engdahl, William 53–54
Equatorial Guinea 32, 123
Erdogan, Recep Tayyip 25
Escobar, Pablo 112
Ethiopia 134
Evans, Jonathan 139

Faarax-Deeq, Ahmed Said Mohamed 141
Fadhli, Tariq al- 61, 64–65
Fallon, Michael 93, 157
FARC (Fuerzas Armadas Revolucionarias de Colombia) 106–108, 110
Farhan, Sattam 40–41
Farrell, Theo 19
Flint, Caroline 159
Foley, James 49
Fox, Liam 1, 31, 58, 70, 99
France 8, 11, 14, 47, 91, 155, 159
  Anglo-French Treaty (2010) 9, 12
  and Iran 56
  and Islamic State 50
  and Libya 32–33
  and Syria 19–20, 23, 25–26
Free Syrian Army 20, 23, 24, 25, 43, 47, 49, 159
'free trade' 2–7, 155
  agenda for Middle East and North Africa 21–22
  in Bangladesh 151–54
'Full Spectrum Dominance' 7, 73–74, 156, 162

Ga'amadheere, Guled 137
Gaddafi, Muammar 12, 14–15, 20, 22, 24, 27, 29, 44, 147, 158, 171n7
Galán, Luis Carlos 113
Gallagher, John 5
Gaviria, César 109
Georgia 48, 85, 88

Germany 23, 47
Gildo, Bherlin 26
Godane/Zubair, Ahmed Abdi 140
Godir, Musa Said Yusuf 141
Government Communications Headquarters (GCHQ) 54, 73, 78–80
Green Berets (US) 61
Green of Hurstpierpoint (Lord) 114–115
Grieve, Dominic 141, 157
Griffiths, Leslie (Lord) 125
Guirtili, Mohamed al- 32

Haftar, Khalifa 30
Hagerty, Devin T. 149
Haiti 9
Haq, Samsul 148
Harati, Mahdi al- 25
Harithi, Qaed Salim Sinan al- 77
Harnetty, Peter 5–6.
Harries, Richard (Lord) 125
Hartley, Aidan 135–36
Harvey, Derek (Colonel) 36
Harvey Nick 71
Hassaine, Reda 140
Healy, Sally 142
Hekmat, Halgurd (Brig. Gen) 45
Hersh, Seymour 25, 26
Hezbollah 50
Hoon, Geoff 76
Hosseinpour, Ardeshir 55
Houthis (ethnic/religious group) 60, 66–68, 70
Howells, Kim 57, 114
Hussein, Abdullah II bin (King of Jordan) al- 70
Hussein, Saddam 13, 34–35, 45, 54

Ijape, Mathias 123
India 4–7, 156
Indonesia 10, 155
  and West Papua 118, 124–25
Ingram, Adam 57
International Humanitarian Law 74–75, 186n16
Iraq 34–5, 17–12, 158, 168n31
  Gulf War (1991) 14, 56
  invasion of (2003) 14, 27
  planned invasion of 30
  sanctions 35
  shock and awe strategy 35
Iran/Persia 52–59, 5, 15, 114, 155
  and Iraq 55
  and Islamic State 43, 49
  and nuclear strategy 54–55
  planned invasion of 30
Ireland 23, 83
Islamic Courts Union 130, 133
Islamic State/ISIS/ISIL/Daesh 13, 15, 155–60
  in Syria 19, 22–23
  in Iraq 37–39
  in Libya 44
Israel 15, 118, 155
  and Iran 52, 55
  bombing of Syria 160–61
  Defence Forces 39
  in Papua 122
Italy 23

Jaish al-Muhajireen wal Ansar 43, 48
James, Lawrence 5
Japan 5
Jayewardene, Junius 97
Johnson, Steve 169n32
Jones, Kevan 121

Jordan 23, 26
Jordan, Adalberto 113
Jundallah 58

Ka'ary, Fathi al- 33
Kadirgamar, Lakshman 99, 101
Karim, Lamia 152
Karuna/Muralitharan, Vinayagamoorthy (Col.) 101–02
Kassem, Abdel 34
Kaszeta, Dan 169n32
Katz, Rita 39
Kearney, Robert 96
Kekule, Alexander 169n32
Kendrick, Kelly (Maj.) 37–38
Kennet, Wayland Hilton Young (Lord) 76
Kenny, Hugh 158
Kenya 91, 140
Khalid, Usama 78
Khalifa, Sheikh Hamad bin Isa al- 70
Khan, Daraz 77
Khan, Jehangir 77
Khan, Mir Ahmed 77
Khan, Mohammad Sidique 49
Khan, Noor 78
Khan, Reyaad 156–57
Khomeini, Ayatollah 53–54
Klein, Yair Gal (Col.) 112
Kolomoyskyi, Ihor 91
Kosovo 23, 73, 76, 139
Koussa, Moussa 30
Kuchma, Leonid 87
Kumaratunga, Chandrika 98
Kurds (ethnic group) 9–10, 43
  and Turkey 166n22
  Peshmerga 45
Kuwait 49, 50, 70
Kyrgyzstan 23

Lammy, David 159
Lang, W. Patrick 20
Laycock, Stuart 2
Lebanon 23, 24, 43
  planned invasion of 30
Libel/defamation 1, 164n2
Liby, Anas al- 29, 158, 204n7
Libya 27–33, 11–12, 19, 23, 27, 70, 157–58, 160, 204n7
  and Islamic State 44
  Libyan Islamic Fighting Group 29–30
  planned invasion of 30
Livingstone, Grace 107, 112, 116
Lloyd, Peter 150
Locarno, Manuel José Bonnet 108
Lubbock, Eric (Lord Avebury) 124, 126, 128
Lyall-Grant, Mark 159–60
Lynch, Rick (Maj. Gen.) 36

Macedonia 23, 76
Macmillan, Harold 60
Magee, Gary 6
Mali 12, 32
Maliki, Nouri al- 34–35, 41, 46
Malloch-Brown, Mark (Lord) 135
Mann, John 115
Mann, Simon 123
Marie, Hussam al- 20
Martin, Laurence 3
Mashhadani, Khalid 38
Masri, Abu Ayyub al- 38, 41
May, Theresa 26
McAleese, Peter 113
McAloon, Aiden 158
McBride, Peter 122

McCafferty, Campbell 139
McCoy, Alfred 111
McGill, Heather 88, 90
McLean, Neil 61
McVeigh, Patrick 158
Melanesians (ethnic group) 118
Melman, Yossi 54
Mengistu, Haile Mariam 132
Mexico 83, 114
MI5 49, 59, 100, 130, 141
MI6 14, 157
  in Bangladesh 147–48
  in Colombia 104, 108
  in Indonesia 124
  in Iran 52–59
  in Libya 29–33
  in Somalia 130, 139, 141
  in Sri Lanka 101
  in Syria 20, 23, 24, 49
  in Ukraine (alleged) 92
  in Yemen 60–62
Middleton, Roger 131, 142–43
Miliband, David 27, 68, 150
Miliband, Ed 27
Miller, Phil 95
Mitchell, Andrew 138
Monbiot, George 129
Montenegro 23
Moonesinghe, Mangala 100
Moreno, Pedro Juan 113
Morocco 5, 140
Mossad 52, 55–56, 61
Mossadeq, Mohammed 53
Mounika, 153
Mowlam, Mo 111
Mubarak, Hosni 21, 171n7
Mujahedin-e-Khalq 55–58
Murray, Patrick 158
Muslim Brotherhood 32–33
  in Iran (Devotees of Islam) 53

Narayana, Kurapati Venkat 153
Nasser, Gamal Abdel 53, 60
National Council of Resistance of Iran 55–56
Navy SEALS (US) 61
Netherlands 23
Newsinger, John 2
Nicaragua 54
Niger 32
Nigeria 10, 28, 73
Nonis, Chris 103
North Atlantic Treaty Organization (NATO) 12, 14, 155, 160
  and Russia 168n32
  and Turkey 166n22
  and Ukraine 83–84, 86, 88, 93
  in Afghanistan 76
  in Libya 27–28, 31,
  in Serbia 75
Northern Ireland, 37, 158
Norway 23
Nuclear weapons/materials 55, 68, 83–86, 156, 160–63

Obama, Barack 31, 45, 75
Odierno, Ray 41
Oman, 60, 70
Omar, Abu 43
Onuch, Olga 90
Operation Able Archer 161–62
Operation Atalanta 142
Operation Clean Heart 146
Operation Mermaid's Dawn 32–33
Operation Overhead 74, 78
Operation Restore Hope 132–133
Operation TPAJAX 53, 55

Pace, Peter (Gen.) 109
Pahlavi, Shah 53
Pakistan 2, 22, 23, 31, 38, 52, 58, 61, 139
Palestine 118
Papua (New Guinea and West) 118–129, 155
  and Bougainville Resistance Army 122
  West 15, 118–119, 124–29
Payton, Gary 165n15
Petraeus, David 26
Pfaffenberger, Bryan 97
Pfeffer, Anshel 169n32
Philippines 22, 23, 91
Poroshenko, Petro 92
Povey, Mike 131
Price, Adam 57
Putin, Vladimir 49, 85

Qaboos, bin Said al-Said (Sultan of Oman) 70
Qatada, Abu 140
Qatar 25, 33, 70

Rahman, Omar Abdul 33
Rajasingham, K.T. 98
Raju, Ashiqul Islam 148
Rama, 153
Ramirez, Francisco 105
Ratcliffe, Barrie M. 4, 6
Rawlings, Patricia (Baroness) 126
Razmara, Ali (Gen.) 53
Rezaeinejad, Darioush 55
Rigby, Lee 139
Robinson, Ronald 5
Rooney, Daniel 158
Rose, Michael (Gen.) 111
Royall, Janet (Baroness) 126
Rupesinghe, Kumar 97
Russia 7, 22, 156
  and NATO 168n32
  and Somalia 133
  and Turkey 160
  and Ukraine 83–94
  and Yemen 61
  in Syria 43, 47, 50
  war with Georgia 48
Rwanda 9
Rycroft, Matthew 157

Sadiq/Belhaj, Abu Abdullah 29, 43
Saleh, Ali Abdullah 60, 61–70
Sallabi, Ali 32
Sallal, Abdullah al- 60
Samarrai, Ibrahim al- 41
Samper, Ernesto 108, 112
Sandhurst Military Academy 70, 99
Saudi Arabia 10, 23, 27, 38, 46, 155
  Bahrain (invasion) 69
  British arms 69–70
  human rights in 69
  war with Yemen 60, 66–70
SAVAK (Iranian secret police) 53
Sawers, John 52, 55, 85
Sayyaf, Abu 44
Scarlett, John 55
Schanzer, Jonathan 46
Schicks, Jessica 152
Search for International Terrorist Entities (SITE) 39, 41
Serbia 14, 23, 75, 87
Serrano, Rosso José 113
Seychelles, 79
Shahriari, Majid 55
Shaw, Tommy 158

Shayler, David 204n7
Shiki, Salem al- 32
Shortland, Anja 142
Siam 5
Singapore 122
Sinhalese (ethnic group) 95–97
Smith, David 113
Smith, Joe
Snowden, Edward 78
Somalia 130–144, 8, 9, 13, 15, 79, 156
  boat people (refugees) 136
  famine 130, 131
  invasion by Ethiopia 134–35
  oil and gas 130–33
  piracy 142
  planned invasion of 30
  war with Ethiopia 132
South Ossetia 48, 85
South Sudan 91
Special Air Service (SAS) 13–15
  in Colombia 104, 107–108, 111–112
  in Iraq 37
  in Libya 23, 30–33
  in Papua 122
  in Serbia 75, 185n8
  in Somalia 138
  in Sri Lanka 97
  in Syria 24
  in Yemen 60, 77–78
Special Boat Service
  in Colombia 104
  in Somalia 138
  in Syria 24
Spellar, John 75
Spicer, Tim 100, 122
Sri Lanka (formerly Ceylon) 94–103, 8, 11, 15, 156
  Army of 8, 13
Steele, John 111
Sterling, Jeffrey (Lord) 130
Stratford, Jemima 79
Straw, Jack 89–90
Sudan 30, 140, 204n7
Suharto, 124
Suna, Mohamed al-Saleh 78
Suskind, Ron 139
Sweden 23
Swire, Hugo 94
Syria 19–26, 11–12, 14, 114, 156–60
  alleged chemical weapons use in 168–69n32
  invaded by Israel 160–61
  planned invasion of 30

Tabuni, Mako 128
Tajikistan 23, 48
Taliban 61, 168n31
Tamil Tigers/Liberation Tigers of Tamil Eelam (LTTE) 94, 97–102
Tamils (ethnic group) 13, 15, 94–103
Taris, Wissam 25
Taylor, Ann (Baroness of Bolton) 121
Thani, Sheikh Hamad bin Khalifa al- (Emir of Qatar) 71
Thatcher, Margaret 53, 97–98, 112
Thiers, Adolphe 4
Thomas, Anna 80
Thompson, Andrew 6
Tomkins, David 113
Torlot, Tim 71
Trevaskis, Kennedy 61
Tripp, Charles 34
Tudeh Party 53
Tunisia 21, 23
Turcan, Metin 20
Turkey 5, 9–10, 160

and Islamic State 45–47, 49
and Kurds 44, 166n22
and Syria 23
Turkmenistan-Afghanistan-Pakistan (TAPI) pipeline 58

Ukraine 83–93, 15, 51, 155
Umma Brigade 25
United Arab Emirates 33, 60
Uribe, Álvaro 110
Uribe, Carlos Castano 115
Uzbekistan 23, 48

Valentine, Douglas 111
Vanninen, Paula 169n33

Waddington, David 98
Waterfield, Gordon 61–62
Watson, David 29
Watson, Tom 76–77, 79
Watts, Dave 143
Wazed, Sheikh Hasina 149, 151
Webb, Gary 111
Wenda, Benny 124
Werritty, Adam 58
Wheeler, Roger (Gen.) 111
White, Dick 61
Willett, Lee 142
Winfield, Gwyn 168–69n32
Wright, Jeremy 157
Wuhaishi, Nasir al- 62

Yanukovych, Viktor 87, 88, 90–91
Yazid, Mustafa Abu al- 62
Yemen (formerly Aden) 60–72, 15, 155
bomb hoax 72
Houthis 66–69
oppression of socialists 61–66
terrorism 73

Young, George 61
Yudhoyono, Susilo Bambang 127
Yushchenko, Viktor 89
Yusuf, Abdullahi 136

Zanders, Jean Pascal 169n32
Zanzibar 5
Zawahiri, Ayman al- 31, 33
Zawi, Hamid Dawud Mohamed Khalil al- 41
Zia, Khaleda 146–47
Zinni, Anthony 133